ON THE BOW

LOVE, FEAR, AND FASCINATION IN THE PURSUIT
OF BONEFISH, TARPON, AND PERMIT

BILL HORN

STACKPOLE
BOOKS

Guilford, Connecticut

To the late Ralph "Mac" MacDonald,
aka "The Devastator"—a fine angler, boatmate,
raconteur, epicure, editor, songwriter, veteran
Tarpon Camper, and great friend

Published by Stackpole Books
An imprint of The Rowman & Littlefield Publishing Group, Inc.
4501 Forbes Blvd., Ste. 200
Lanham, MD 20706
www.rowman.com

Distributed by NATIONAL BOOK NETWORK

British Library Cataloguing in Publication Information available

Library of Congress Cataloging-in-Publication Data

Names: Horn, William Pierce, 1950– author.
Title: On the bow : love, fear, and fascination in the pursuit of bonefish, tarpon, and permit / Bill Horn.
Description: Guilford, Connecticut : Stackpole Books, [2021] | Includes index. | Summary: "Veteran saltwater angler and Keys resident Bill Horn shares his years of experience pursuing tarpon, permit, and bonefish and captures the magic and mystery of flats fishing around the world"— Provided by publisher.
Identifiers: LCCN 2020053430 (print) | LCCN 2020053431 (ebook) | ISBN 9780811739542 (hardcover) | ISBN 9780811769532 (epub)
Subjects: LCSH: Horn, William Pierce, 1950- | Saltwater fishing—Florida—Florida Keys. | Bonefishing—Florida—Florida Keys. | Tarpon fishing—Florida—Florida Keys. | Permit fishing—Florida—Florida Keys. | Fishers—Florida—Biography.
Classification: LCC SH457.3 .H67 2021 (print) | LCC SH457.3 (ebook) | DDC 799.1609759/41—dc23
LC record available at https://lccn.loc.gov/2020053430
LC ebook record available at https://lccn.loc.gov/2020053431

♾™ The paper used in this publication meets the minimum requirements of American National Standard for Information Sciences—Permanence of Paper for Printed Library Materials, ANSI/NISO Z39.48-1992.

CONTENTS

ACKNOWLEDGMENTS

A veritable legion of family members, friends, and associates helped make this book a reality. It was a far larger task than my first venture into authorship, and I needed every bit of assistance offered by lots of willing helpers. I should start with my hard-bitten sailor father, Bill Manz, who made the mistake of taking me onto an Islamorada dock—fishing rod in hand—in 1957. Sailing was cool but fishing, for me, was the real deal; neither of us could have ever foreseen how much that first small fish would influence my life. Thanks, Dad.

Inspiration to write another book, as well as very helpful reviewer services, came from a bunch of good friends, boatmates, and professional acquaintances including but not limited to (a little lawyer jargon there) Stu Apte, Liz Bain, Frank Carlton, George Conniff, Doc Frangos, Rick Hirsch, Steve Huff, Joe Kelley, Paul Kiessling, Mike Lawson, Jim McDuffie, David Olson, Jim Reinertsen, Nick Roberts, and Paul Turcke. They helped me add needed depth and texture while steering me away from a lot of steep cliffs.

Special thanks to the interviewees and fishing guides: Steven "Kiki" Adderley, Bus Bergmann, Richard Black, Scott Collins, Guy Fullhart, Leslie Greene, Dustin Huff, Richard Keating, Albert Ponzoa, Justin Rea, and Alex Zapata. Even after years of fishing with and knowing these great guys, I learned a lot during our interviews and hope you do too.

The Bonefish & Tarpon Trust science guys were very helpful, and it's a real pleasure to present many of their important findings. My appreciation to Aaron Adams, Ross Boucek, Jake Brownscombe, Andy Danylchuk, Luke Griffin, and Jon Shenker.

Assembling the photographs took some real effort, and I must extend my gratitude to Aaron Adams, Stu Apte, Bus Bergmann, Brad Bertelli (Florida Keys History and Discovery Center), Brooke Black, Bonefish & Tarpon Trust, Jacqueline Chapman, Stephen Davis (Everglades Foundation), Guy Fullhart, Luke Griffin, Heather Harkavy, R. He, Mike Lawson, David Olson, Justin Rea, Robbie Roemer, M. Roffer, Neal Rogers, Jon Shenker, Jerry Wilkinson, Ian Wilson, and X. Zeng for their contributed photos.

Jay Nichols, along with his team including Stephanie Otto and Ellen Urban, was once again willing to take a chance with my manuscript and expertly shepherd it into this finished product. I can't thank them enough.

And saving the best for last, my deepest appreciation and heartfelt thanks to my spouse, Jeannette Chiari. Not only is she the star of a lot of the pics, but this book simply could not have happened without her counseling, handholding, help, inspiration, superlative computer and organizational skills, and endless patience. Thank you, Sweetie!

Bill Horn
Marathon, Florida

CHAPTER ①

Taking the Bow

The skiff drops off-plane and glides to a stop. With the outboard shut down, silence descends except for the harsh croak of a passing cormorant. Five feet under the hull, bright sun and clear water reveal small frightened fish dashing under purple sea fans and tan mottled sponges. The two men aboard go into action. One unclips a black boat pole and clambers up on the stern poling platform. The other slides a fly rod and gold-finished reel from under the gunwales; the reel hums as 60 feet of fly line is stripped out. A hundred yards away an audible sigh and a splash alert the two and both catch a glimpse of a broad green back disappearing in a big boil. In unison they pronounce, "Tarpon." The angler steps up on the bow, the pole dips into the water, and the boat slides ahead. The hunt begins.

My spouse, Jeannette Chiari, jumps a Florida Keys oceanside tarpon during the annual spring migration.

1

Hunting fish on the flats is like visiting an aquarium, revealing creatures like a lurking, alien-looking stingray or rolling tarpon.

Commanding the bow of a flats boat opens the window to a fascinating aquatic world. Eyes probe transparent shallow waters in search of elusive bonefish, tarpon, and permit. You look hard for bits of color, moving shadows, or the spectral outline of fins and tails among a welter of sea life. Coral heads deceive and comical aqua trunkfish register briefly as "Bones!" Alien-looking stingrays pulse mud devouring hapless crabs, and shadowy silver-and-black barracudas hang motionless in green sand holes.

Sinuous sharks cruise over turtle-grass bottoms, and breathing, rolling bottlenose dolphins are mistaken for tarpon. Your heart surges as a black sickle tail waves up where a permit pins a crab or a small puff of smoky mud betrays a feeding bonefish. Untrained eyes can miss these often-subtle clues. Then "no doubt" signs assault the senses like a 100-pound tarpon exploding on mullet.

This hunt for fish occurs in a stunning, ever-changing environment. A blazing, bright tropical sun lights up shallow salt waters, giving the flats a special luminous quality. At deeper tarpon depths, add a light breeze and the water sparkles and flashes in the sun.

The quality of the light changes constantly from a brilliant yellow sun in clear blue skies to a hazy orange orb rising on a still, humid morning. Other days feature stiff winds and clouds turning waters pewter, streaked with white foam lines. There are seasonal changes as well. Winter anglers battle brisk north winds—refreshing if you're not a flats angler. Summer on the flats carries the forced torpor of wilting heat and air thick enough to cut with a knife.

All senses come into play. The nose takes in clean salt air as well as the low-tide smell of marl mud and wet sea grass. Mangrove cays laden with roosting cormorants and pelicans emit a guano reek. Deep into Everglades waters, there is the rank fecundity of thick mangrove jungles. Ears pick up the ripping sound of showering schools of baitfish or the crash of diving pelicans. Tailing bonefish, revealed by water splashing, can be heard on still mornings in remote Andros Island bays.

Imagine it's spring in the Florida Keys. The great tarpon bacchanal is under way, and a group of anglers assembles to pursue the silver king: a couple of graying veterans, a young

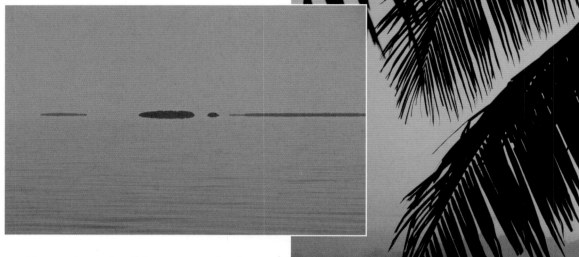

rookie, and a pair of 'tweeners who have somewhere caught a few bones or poons but are enamored with and deeply curious about the world of flats angling—the fish, fishing, people, and places. Bad weather blows in. Flags are starched out straight, and black squall lines carrying noisy, gray sheets of rain march across the narrow islands. No one is fishing today.

By afternoon there are no more flies to tie, leaders to rig, or reels to oil. A bottle of fine añejo rum appears, enlivening a long, meandering conversation about why this fishing is so addictive. What makes it so alluring? Why do the angling history, mysteries of the flats, and the great fish elicit such curiosity? Why are the colorful characters encountered there—guides, old friends, and anglers, good and bad, and the occasional jackass—so compelling? What are the best places to get on the bow of a flats skiff? And throughout, fish stories abound, some of suspect veracity. Welcome to this book. Pour your own añejo, if you wish, and join in.

Fishing the subtropical and tropical flats is a lyrical mix of fish, fishing, people, and places. Chasing bonefish in the Florida Keys and the nearby Bahamas gave birth to flats fishing in the 1930s and '40s. Northeastern anglers, experienced in using split-cane fly rods for trout and Atlantic salmon, took readily to casting to 2- to 8-pound bonefish in the shallows. Famous author of western novels, Zane Grey, popularized bonefishing, plying the waters around the Long Key Fishing Club in the Middle Keys.

The bonefish legend grew rapidly in the 1950s, and it continues to be the number one flats fish around the world. You must remember to breathe while stealthily stalking a big bone in inches of water. A visible dorsal fin and silver tail ooze along as the fish nears your waiting fly. You give it a twitch, the bonie pounces, its dorsal flares, the hook is set, and the fish streaks off with the fly line ripping a visible, and audible, rooster tail in the water. Adrenaline rushes into your veins, and you wonder if you have enough line on the reel. You're hooked—literally and figuratively.

Calm mornings and slick, lazy days offer great chances for laid-up tarpon or tailing bonefish. Storms make angling difficult if not impossible.

This is the famous Long Key Fishing Club, where bonefishing was invented, before it was destroyed in 1935 by a monster hurricane. (Courtesy of FloridaMemory.com)

A stealthily presented fly gets taken aggressively by a tailing bonefish.

Big silver-sided, green-backed tarpon were readily evident to early Keys flats anglers. In fact, tarpon fishing—with conventional tackle or harpoons—was already a major attraction in southwest Florida in the 1890s. But fly fishing for the great beasts did not develop for another 60 years, until technology in the form of fiber-glass rods, nylon monofilament, and bar stock aluminum fly reels gave anglers a fighting chance at hooking and landing the *Megalops atlanticus*. Pioneer guides and anglers such as Stu Apte (a Navy fighter pilot before he was a guide), George Hommell, and J. Lee Cuddy learned the tarpon's haunts in Keys shallow waters and through painstaking trial and error figured out how to catch the big girls (almost all of the big, 100-plus-pound tarpon are female). Tarpon fishing in the Keys remains excellent.

But years of fishing pressure, and catch-and-release, have educated these long-lived fish, requiring anglers to bring well-honed skills to the bow. Whether it's stalking laid-up single fish in the Keys backcountry or intercepting hundreds of ocean swimmers during the annual spring migration, the pursuit of tarpon remains an incomparable experience.

Permit were last to the flats fishing party. Their affinity for small blue crabs was known for years, and a handful of individuals chased them on the flats with crabs and spinning rods starting in the '50s. An odd perm or two fell to flies, mostly buggy-looking tarpon flies, but a permit on the fly was a rare achievement. Lefty Kreh's seminal 1974 book, *Fly Fishing in Saltwater*, noted that "fewer than one hundred of these fish have been taken on a fly rod." In the '80s, however, legendary Keys guide Captain Steve Huff and frequent client Del Brown concocted a new crab imitation—the Merkin—and perfected the "hit 'em on the head" presentation to start catching perms in unprecedented numbers. Before Brown passed away, he notched 513 fly-caught permit, setting a record unlikely to be equaled or surpassed. Having demonstrated that fly fishing for permit was in fact viable, lots of hard-bitten permit addicts took up the challenge, inventing new patterns and techniques to fool the hyper-wary fish. And what started in the Keys expanded quickly into the permit-rich waters of Belize, Cuba, Honduras, and Mexico.

The explosion of flats fishing in the Keys coincided with unfortunate declines in the Florida fisheries for bones, poons, and perms: the big three. Bonefish numbers began to slide in the late 1980s following the first of successive water-quality catastrophes in Florida Bay; the Bay is wedged in between mainland Florida to the north and the arc of the Keys south. Fifty years of damming, diking, and diverting the Everglades starved the wetlands, and adjacent Florida Bay, of clean fresh water. The combined water quantity and quality crises began to destroy the Bay, and a hoped-for recovery is still on the horizon.

Nine Mile Bank is a massive grass flat along the western edge of Florida Bay. For decades it was bonefish central, and big schools pushing wakes were a common sight, exciting even the most jaded anglers. Those schools became harder to find in the '90s and virtually disappeared by 2010. When that domino fell, it seemed to trigger the collapse of other historic bonefisheries throughout the Middle

A big tarpon unhooks herself at boatside—note the purple Mouse fly.

A big permit is ready to swim off after its encounter with a happy angler.

and Upper Florida Keys. The only good that came out of this debacle was the 1997 founding of the Bonefish & Tarpon Trust (BTT). It embarked on the critically needed research and development of conservation strategies to restore the bonies.

Decades of research into tarpon and permit have also produced discoveries essential to conservation and angling. Neither species suffered declines comparable to Keys bonefish, but Florida's swelling population, shoreline development, water-quantity mismanagement, and declining water quality raised red flags for both fish. Florida's problems may create regional trouble, as highly migratory tarpon don't confine themselves to the Sunshine State. The late famous tarpon hunter Billy Pate spoke for all anglers when he asked, "Are their tarpon our tarpon?" Does Florida share its tarpon population with other Atlantic and Gulf of Mexico states? Does the United States share its tarpon with Cuba and Mexico? Focused research has begun to answer these questions, revealing that Florida tarpon range widely, visiting states as far north as Maryland and west to Louisiana.

Moreover, all Atlantic tarpon—from west Africa to the US east coast—are linked genetically.

The habits and spawning movements of permit were similarly unknown. Innovative permit acoustic-tagging programs within the Keys have determined that the black tails on the flats are the same fish found in large spring spawning aggregations on offshore reefs and wrecks. Successful permit conservation must encompass these habitats and regulate fishing inshore and offshore.

Understandable focus on the big three species—they are simply spectacular gamefish—should not distract from other outstanding flats fishing opportunities. Plenty of other hard-fighting big fish are available in the shallow waters. Blacktip and spinner sharks are commonly found on Keys flats, especially in Florida Bay and the Gulf of Mexico. These athletic species will run deep into your backing, jumping en route. Hanging a butterfly-filleted bonito or jack carcass over the side brings in the sharks, and when the scent and commotion get them fired up, they will munch big, flashy orange flies.

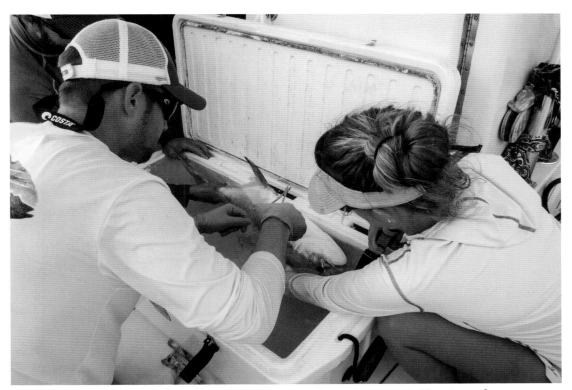

Bonefish & Tarpon Trust's Science Team inserts an acoustic tag in a permit. (Courtesy of Jacqueline Chapman)

Catching a jack crevalle or two is another way to put a big bend in a fly rod. Resembling permit but with a yellow rather than black tail, jacks are utterly tenacious fighters and usually very aggressive eaters. What they lack in cachet is more than made up for by a proclivity to bite and brute strength. And there are more-glamorous species to be caught on the flats: cobia and mutton snappers. These are deeper-water fish that infrequently cruise into the shallows but can be induced to take a well-presented fly. Both are strong and stubborn fighters, and many veteran anglers rank a fly-caught flats mutton snapper higher than permit.

Snook and redfish can also be pursued on the flats. In the case of snook, most but not all of the action is along tangled green mangrove shorelines in Florida and Yucatan Peninsula fisheries. The silver snook sports a sloping head, yellowish fins and tail, and a distinctive single black line down its side; hence the nickname "lineside." A snook fight is short and savage. Keep the charging, jumping lineside out of the mangroves and it can be landed quickly; if

the fish gets to its tangled sanctuary, the game is over. Reds are highly popular along the Gulf of Mexico coast from Florida to Texas and up the Atlantic to North Carolina. Those found in the shallows run smaller, with big bruisers lurking in deeper Gulf waters.

Angler wanderlust and improved travel added lots of other tropical and subtropical locations to our contemporary fishing itineraries. Bahamas out-island fisheries, such as Andros and Bimini, sprung up coincident with the Keys. Big-game fishing for massive bluefin tuna and marlin in the Gulf Stream waters west of Bimini was under way in the '30s. Bonefish were caught to be used as trolling baits, and a few people discovered catching the "bait" could be a lot of fun. Locals realized they could earn a few bucks guiding the visiting sports to the bonefish. At the same time, wealthy American visitors to Andros—there to shoot white-crowned pigeons—found bonefish too, and enterprising Androsians entered the flats guiding business. Eight decades later the Bahamas abound with excellent flats fishing lodges and guides.

Yucatan Peninsula waters of Belize and Mexico joined the ranks in the '70s. The expansive flats of Mexico's Ascension Bay teem with 1- to 5-pound bones but are better known and revered for oodles of permit—perms much more willing than their Florida cousins. Similarly, the tumultuous flats inside Belize's barrier reef are favorites for bones and permit. Tarpon are also found along the Yucatan. Most are "juniors" from 1 to 20 pounds in hidden mangrove bays, although bigger fish can be found, especially in Belize.

Not long thereafter, the Pacific got into the act. Remote Christmas Island became extremely popular for bonefish and giant trevally. Then some sharp-eyed Hawaiian locals realized big bonefish cruised deeper flats, particularly off Oahu and Molokai. Anglers in Hawaii toted stepladders into 3- or 4-foot-deep waters and perched on the top for better visibility and casting angles. By the turn of the century, bonefish guides were available in a unique fishery for what I think are the world's spookiest bones.

More exotic locations get added to anglers' itineraries every year: the Indian Ocean, South Africa, and west Africa, to name a few. Time and money are the only barriers (except for an occasional pirate incident) to boating or wading the flats at places most of us had never heard of just a few years back.

Visiting these locales with a fly rod in the luggage opens the door to extraordinary people and places missed by tourists holed up in a resort or mooing down the ramp of a cruise ship. How else could I have met in Hawaii a 350-pound former LA bodyguard who tucked his dreadlocks into an industrial-size shower cap before heading out for bones? And visitors to some Vegas-style hotel in Nassau never hook up with local guides to learn about Chick-charneys on Andros Island. Absent bonefish I sure wouldn't have known of a great sunset spot on a Bahamas out-island to propose to my future spouse. Even close to home in the Keys, fishing reveals interesting bits of lore. You can stake out for tarpon by small Indian Key, sporting a few 175-year-old ruins, that once was the Dade County seat (now Miami). And when your search for bonefish takes you to the "Dog Dick" Flat, you wonder how did it get that name?

Interaction with fascinating people is a major part of the flats fishing experience. Solo angling is uncommon, as most anglers get on the water with a guide and a good friend to split the costs. Guiding is a unique profession attracting a range of personalities and grade A characters. Any reference to guides requires I tip my hat to my four good friends and Marathon neighbors and outstanding guides:

Anglers board a flats skiff, ready to pursue bonefish, at the Mangrove Cay Club, Andros Island.

Captains Bus Bergmann, Scott Collins, Richard Keating, and Albert Ponzoa. Far more to me than excellent guides, these guys became friends of the first order, always willing to share hard-earned knowledge and explain why a certain spot works, or does not, and how all the variables come into play when selecting where and when to fish on a given day.

Their decades-long graduate course in fishing dynamics, conducted mainly while I stood on the bow of their skiffs, was (and is) utterly invaluable. I can never thank them enough.

Guides are among those whose lives are built around the flats, the fish, and the fishing. That's a more difficult choice for anglers, given the time and costs needed to really learn the

Captain Bus Bergmann looks for laid-up tarpon in the Keys, circa 1998.

Growing populations and affluence have put many more people on the water compared to the "good ol' days." More people mean more interactions, good and bad. Simple numbers, as well as conflicting uses and users, generate controversial resource management issues. Conserving the environment is at the top of the list, but regulations to manage user conflicts create the most political heat. Unfortunately, there is no escaping these matters if we want to maintain quality flats angling as our population of over 330 million people keeps growing. Today's committed flats angler should not simply take from our sport without giving back. It is crucial that an angler care—and act—for the future of the fish and the fishing.

Flats fishing can be serious business, hard, and demanding. The challenges and curiosity create a deep love or passion—spilling into obsession—for the sport. But it is still recreation. No one starves when an angler comes up empty-handed—as is more often than not the case. Sometimes the best advice, especially during a difficult fishless spell, is relax and stop trying too hard.

Humor is necessary to absorb the mishaps and blows to the ego that come with being humiliated by critters with pea-size brains. One day, the combination of hot weather, largely AWOL tarpon, and a beer for lunch had my boatmate sitting on the bow casting platform with a nodding head and an odd snore or two. A pair of unexpected tarpon appeared, and the guide called out, "Two o'clock! Two o'clock!" A sleepy head snapped up and a befuddled angler looked at his watch. The guide and I busted up and so did the snorer. Another day at another venue, my spouse, Jeannette, and I were after bonefish that were very few and far between. Smiles were in short supply. I finally hooked up and brought in a small schoolie. Jeannette handled the unhooking honors, struggled with the hook, and griped, "It's in there hard." I couldn't resist a quip, "That's what she said." Our guide and my spouse damned near died laughing, turning a tough day memorably funny.

Fishing is experienced in three stages: anticipation, execution, and remembrance. Think of a long-awaited trip. Anticipation starts building the day you book the lodge or the guides or plan an outing. A month out, packing lists are written and rewritten. New "must-have"

fisheries. The learning curve in the salt seems much steeper compared to trout. But making the flats a major feature of one's life is possible and rewarding. Becoming a predator (even if it is overwhelmingly a catch-and-release fishery) and tuning in to the world of the fish reaches deep into our souls, creating a satisfying connectedness with things elemental.

gear gets bought. Rods and reels are examined for the umpteenth time. Fly boxes are checked and rechecked and more flies are tied so you won't get caught short (and you end up with enough flies to outfit a regiment). Two weeks from departure, long-range weather forecasts are looked at, even though you know most such predictions are worthless. The intensity ramps up almost by the hour as D-day (departure day) approaches. All goes smoothly and now it's the night before getting on the water. Sleep comes hard like it does for little kids on Christmas Eve.

The actual angling is terribly short: Spotting, casting to, hooking, landing, and releasing a trophy fish is at most a 30- to 60-minute exercise. A whole trip gets measured in two, three, maybe six days.

The memories and reflections, however, are infinite. They get refined, polished, and "pulled out" to be enjoyed over and over again and shared with best friends. Most of us can put a room to sleep with a second-by-second recounting of a memorable (to us) fish—taken 20 years ago! The precious nature of anglers' memories, some not so accurate, prompts many jibes and we laugh along graciously. Deep down, though, it makes me recall an aging friend's observation: At the end you possess three things that matter—family, friends, and memories of grand experiences. Two of those can be provided by a life on the flats.

Nearly 50 years ago, I took my first steps onto the bow of a flats boat. The quarry that day was bonefish in the Keys backcountry, and we succeeded beyond my expectations. An addictive experience, it granted me access to spectacular fish that I came to love, colorful angling history, a fascinating environment, unique people, and wonderful off-the-beaten-track places. Incomparable experiences also built the foundations of apprehension and fear about tomorrow as well as commitments to conserve and restore what we now enjoy. Without flats fishing my life would have been less rich and concern for its future uninformed.

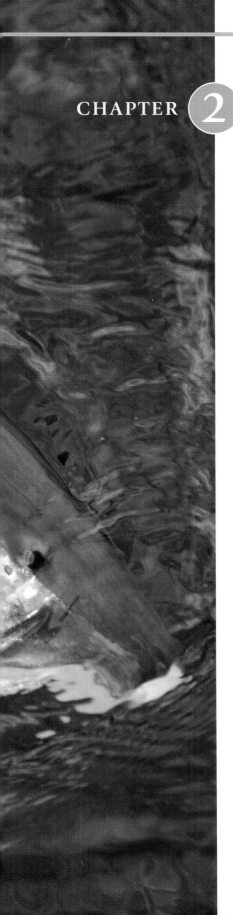

CHAPTER 2

The Fish and Fishing

Traditional saltwater flats angling is special because of the storied fish pursued in subtropical and tropical shallows: bonefish, tarpon, and permit. These are relatively new fisheries with angling techniques evolving rapidly to cope with the twin challenges of declining fish numbers and the prey made warier by fishing pressure and catch-and-release. Mystery has also surrounded these species with next to nothing known about their life cycles, spawning, rearing habitats, and migrations.

Passionate pursuit of the "big three" has generated major technological advances in rods, reels, lines, hooks, and flats boats. It has also led to innovative fly patterns and ways to present the flies to often lockjawed critters. And although this kind of fishing was first confined to the Florida Keys, the three species are now sought in worldwide venues. Lastly, angler sponsored research has finally begun to answer many scientific questions about the species. These fascinating fish (at least to flats fishers) are explored in this chapter.

Bonefish

Why bonefish? It's an unprepossessing creature: modest size, head a little too big, very subtle coloration at best, and that underslung mouth. The uninitiated look and ask, "Is that some kind of sucker?" It swam largely unmolested by humans for thousands of years. Trout and salmon were pursued by anglers in the Roman Empire and gave birth to English angling literature beginning in the 15th century. In contrast, there was no fly-caught bonefish until the 1920s, and that was by mistake. But on closer examination, it piqued curiosity. Here was a fish scurrying around transparent shallows, waving its forked silver tail above the waters, and exploding to race off when spooked. When hooked it became a formidable opponent, testing light tackle to the max. The fish also happened to occupy warm tropical waters when early sports were escaping the cold and snow of Boston or New York, and Henry Flagler's recently completed Railroad That Went to Sea (in reality, Key West) could take you there directly.

About 8 pounds of Middle Keys bonefish poses before release.

Chasing bones is quite different from taking on permit or poons. Bonefish are usually numerous enough to provide multiple shots, the fish eagerly take flies, and battling a 5-pound fish is enjoyable but not fraught with anxiety (permit) or a sweaty, arm-cramping grudge match (tarpon). Bones can inspire whimsy—a word never associated with the other two fish. In fact, poems are written about bonies; mostly unprintable comments get made about permit or lockjawed tarpon. Bill Levy was a dedicated bonefisher who plied Keys waters for many years before he passed. A very competent guy on the bow, he maintained a "joie de vivre" about the gray ghost, penning a great little poem (courtesy of Captain Bus):

> What a wonderful fish is the bone
> The gray ghost of the flats he is known.
> You are out on a flat
> And off he scats,
> And you're standing alone
> And he is gone.

Decades later it is still the perfect saltwater fish for the fly rod. One of my angling journal entries encapsulates the complete experience:

FEB. 22, ANDROS ISLAND, MOSTLY SUNNY, 80, WIND 15+ E. After lunch Capt. Leslie [Greene] had us hunting big boys on a luminous green flat between two deep blue channels. He poled SW with the stiff breeze whistling in on our left. When the boat pivoted 90 degrees and Leslie started pushing intently, I knew he had seen something. Sure enough 150 feet out a sizeable greenish shadow ghosted our way over the pale marl bottom. The distance closed but the fish turned away; Leslie tracked it keeping 100 feet back, figuring it would eventually turn right for the channel. And it did. He got us to 90 feet; I let the fish move ahead a bit then delivered a 70-foot throw, putting the fly 10 feet ahead of the bone. Let the fly settle and when the fish was four feet away the good Capt. instructed "long smooth strip." I did, the fish charged ahead, tipped and curled, I stripped long, and the line snapped tight. The big fish screamed off to the NE and kept going and going. A bona fide 175 yards of chartreuse backing melted off the 3N

and we were within seconds of giving chase with the motor. The longest bonefish run I've ever seen. Mr. Bone was incredibly stubborn and stayed away, shaking its head and taking whatever backing I recovered. Leslie muttered "That fish is on steroids." Unsaid was that this might be a giant bone. Patience prevailed and a long 15 minutes later we had it in hand—27" to the fork and 14" girth—probably a nine-pounder. An absolutely classic bonefish. ●

Albula vulpes (white fox) is the scientific name. It is part of a family of "bony fishes" that have been on the planet for approximately 100 million years. Our bonefish's ancestors evolved in the Jurassic period; modern bonies arose in the Miocene epoch roughly 15 million years before humans appeared. Scientists describe bones as exhibiting an inferior mouth (i.e., underslung) and a conical nose. The body is torpedo shaped, and coloration is usually described as a blue greenish back with bright silver scales on the sides as well as darker cross-bars on the back. Behavior and feeding habits are most important (at least to anglers), and the scientists note bonefish forage primarily on the flats, entering shallow water on rising tides and feeding on benthic and epibenthic prey, often in water less than 12 inches deep. The prey includes crustaceans, mollusks, polychaete worms, and fishes, primarily the gulf toadfish. Toadfish are more often found in the stomachs of bigger Keys bones, while Bahamas fish appear to prefer bivalves.

Creative anglers concoct all varieties of flies to imitate "benthic and epibenthic prey" and convince the fish it has found something worth eating. Because prey differ in locations as disparate as the Bahamas, Belize, and the Indian Ocean, patterns are as varied as the things bonefish will eat. Some flies have interesting names and histories: the Nasty (now Crazy) Charlie, Clouser Minnow, Gotcha, or the Frankee Belle. Once invented, the patterns get tweaked endlessly, adding a new bit of color (Gotchas now come in at least pink, red, and orange versions) or larger eyes, or scaled up or down in size.

Recent studies, many sponsored by the Bonefish & Tarpon Trust (BTT), found that there are at least 12 species of the genus Albula scattered around the globe. *A. vulpes* supports

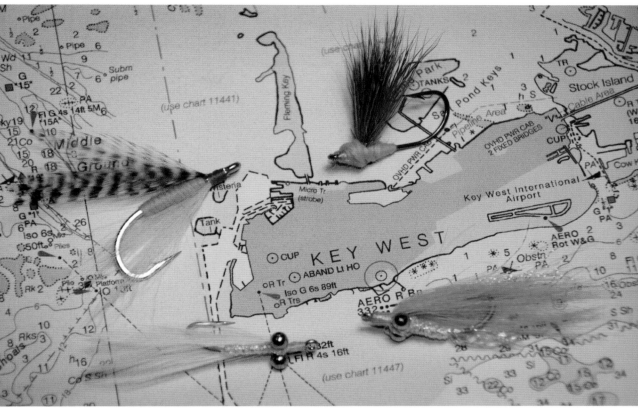

These are classic bonefish flies developed in the early years of the sport: Frankee Belle, Horror, Gotcha, and Nasty Charlie (clockwise from top left).

the various Atlantic and Caribbean fisheries, although fish caught in deeper water or a bit to the north are likely *A. goreensis*. The Pacific and Indian Oceans include another seven species. *A. glossondonta*, called the roundjaw bonefish, appears to support the fisheries in Hawaii as well as the Seychelles. All these species look very much alike, and laboratory work is needed to identify which fish is which.

When Keys bonefishing began to suffer 20 years ago, anglers wanted to know why and what might be done to turn things around. It was quickly realized that very little was known about these prized fish. The bonefish life cycle was a complete mystery, with no one knowing when and where they spawned, how they spawned, and where little bonefish go to grow up. Ancillary questions focused on whether the various populations of bonefish in the Bahamas, Florida, Cuba, and the Yucatan were connected or related. Early, BTT-sponsored surveys looked in the Keys for young bonefish as well as groups of spawning adults and came

up empty on both counts. Limited bonefish tagging also produced perplexing results. Most tags showed that bonies were homebodies, generally using a small set of flats. Nearly 90 percent of tagged fish were recaptured within 12 miles of where they were tagged; over 50 percent were recaptured within 2 miles of the tagging site. However, a few fish were detected far from home. A couple of Biscayne Bay (Miami) and Key Largo bonefish were found near Key West, 100 miles to the south and west. None of it made sense.

The scientists scratched their heads and figured they should look instead in the Bahamas, where there were robust bonefish populations. That commenced years of investigation that paid off in 2011 when the first confirmed aggregation of spawners was found off Abaco Island. Turns out bonefish will travel quite a way to take part in their nuptials. A few days before a full moon from November through April, bonefish will school up and swim along shorelines toward a special meeting spot a

A typical Keys oceanside bone shows off its colors: silver, olive, and aquamarine.

little way offshore in maybe 20 feet of water. Thousands of fish may join in this aggregation, and some fish will travel 100 miles to reach the magic spot. On a full moon night, the fish will swim out beyond the reef into hundreds of feet of water. There the fish, especially the females, swim down to as far as approximately 400 feet. Going deep may use water pressure to squeeze the eggs toward release, but newer research indicates the fish could be seeking denser, more saline water that keeps the fertilized eggs from sinking into the deep. After a period of down-and-up dives, the fish ball up between 100 and 200 feet, the females expel their eggs, and males release clouds of milt. Sperm cells in the milt find an egg, and the life of a new bonefish begins.

Adult bonefish return home to the flats, and within 25 to 28 hours the fertilized egg hatches into a tiny, translucent, strange-looking eel-like creature called a leptocephalus. Large (for a tiny larva) ferocious-looking teeth and a big mouth enable it to capture "marine

snow"—nutritious plankton-like material that feeds marine microorganisms. The little "eels" can barely swim and are at the mercy of ocean currents. They remain in this odd form for the next 41 to 71 days before they change into tiny, 1-inch-long bonefish.

The little bones head for protected, sandy flats and shorelines, where they mix in with schools of mojarra (called shad in the Bahamas) for protection from predators. A year later, the little bones are about 8 to 10 inches long and school up with other bones, taking refuge back in tidal creeks and other protected environments. When the bonies reach 2 to 3 years old, they are in the 16- to 18-inch class and weigh 2 or more pounds—ready to bend a fly rod.

The leptocephalus stage and its weak swimming ability are important. During this approximately two-month period, the larvae can be carried far and wide by the currents. This is common among many marine species of fish and crustaceans. For example, Florida harvests about six million spiny lobsters each year, although few if any are spawned in the state. Lobster larvae drift in the currents for up to six months, and the Keys are supplied with larvae each year from as far away as the waters off Nicaragua and Honduras. The currents that form the Gulf Stream begin there and carry the larvae north and east to Florida. I speculated in a 2015 article that the Keys might receive bonefish in the same manner, but this got pooh-poohed then by some fishery scientists. Shortly thereafter, updated current modeling provided evidence that bonefish larvae from Belize, Cuba, and Mexico could end up in the Keys. Similarly, currents could create an interchange of larvae between the Bahamas and Cuba and among the Bahamas' many islands. An extensive BTT-sponsored bonefish DNA study (over 11,000 bonefish fin clips were analyzed), completed in 2018, confirmed the current model results and demonstrated connectivity among these bonefish populations. The study also revealed that approximately 40 percent of Keys bonefish are spawned off Belize, Cuba, and Mexico.

With these results in hand, it was time to look again at the Keys. The presence of those Biscayne and Key Largo bones by Key West now made sense: They were likely on a spawning run to some unknown site in the Lower Keys. Years ago, large schools of big bonefish would cruise south along the Atlantic shoreline of Key Largo, mostly in February and March. With hindsight, we now realize those were likely bones on a spawning run. Unfortunately, despite intense searching, no positively identified spawning aggregation sites have yet to be found in the Keys (although a few potential spots have been located). However, multiple aggregation and spawning sites have been discovered in the Bahamas and Yucatan, and efforts are under way to protect these critical locations.

Current models also pointed to the Lower Keys as a place for Florida bonefish to spawn. Bonefish larvae hatching there would float into the waters near Key West. In contrast, bonefish spawning in deep waters off Key Largo would produce larvae carried away north by the powerful Gulf Stream. The Keys were also searched for larvae and tiny bones, with mostly disappointing results. Only a couple of leptocephali showed up, some tiny bones were species *A. goreensis*, which does not support the fishery, and a few other baby *A. Vulpes* were found in an odd corner of Florida Bay.

Anglers knew from the collapse of the Keys bonefishery that something was very wrong. But anecdotal information and stories don't cut it with state and federal agencies when it comes to taking action. The decline needed to be documented with hard data that could withstand scientific scrutiny. So, BTT and its partners at Florida International University went to work to document and verify what anglers and guides already knew. Sure enough, this multiyear effort confirmed empirically that the Keys bonefish decline began in 1985–1990, accelerated after the turn of the century, and nosedived following the 2010 record cold snap. Catch rates declined nearly 50 percent, with a more acute fall-off occurring in Florida Bay (and places like Nine Mile Bank).

Other studies were commissioned to find the culprits behind the decline. In 2018 the threads of these studies came together to weave a tapestry showing what happened to Keys bones. Water-quality problems were prominent. Everglades water mismanagement had first reared its ugly head in the late '80s by crippling Florida Bay, and it was no coincidence that this started Keys bonefish on their downward spiral. Another Bay water-quality crisis arose in 2015, caused by the very same mismanagement issues from the '80s, killing thousands of acres of vital sea-grass beds and fouling thousands of acres of water with stinking clots of pea-green algae. Recent surveys indicate that the Bay's three primary species of sea grass have declined 28 percent, 88 percent, and 92 percent over the last 35 years courtesy of the water-quality mess. Until the Everglades are in fact restored with better clean-water flows—as authorized by federal and state law in 1988 and 2000—the chances of a bonefish rebound in Florida Bay are slim.

Polluted waters still plague the Bay as well as the Upper and Middle Keys. Following Hurricane Irma in September 2017, fouled Bay water could be seen (and sometimes smelled) flowing through the Long Key, Tom's Harbor, and Seven Mile bridges. Bonefish were forced out of much of the Bay beginning in the late '80s and have not returned in historical numbers.

BTT's bonefish DNA study (from bonefish fin samples) and ocean current modeling revealed that bonefish spawned in places like the Yucatan (the aqua square), and the dark blue depicts areas where the drifting larvae can be carried by the currents. X. Zeng, A. J. Adams, M. Roffer, and R. He. "Potential Connectivity among Spatially Distinct Management Zones for Bonefish (*Albula vulpes*) via Larval Dispersal."*Environmental Biology of Fishes* 102, no. 2 (2019): 233–52.

And since the Bay fish traditionally migrated to warmer oceanside waters off Key Largo and Islamorada in the cooler months, few fish in the Bay means few Atlantic bones in the Upper Keys.

Hypersalinity remains a problem too. Studies show that tiny young bonefish rely on estuarine low-salinity environments. The extensive creek systems and freshwater flows in places like Andros Island may be one factor in sustaining its outstanding populations of bonies. Of course, young Florida bones encountering extra-salty water in Florida Bay (because there's not enough clean fresh water flowing through the Everglades) may face death without ever becoming part of the adult population sought by anglers.

Unusual cold weather in January 2010 was another culprit. A record cold snap of unprecedented length caused water temperatures in and around the Keys to plunge into the 40s. Consequences were devastating, with untold thousands of subtropical fish killed by the chilled waters. Permit that survived sported red, bleeding tails—some kind of disease rot caused by the cold. Fish with injured tails don't survive long among the sharks and barracudas. Bonefish carcasses floated ashore along the Middle and Upper Keys, and dead tarpon littered the margins of the Everglades. Snook took a terrible hit, causing Florida to close snook fishing for the following two years. Fortunately, the fisheries proved resilient, with all of them bouncing back in the following eight years. The bonefish recovery, however, trails the other species.

Contaminants in south Florida waters are yet another source of worry. Copper sulfate is used extensively to control water weeds in the state's canal systems as well as on agriculture lands, golf courses, and lawns. Copper residues can be deadly to many fish species, and the presence of such residues in Biscayne and Florida Bays may be a looming problem. Similarly, untold quantities of prescription drugs are flushed down toilets throughout south Florida, and these chemicals are not treated in sewage plants. The result is growing drug residues in the state's waters. Drugs—especially birth control pills—are causing serious fish deformities in many locations across the United States. No one knows yet if the drugs will cause comparable problems in bonefish and other flats species, but the presence of a retrovirus in Keys bonefish has set off an alarm. This retrovirus has not been found in bonefish in the Bahamas or Cuba.

Despite this depressing news, Keys bonefish populations from Islamorada (in the Upper Keys) to Key West (Lower Keys) have been staging a comeback in the last few years. Most of the returnees are now 4 pounders approximately 2 to 4 years old; 20 years ago, the average Keys bone weighed in at around 5 or 6 pounds (5 to 7 years old). There are now enough of the small guys, and a few bigger ones, to once again target bones with good odds of success, as revealed by another angling journal excerpt (as I have decades of entries, expect to see more from the journals):

NOV. 22, CONTENT KEYS, CLEAR, 80, WIND ENE 10. Capt. Scott [Collins] and I had enough Hurricane Irma (2017) recovery chores behind us (Scott and his family lost their house) to finally sneak off and see how the fish survived the Cat 4 storm. They did great but the backcountry islands did not—shattered, uprooted black and red mangroves were stripped bare. After exercising a bunch of 10-pound tarpon, we hit the Gulf edge on an incoming tide. During the next two hours, and two passes down a big flat, we encountered about 60 bonefish and a dozen grumpy permit. We took turns poling and fishing and got half a dozen bones all about three pounds; I blew a shot at a trio twice that size. This was the best sight fishing for bones in quite some time. ●

No one is sure where these smaller fish are coming from, but some speculate that diminished inshore gillnetting in Belize, Cuba, and Mexico has allowed more bones there to survive, spawn, and send some of their larvae to Florida. Whatever the source(s), it's a start toward broader restoration of the Keys' historic bonefishing. The hope is that serious progress on Everglades restoration, better water quality in Florida Bay and around the Keys, and continuing efforts to control bonefish netting in Belize, Cuba, and Mexico will let the bones rebound. Netting control remains a major issue, demonstrated by recent research indicating approximately 20 tons of bonefish are being netted annually from one port on Cuba's north shore.

No discussion of bonefish research and conservation is complete without a tip of the hat to the founders of BTT. Two committed Key Largo bonefish anglers noticed the steady decline in bonefish numbers in the Upper Keys and quickly found that no one knew why or what could be done to reverse the slide. Instead of simply lamenting this sorry state of affairs, Tom Davidson and Russ Fisher went to work corralling fellow flats adherents and establishing in 1997 Bonefish & Tarpon Unlimited. The plan was to conduct the needed groundbreaking research to answer the oh-so-many questions surrounding bonefish and tarpon (and later permit). They passed the hat and made incredibly generous personal donations to get the fledgling entity up and running with a goal all of us can subscribe to—restoration of the Keys bonefishery (and conservation of the flats fisheries in places like the Bahamas, Belize, Cuba, and Mexico). Twenty years later Tom and Russ handed off their leadership batons as chairman and vice chairman of the re-designated BTT, having grown it into the respected organization it is today. These two guys earned the enduring gratitude of flats anglers everywhere.

A full-scale return of Keys bonies would be a welcome event, bringing back genuine good old days from over 20 years ago:

APRIL 29, SUGARLOAF, SUN AND CLOUDS, 80, WIND ESE 10. Capt. Bus [Bergmann] had us looking for tarpon in the Lower Keys, and the big fish were stubbornly absent. Bus looked at his watch, pulled out his tide book, stared toward a nearby key, and asked, "Want to try for some bonefish?" I was game for anything and asked about our chances. He pointed with the boat pole and offered the coral bar protruding from the east side of "Blue Roof Key" could be good on this tide. A big house with a very bright blue tin roof occupied the small island. As he poled toward the bar, I stowed the tarpon rig and grabbed a 9-weight with a strange bright orange Clouser on the leader. My apprehension must have been evident, prompting Bus to explain, "That's the Navel" (as in navel orange), adding it was an experimental fly that worked well at Key Largo. I said "OK" without conviction. Started down the south edge of the bar looking hard in the morning light for signs of fish. It didn't take long before I heard "10 o'clock, 60 feet, sliding right." Stared hard, catching a glimpse of gray/green moving to 12, got the rod in motion, and put the fly 10 feet ahead of the bone. Let the fly sit for a moment and then gave it a hop, hop. Mr. Bone accelerated ahead, stopped on the fly, Bus commanded "strip," I complied, and the hook went home. The fish wanted none of this and burned off, taking

Jeannette and Captain Bus get ready to release a small Florida bone, part of the post-2010 recovering population.

line at a frightening rate. Out there a genuine 150 yards, the fish stopped and started shaking its head, making the rod buck. Bus and I looked at each other and said together, "A good one." Played it carefully through the subsequent runs and let the rod absorb a series of head shakes before Bus got it in the net. The scale read 10.2 pounds—my first [and only] 10-pound Keys bonefish. We followed this trophy by sticking another four or five— the bar was crawling with bonies until the current slacked. ●

Fly fishing for bonefish, particularly in the Keys, breaks down into roughly four types: regulars, mudders, tailers, and chummers. The "regular" bonies are hunted on 1- to 3-foot-deep flats covered with luminous trans-parent waters over mostly dark green turtle grass in the Keys, pale marl in the Bahamas, or mixed in the Yucatan, where the fish cruise about in search of a meal.

Smaller fish travel in packs or schools of up to 20 fish; the big double-digit trophies are mostly by themselves, but a two- or three-pack

A hefty Keys bonefish is revived. Note the torpedo shape and the barred, camouflage back.

is not uncommon. When the fish are 30 to 80 feet from the boat (or the wading angler) the fly is delivered a bit ahead of the fish. The precise distance is a function of the depth, the speed of the fish, and the bones' sensitivity to a plopping fly. On good days, the sound brings them charging in; on others, the sound sends them fleeing for their lives. Standard weighted flies, typically with bead-chain eyes in shallower waters found in the Bahamas or Mexico, or small lead eyes for slightly deeper Keys flats, are the ticket.

Chasing mudders is a form of angling voodoo. Clouds and wind turn clear waters an opaque gray, pushing bones into deeper waters, say 3 to 5 feet; at those depths and curtailed visibility, the fish are damn near invisible. Fortunately, their feeding behavior gives them away. Digging in the bottom for prey, the bones kick up saucer-sized puffs of smoky mud that a trained eye can detect. Throw at the puffs and an unseen hungry fish will often jump on the fly. The best situation is to spot one puff, then another, guess where the next will appear, and drop your fly there. Heavier flies are needed to get down quickly, so patterns with bigger lead eyes get affixed to the leader. These tactics work:

MARCH 11, CLOUDS AND SUN, 75, WIND ESE 15–20. Relocated to the east side of a Gulf-side mangrove cay torn up by Hurricane Charley. A sailboat was way up in the groves and the tilted mast will be a landmark for a while. Tide was rising and saw some bones, but we were fighting clouds and got no shots. Then a pair of mud puffs blossomed 50 feet out at 2 o'clock. Looked hard for the next, got it also catching a glimpse of a couple of gray/green shadows. Delivered a low sidearm cast under the wind, dropping the lead-eyed Brown/White Clouser on our side of the last puff. Started hopping the fly and on the third felt resistance, stripped hard, and hooked up. A classic bonie fight followed and got the good fish—about eight pounds—in the net. ●

Flats come in a variety of forms: sand/grass combinations in the Florida Keys (above) or bright sand in the Bahamas (below).

"Tailers" are the acme of bonefishing. The fish are highly visible in the shallowest of waters. They're on high alert, ready to bolt from a small splash, an errant shadow, or sprinkles of water from a fly line.

The olive back with faint bars sticks up, as do the dorsal and upper lobe of the silver tail; creeping and crawling defines the motion better than swimming. Seeing or scenting prey, a bone will dash ahead furrowing the water, pounce on the hapless shrimp or crab, and the tail waves up as the nose pokes down. If you can show it the fly, without scaring it off, the fish wants to eat. Breathing is hard, anxiety constricts your throat, and the game is at its absolute best:

NOV. 12, ANDROS SOUTH BIGHT, CLEARING CLOUDS, 75, WIND NW 5–10. We worried that conditions would be poor on the backside of a weak cold front, but we dodged that bullet. Consulted with Capt. John and off to the South Bight we went. Got on a lee shoreline edged with high black mangroves against which visibility was good. The flat was a great mix of hard bottom, golden coral outcrops, and little embayments with white sandy bottoms. At low ebb tide, we found plenty of bones crawling in the skinny shallows with exposed dorsals, backs, and tails. Classic stuff. Lengthened the leader to 14–15 feet and tied on a #4 plastic-eyed Red Headed Gotcha [RHG] with some extra silly legs. We picked up a pair of three- to four-pound green-backed, aqua-finned beauties and then a pair of very memorable fish—one good and one not so good. The good one tailed 150 feet ahead, then ghosted across a tongue of sand to tail again at 90 feet. It meandered our way with fins up in six inches of water. John stopped the skiff, and I made a backcast to 10 o'clock, landing the fly eight feet ahead. When the fish closed on the fly, I made one smooth strip, the bone darted, sucked up the fly, and I got tight. Mr. Bone exploded, racing along the shoreline trailing chartreuse backing. It turned for the mangroves and a break-off was imminent. I released the pressure, John poled hard to get closer and angle out. The fish slowed, stopped short of the roots, then I muscled it away from disaster. The tactics worked and John grabbed

a wonderful six-pound "ocean"-colored dark green bone. Then came the bad juju. John located a much bigger tailer moving in and out of flooded red mangrove roots. I made a pretty good throw, but the bone wandered back into the roots and never saw the fly. Then it turned back out, we guessed its heading, put the fly 10 feet ahead in a little sand spot and waited. The bone got about three feet away from the fly, I twitched it. The fish surged ahead, with flared dorsal and nailed the fly. Hook up! A good eight-plus trophy rocketed down the shoreline with line and backing snapping out the guides. Way out it stopped, shook its head, and the line fell slack. Damn! Despondent I pitched the rod and reel overboard. ●

In contrast, chumming is a dark art—at least according to the purists. I did my turn as a purist, checked that box, and decided catching fish was more fun. When the weather turns bad in the Keys and visibility goes to hell, pitching broken-up shrimp into a sand hole, and waiting for the "chummer" bones to come, is the only real option:

AUGUST 31, BIG PINE BACKCOUNTRY, HEAVY CLOUDS, SQUALL LINES, WIND ESE 20+. Tropical storm conditions in late afternoon. Capt. Albert [Ponzoa] and I are crazy. Despite an approaching TS we decided the morning was just fishable and went for it. Ended up on a good sand patch where the current was running strongly S. Staked out and tossed the broken shrimp bits down current. And the bones showed quickly. I missed the first then we got six in a row—three apiece. Albert picked up the best, pushing seven lbs. We released fish #6 and saw a low black ragged squall line bearing down on us. Jumped into our rain gear and ran like hell for the ramp. ●

Solo anglers also resort to anchoring and chumming, as poling and fly fishing for bonefish—simultaneously—is damn near impossible. And, like any form of angling, there are some real tricks to successful chumming. Good current and the ability to anchor/stake out about 35 feet upcurrent of a sand spot are the basic requirements. Break up a dozen shrimp (fresher is better), and use your best fastball

Bonefish have a hard time hiding in skinny water.

Comical trunkfish, which fight surprisingly hard, are frequently mistaken for bones.

delivery to get the shrimp into the hole and wait. Often enough bones will appear before you pull the fly rod from under the gunwales. If, however, the fish are a no-show after 20 minutes, move elsewhere.

Current and shrimp are powerful attractors to lots of other finned creatures. In fact, a big part of the fun is all the other stuff that will show up: stingrays, bonnethead sharks, jacks, trunkfish, and even the odd permit. The strange-looking, boxy, aqua trunkfish can be a hoot on a fly rod. Tiny rubber lips over beaky teeth make them hard to hook on flies. When a hook does stick and stays in, the fish are surprisingly strong, and bigger ones will get into the backing. How they generate power with their funny little tail is beyond me, but a gang of trunkfish can be entertaining.

Bonnethead sharks are little cousins of the great hammerhead. Bonnies, 2 to 4 feet long, are everywhere on Keys flats. They will take flies, but cutoffs are quick unless you get lucky and the fly lodges in the corner of the mouth. Hook a good one and the backing will make an appearance. Better odds come with small bait-tipped jigs on a wire trace. There is

no better way to introduce kids to flats fishing than chummed-up trunkfish and bonnethead sharks.

Successful anglers must also practice good catch-and-release techniques. BTT studies done in recent years revealed that bonefish handled with dry hands or taken out of the water for more than 30 seconds fared poorly after release. All those fish from years ago that we pulled aboard the boat, manhandled during unhooking, held proudly for the traditional hero shot, and seemingly swam away none the worse for wear likely succumbed, many to barracudas and sharks. However, fish left in the water and handled minimally almost always survive post-release. Hence, the modern hero shot should have the angler gently keep the fish in the water, the camera readied, the cradled fish lifted for a couple of seconds, the picture snapped, and the fish returned immediately to its environment. Fish not worthy of the hero pic can simply be unhooked in the water using wet hands or any number of dehooking tools. Some of the older photos in this book predated this knowledge, while others depict proper unhooking/release techniques.

Keeping a bonefish in the water and not touching it while the hook is removed is a quality release.

Don't "trout set" a bonefish: Strip-striking requires you to keep the rod tip down.

Weather and bonefish are a source of endless conversation. Keys fish can usually be found in all kinds of weather except the extremes. A cold winter day drives them off the flats, and broiling under an August afternoon sun does the same. Scientists tell us the optimal temperature range is 70 to 85 degrees F. This explains why early morning trips are necessary in high summer and a late afternoon outing works better during the cool months. Bonefish are very tolerant of wind or the lack thereof. Wind in Florida affects fishing but apparently not so much the fish. Bones are available—if the temperatures (and tides) are right—whether it's slick calm or blowing 25 mph. Getting a fly near them at either end of the spectrum is the challenge—the cast can't be too long when dead calm settles in, and making a cast at 25 is an exercise in survival. It's a different story in the Bahamas, at least on Andros, but more on that later.

A well-presented fly, in any of these scenarios, is only part of the equation. Recognizing precisely when a bonefish eats the fly is a valuable skill. Bonefish almost always stop on a fly to suck it in, explaining why the typical guide instructions are "strip, strip, stop . . . long strip." The strips catch the fish's attention, the stop prompts the take, and the long strip sets the hook. Bonefish signal a take with other tells. A flared dorsal is a giveaway, especially with very shallow tailers. Another is the curl or scrunch. As a bone goes down to take a fly, it will curl a little. Careful observation will reveal a kind of scrunch with the shoulders/back curving a tad. It must have something to do with punching prey, or a fly, into the bottom and is very distinctive. Learning to see these signs is key to do-it-yourself (DIY) bonefishing and, when fishing with a guide, makes you less dependent on instructions and more reliant on what you see.

Keys bonefish can be difficult, especially the hard-pressed ones in the Upper Keys. But in my experience, Hawaii's bones have been the toughest to fool. It may be the deeper water, or fishing pressure, or the Pacific species. My theory is that generations of Polynesians throwing cast nets bred a species of bones hypersensitive to anything above the water. I fished there twice—once on Oahu and later on Molokai—and recall my guide insisting that I cast sidearm to keep the fly line low and out of sight. When conditions forced a traditional higher cast, the targeted fish spooked hard.

Bonefishing in Hawaii offered up lots of unique features. Flats geology was far different from Atlantic/Caribbean destinations. Oahu's north shore had a big, mostly waist-deep "flat" out in the middle of large bay. A bumpy boat ride—in the teeth of the northeast trade wind—got you there and woe if the boat drifted away. The pancake-like flat was surrounded by hard, jagged corals, and sandy runways or ramps led from deep water up onto the flat. Bonefish came and went via these sand strips. I wondered out loud about keeping hooked fish from the sharp rocks and was directed to modify my leader using 20-pound-test hard Mason for the tippet—the tough stuff we use for tarpon leaders in Florida. I thought it was overkill—it was not. The first bonefish ate an orange pattern, supposed to imitate some kind of mantis shrimp (the Navel would have worked here), and it was a struggle to keep it off the coral. That 5-pounder surprised me. Then we spotted a much bigger fish cruising up on the sand strips. Got it to eat, muscled it away from the coral on the first run, but it was very determined when it took off a second time. I held as hard as I could, and the 20-pound tippet let go. Strong fish.

Our Oahu guide, Ollie Owens, was a trip. We had emailed and phoned each other before our Oahu outing and agreed to meet in a parking lot north of Honolulu. A nondescript van pulled in, and a very large black guy stepped out. About 6 feet, 5 inches and 350 pounds, thick dreadlocks cascaded down his back—not exactly my image of a Hawaiian bonefish guide. A booming basso profundo voice asked, "You're Bill and Jeannette?" We nodded yes and a giant paw engulfed my hand. He introduced us to his sidekick "Maholo Bob" and off we went. Getting into a rickety boat on Kaneohe Bay, Ollie stuffed his dreads into an enormous shower cap. Stu Apte and the lean military, khaki look it was not.

A year later we were back, this time on Molokai. Ollie was waiting for us at the airport, where he squeezed into our rental car and headed for the condo we rented. He insisted 20-pounders could be found there (a world record 18-pounder was caught on Molokai in 1948). Unfortunately, our timing was bad and the weather and tides were marginal. We waded a big, deep flat that extended from the southeast tip of the island. The flat ended abruptly, dropping precipitously into deep blue waters. On the other side, the islands of Lanai and Maui reared up from the Pacific depths. Humpback whales were present, and looking at breaching, rolling, and tailing whales—while wading for bones—was a once-in-a-lifetime experience. Part of me would love to return, but we found Molokai to be a chilly place. Tourists were not welcome, and it seemed most visitors disappeared behind big gates fronting guarded resorts or condos.

Mexico is a different experience. Cancun is a giant tourist trap, and the airport is a mob scene of pasty northern tourists arriving for a week of sun, poolside margaritas, and blackjack tables at the monstrous beach hotels. The odd fly fisher sneaks away, dodges the condo hawkers at the rent-a-car counters, and heads south for the end of the road—Punta Allen. The big highway ends near Tulum and its beautiful oceanfront Mayan ruins. A narrow road winds farther south where pavement disappears, and the last 20 miles is a bumpy, sandy affair with gorgeous views of blue water, empty white beaches, and swaying palm trees.

It ends in little Punta Allen, perched on the north edge of Ascension Bay. Four or five small fishing lodges dot the town; fishing pangas line the beach. Most of the power goes off at 10 p.m., but wandering the town's sandy streets and its collection of funky open-air bars and restaurants beats the hell out of Cancun's hermetically sealed, air-conditioned imitations of Las Vegas.

Bonefishing can be genuinely easy in Ascension Bay. Small bays and coves can be loaded with 1- and 2-pound bones eager to take your fly. The first one I waded into showed dozens of waving, glittering tails and waking schools of fish. It was simple to wade to an intercept position, make a 35- to 40-foot cast, twitch the fly, and hook up. Most of the fish lacked the

Punta Allen, a small Mexican beach town, where fishing pangas are launched from the shore, sits on bonefish-and-permit-filled Ascension Bay at the end of the long sandy road.

A pod of Atlantic bottlenose dolphins swim the North Bight, Andros Island.

size to get into the backing, but they were still hard-fighting bones—just little ones. Working more-open waters for slightly bigger fish was a shock to an angler schooled in the Keys and the Bahamas, where the angler takes the bow solo and the single guide handles the boat from the stern. Leaving Punta Allen's beach, four of us got into the 20-foot-long panga: two anglers and two guides.

The fishing angler stood in the bow—with a guide at his or her side—while the other guide poled. Silence is the order of the day per the guides—a rather unique rule compared to other locations where running banter is part of the charm. If a typical Mexican school of small bonefish showed up, the guides let you cast from the boat. If a bigger bone or two or a permit appeared, the panga was stopped a hundred feet away and the angler and guide hopped out to wade after the fish. I found it a bit disconcerting, but the Yucatan guides swear the bigger bones and permit demand the extra level of stealth.

Wherever bonefish are pursued, the species has been shaped by its shallow clear-water environment and the predators found there.

A bonefish's speed is a function of avoiding its dominant predators: barracudas and sharks. Just as speedy antelopes gave rise to speedier cheetahs, bones no doubt contributed to the evolution of cudas. A healthy bone can almost always outrun a shark, but the sharks are relentless because enough bonefish will make a mistake and become a meal. Sharks in the Bahamas have demonstrated some smarts by shadowing skiffs, waiting to take a shot at a hooked or released bonefish. In fact, you rarely find bones on flats lacking either of the two predators.

Dolphins also savor bonefish. A fall day in 2003 is exhibit A. We were far back into Andros Island's North Bight, finding good numbers of bonefish along a scrubby mangrove shoreline. Schools were going by us into a sickle-shaped cove when a pod of five dolphins appeared outside, rolling and blowing. The five seemed to assess the situation, with a couple of them racing for the shallow shoreline and scattering bones like baitfish. With intelligence gathered, the dolphins made a plan. Three patrolled the cove's water perimeter herding the bones in the cove, while two raced in to grab a few panicked fish. The two then swam out and took the perimeter, and two others raced in to eat. They rotated their positions and roles for an unbelievable half hour before the bones were too scattered. The well-fed dolphins then swam off placidly. An utterly awe-inspiring event.

Tuning in to species interaction is an important attribute of successful flats angling. Palolo worm hatches trigger tarpon feeding frenzies. Floating molting crabs prompt permit to cruise the surface, looking to slurp in a tasty meal. Big sharks often have a retinue of jacks or cobia in tow. Bonefish are no different and have an affinity for stingrays. The rays flap along the bottom, stirring things up and dislodging all manners of crabs and crustaceans from their hidey holes. Bonefish know this and will frequently be found in the vicinity of rays, particularly those that are "mudding." A ray will wriggle its way into the bottom, trying to suck up a crab or small lobster, and pulsing wings kick up mud that forms long gray streaks on flats. Coming onto a flat streaked with ray muds means the flat is "alive" and likely to have feeding bones—or permit.

Interestingly, bones rarely show interest in eagle rays—a very common species in the Keys. These rays—in their spotted or solid color phases—are not bottom-oriented like stingrays. Instead the 4- to 6-foot-wide eagle rays glide along in stately fashion, usually in deeper waters adjacent to flats. One day broke all these rules:

MAY 3, MIDDLE KEYS, MOSTLY CLEAR, 80–85, WIND ESE 5–10. Tarpon had disappeared on the tide change and we had a couple of hours to kill before we resumed looking for the big fish. Capt. Albert suggested checking a nearby flat for bones and permit before we had to run west. Mac and I concurred. Light was great and as we poled onto the flat we encountered an eagle ray convention. The rays were banking and gliding in the current. More importantly a closer

A spotted eagle ray, about 4 feet across, cruises under the skiff.

look showed coke bottle green forms over the back of a ray and Albert cried "Bonefish!" Mac had the bow, fired in a #1 pink Gotcha, and hooked up almost immediately. A spirited five-pound bone raced off that he caught. My turn, spied more bones on eagle rays, and I quickly notched another. Mac got back up, Albert poled over to a ray with three bones darting over its back, Mac cast and hooked up again; this time with a slightly bigger fish. This was great. As I retook the bow, my cell phone rang with an emergency call from a law client. Boo. The damn call lasted 30 minutes while my smiling boat mate got two more bones. He decided that sharing a skiff with a [then] practicing attorney wasn't all bad. ●

Bonefish also respond to human predators. Unpressured fish can be downright dumb, as we discovered one day in a remote corner of the Bahamas. A long boat ride took us to a virtually unfished locale teeming with 2- to 4-pounders. The fish were pushovers, prompting an experiment or two. We tied on oversize flies that we could see clearly on the bottom 40 feet from the boat. Fish would appear, the fly would be placed about 15 feet away, and the bones would beeline for the fly and eat it. We decided to not set the hook; the bone would mouth the fly, then spit it out, only to have one of his buddies suck it in. Our record was three eats/spit-outs on one cast.

The other side of the "experiment" is the fishery at the mouth of the Middle Bight in Andros Island: the Fever Creek–Little Moxey Creek–Moxey Creek complex. Twenty years ago, it was lightly fished. Lodges from North Andros would occasionally make the long, choppy run to fish the area. The bones were never stupid, but a decent presentation with a Gotcha almost always got a take. Fast-forward 20 years. In the intervening years, the Mangrove Cay Club was built on the Middle Bight and a corps of independent guides began fishing the area regularly. The North Island guides kept coming over too. The result was an incessant bonefish educational seminar. Today the local bonefish are spooky, sensitive, and picky as hell regarding flies. I regard the Fever Creek fish, especially the better fish of 5 pounds or more, to be more challenging than anything I chase at home in the Middle Keys. It is damn

near impossible to throw a fly directly to a cruising fish—anything that lands within 15 feet sends the bonie racing in the other direction. A successful presentation entails using a small fly (a size 4 crab pattern is good) and a 15-foot leader, and putting the fly 20 feet or more ahead of the fish, guessing where it might go. If in fact it nears the fly, a couple of subtle twitches are in order. Any more than that and it's adios fish. This is technical, close-quarters bonefishing at its best.

Equipment, tackle, and flies to catch bonies have evolved substantially in 50 years. An early '60s bonefishing book by Stanley Babson complained that a split-cane bamboo fly rod, when used for bones, had to be expensively refinished

Great bonefish spots, Fever Creek, Little Moxey Creek, and Moxey Creek (left to right), are found near the mouth of the Middle Bight on Andros Island.

after exposure to the salt. My first saltwater fly rig—in 1973—was a heavy, slow 9-weight fiberglass rod paired with a Scientific Anglers "System" reel. It was hard to throw good tight loops with the rod, and the reel had only a click drag. The first time I took it to the Keys—to try for blackfin tuna and bonita—the guide chortled and stuck a spinning rod in my hand.

A lot of guys, including Captain Keating, took their first bonefish on an old black-and-white Pflueger Medalist. Rich told me a counterweight needed to be hammered or screwed onto the spool to keep the reel from shimmying apart, like an unbalanced tire, during a big

bonie's opening run. You would never confuse the setup with a modern Abel or Tibor. If you were very well-heeled, you bought a Fin Nor "wedding cake" reel, and real insiders could score a Seamaster built by Captain Bob McChristian in Miami. But most limped along with reels that were barely up to snuff.

There was one choice of line—a standard weight-forward taper that was sold to bass anglers and saltwater types alike. Since the changeover from the old letter/diameter system for denoting fly lines to the modern American Fishing Tackle Manufacturers Association (AFTMA) numerical weight system had just

Saltwater fly reels evolved from simple reels with click drags to sophisticated barstock models with strong, smooth (cork or nylon) drags—Pflueger Medalist, SA System, Seamaster, Abel, Tibor (clockwise from bottom left).

occurred, lines were marked both ways. My first weight-forward 9-weight (WF/9) was also a "GAF," denoting lettered diameters of different sections of the tapered fly line. Leaders were constructed of nylon mono and in the finer diameters had about half the strength of today's products. Weaker, more-suspect leader material was one reason 100 percent knots like Bimini twists were so crucial for fishing the salt.

A contemporary flats angler has an enormous array of tackle choices. Rods come in an indecipherable range of actions and a variety of graphite or composite materials. No one buying a rod in 1973 ever heard the word "modulus." Any modern rod is lighter than its historical counterpart, and this has enabled anglers to go lighter. The 8-weight rig is the standard for bonefish—a 9 held that spot decades ago. Besides, modern rods are more than capable of being cast and fished effectively underlined or overlined. Many rods are too stiff for effective close-range fishing. I routinely choose a line weight heavier than recommended to make quick, short casts easier.

The revolution in lines is truly staggering. You cannot simply buy a "weight-forward."

Lines are marketed specifically for "bonefish," "permit," "tarpon," "redfish," "saltwater," etc. Within a group of ostensibly species-specific lines, you have to decide if you want a long head, a short head, a triangle, or any number of particular back and front tapers. And you can't simply purchase an "8-weight." Per the standards, an 8-weight line is supposed to weigh between 202 and 218 grains. Some 8s weigh in at 243 grains or more; others are at the bottom of the range. Trial and error with different rods and different lines is the only reliable way to find a setup that suits your casting skills and style of fishing.

Rod manufacturers have taken a page from the golf club industry in trying to convince customers that they can buy casting skills—ain't going to happen. Effective, efficient saltwater fly casting is an acquired skill that must be learned, practiced, relearned, and practiced, practiced, practiced. Quality equipment is a joy to use, but it will never be a substitute for learning a good casting stroke. Besides, the incremental changes from fly-rod model to fly-rod model are barely detectable except by a tiny handful of genuine casting gurus. Find something you like and stick with it. My go-to bonefish rod is a 20-year-old model on its third or fourth set of guides. It's great fun to visit fishing shows, test-drive the new rods, look at the sticker, and realize spending $1,000 for a new rod isn't necessary.

Having said that, use the money to buy fresh fly lines—regularly. A fresh, slick, semi-stiff fly line is almost always good for an extra 5 to 10 feet on your cast compared to a tired, old, scuffed-up line embedded with dirt. Those few feet often make the difference between a good presentation—that gets bit—and one that falls agonizingly short. Recently, I shared a skiff with a guy in Andros. The guide and I couldn't figure out why his casts kept coming up short until I went to restack his line; it was limp, frayed, curled, and filthy. We asked about the line and he admitted it was at least five years old and hadn't been stretched or cleaned in quite a while. I had an extra new line with me (because barracudas have bitten my fly lines being zipped through the water by a running bonefish) and spooled it up for him, and the casting woes evaporated.

One other fly line suggestion learned from expensive experience: Always strip line from a reel straight ahead or parallel to the rod; stripping down drags the line across the fly reel crossbar with bad results. The latter can peel the finish off a brand-new line and cause it to twist and curl too. At nearly $100 or more a pop, fly lines should be treated gently, like keeping them away from sticky sunscreen or line-eating bug repellent.

Leaders have improved vastly. All kinds of strong nylon-based material can be had in almost any fly shop. Fluorocarbon also has its adherents. I still use hand-tied leaders because I can tailor them to specific conditions. For example, my "wind" leaders are shorter (9 feet) with a steep, sharp taper to punch through a stiff breeze; tailing leaders at 16 feet long have a very gentle taper, promoting a softer delivery of the fly. My regular bonefish leader is 12 to 14 feet long. Learning to handle longer leaders really improved my angling for all species, and to the degree that I have any "secrets" worthy of sharing, this is it. Standard nylon makes up all of these leaders except the tippet—the last 2 or 3 feet—which is fluorocarbon. It is more abrasion-resistant and stands up better to coral

or mangrove shoots than regular mono. I have never seen a need to use the pricier fluoro for the full leader. Just be aware that joining mono to fluoro requires very carefully tied and tightened knots.

Other equipment has also been revolutionized. Polarized sunglass choices were skimpy in the '70s. Ray-Ban Aviators with gray or green polarized lenses were the cat's meow. For those of us with thinner wallets, plastic gray polarized sunglasses from the drugstore carousel were the best option. Only later was it discovered that brown to copper tints were optimal for seeing flats fish. A plethora of good glasses are available now from glass to high-quality plastic in shades never thought of years ago. I get anal about sunglasses and have four pairs in copper, light brown, amber, and rose for all light conditions. You need to see the fish before you can make a good presentation! Plus, my eye doctor lectures me about UV protection and flying hooks, so I'm just following orders.

Maybe the greatest changes influenced flats boats. Keys guides started in the '40s and '50s with simple skiffs and a wooden pole. Since lightweight high-powered outboards did not exist, standard procedure was to tether the skiff behind a commercial fishing boat, head out to the flats, then use the skiff to access the shallow water. Grainy old black-and-white films show early Islamorada guide Jimmie Albright and legendary fly angler Joe Brooks doing just that to target bones in the Keys backcountry right after World War II. Down the Overseas Highway (US 1) in the Middle Keys, the same tactic let guides take sports out to the then-distant Content Keys.

Growing interest in bonefishing and a growing cadre of Keys guides created a need for a better boat to fish the flats. Willy Roberts pioneered in the late '50s the first specifically designed flats boat. Roberts was bona fide "Conch" (born and raised in the Keys), having been born in Key West in 1914. His new boat was made of wood and had the lines we still see today, although the boat was deeper. The stern and bow were decked to be manned by an angler and guide. The boat was run from a center console, and one or two captain's chairs were set forward of the console for the clients. Wooden boats were fading from favor when Roberts built his first flats boat, and when

Captain Richard Keating mans the pole on a modern flats skiff.

pressed about using fiberglass he reportedly groused, "When fiberglass trees grow, I'll build a fiberglass flats boat." Even with the heavier wood, the design was a winner, and his boat was very popular among Keys guides through the 1960s. I see occasionally a beautifully refurbished model off Marathon.

Bob Hewes was next out the blocks with a fiberglass flats boat in the early '60s. He tinkered with the original design, creating what became the famous Hewes Bonefisher. The ensuing decades saw Maverick, Dolphin, Hell's Bay, Chittum, and others enter the ranks. The modern boats are marvels of nautical engineering, able to run dry and safe through a mean chop and still pole silently in inches of water.

One of the other great flats innovations was the poling platform. The late Captain Bill Curtis started guiding in Biscayne Bay in the '50s. Common practice was for the guide to pole from the bow, as it was a bit higher than the stern, with the angler taking the stern deck. I recall fishing from the stern and dodging the outboard when I took up flats angling in 1974. Curtis came up with an alternative—a cooler

buckled into place on the stern, which he stood on to pole. He gave it more thought and concocted the metal-framed tower/platform, which elevates the poler above the outboard engine. The first one was made for him in 1975 and bolted onto his Hewes Bonefisher. It was a winner, and everyone quickly followed suit, making the poling platform a signature feature of virtually all flats boats.

And the material advances that produced graphite fly rods transformed boat poles. The originals were wood, replaced for many years by fiberglass. Compared to today's graphite versions, fiberglass was thick, heavy, and bendy. No one could handle one longer than 16 feet. New graphite poles are light and stiff—and some guides wield 21-footers on the poling platforms, which can be a big advantage when chasing tarpon in deeper water.

Fly fishing, of course, is all about flies. The transition from trout flies imitating insects to shrimp, crabs, and baitfish is the heart of saltwater fly fishing, whether it's bonefish on the flats or northeastern stripers in the surf. Early bonefish flies featured hook-point-down designs such as the Franke Belle—named for Jimmie Albright's wife. Joe Brooks's shrimp fly was similarly designed. You couldn't let them sink down to the turtle grass, or a hang-up was almost guaranteed. The first hook-point-up pattern I saw in the '70s was the Horror, invented by an enterprising guy in Bermuda. A fairly thick deer hair wing would invert the fly, making it easier to fish smack on the bottom.

The big breakthrough occurred on Andros Island in a collaboration between local guide Charlie Smith (recently deceased) and angler Bob Nauheim. Popular history says Charlie (or Bob) affixed bead-chain eyes to the top of the shank, and up near the eye, to flip the fly over so it would ride hook up. The bead-chain eyes also take the fly quickly to the bottom. Surprisingly, the first version had a silver/white body and a white wing; Charlie told me it was designed to imitate a glass minnow. I expected it was trying to imitate a shrimp. He and Nauheim called it the "Nasty Charlie" and it was killer on Andros bones and elsewhere. Later Orvis bought the rights to the fly, apparently didn't like the name, and rechristened it the "Crazy Charlie," which is how we know it now.

That basic design, with bead-chain or lead eyes, is the standard bonefish fly from Christmas Island to the Bahamas and points in between. Jim McVay changed the color scheme to create the original Gotcha, also on Andros. The legend claims he plucked yellowish fibers from a fraying Andros taxicab rug for the wing, wrapped diamond braid to create the body, added pearl flash on top of the wing, and tied the fly with coral pink thread, showing a prominent pink nose or head. It didn't have a name, but the fish didn't care, eating it aggressively. Each time a bonefish grabbed it and hooked up, McVay's guide Rupert Leadon reputedly cried "Gotcha!" and the name was born. Rupert guided me on my first day at Andros and "verified" the tale. Regardless of the origin, the classic pink Gotcha is a killer fly throughout the Bahamas and in the Keys. A red-headed version was created farther south on Andros at the Mangrove Cay Club, and I like it better than the original. Not only do bones love it, but permit will eat it too.

Back across the Gulf Stream, inventive Keys fly tiers were concocting new patterns as well. Chico Fernandez whipped up his classic Bonefish Special (apparently a snapping shrimp imitation). Harry Spear played with epoxy to create the Mother of Epoxy (MOE). Essentially a bland brown fly, an epoxy head was formed over and around bead or lead eyes, creating a fly that would sink like a rock. It was a big success. Outstanding bonefish guide Rick Ruoff came up with his Flea series of flies—and they worked too. Later Islamorada artist and avid angler Tim Borski developed a great series of buggy, natural-looking patterns relying heavily on deer hair, grizzly hackles, and craft fur—barred with a marker to look shrimpier. The Chernobyl Crab, the Butterfly, and the Slider are tested patterns.

Anglers tuned in to bonefish feeding, and prey research noted that Gulf toadfish were prevalent in the stomachs of big bones. Spear took note and produced the Tasty Toad to imitate the toadfish. Interestingly, Gary Merriman, an Atlanta fly shop owner and Keys regular, modified it into the popular Tarpon Toad. Subsequent bonefish patterns that appear to imitate the toadfish include the Kwan. Lots of Upper Keys bonefish tournament participants favor these patterns.

Another classic pattern was developed first on the Susquehanna River for smallmouth bass: Bob Clouser's minnow imitation. The fly can be tied with bucktail or synthetic fibers and in a wide array of colors. It is commonly accepted that the Clouser is the universal fly, catching an enormous variety of species—fresh and salt. The two most widely used colors for bonefish are brown bucktail over white and chartreuse bucktail over white, tied on size 2, 4, and 6 hooks.

Of course, bonefish eat crabs, and virtually all of the crab patterns used for permit will take bonies. I have found that scaling down the classic Merkin crab fly to a size 4 hook makes a deadly bonefish fly. Going to lighter colors—making the body with a mix of cream and ginger/brown yarn strands—imitates the little crabs found on sandy and coral bottoms in the Keys and Bahamas. In Andros, bones will punch these little flies into the bottom with aggressive tailing takes. The guides there raid my fly box for them when I leave. Florida's Chico Fernandez strongly recommends little crab patterns in his excellent *Fly-Fishing for Bonefish*.

Choosing Bonefish Flies

Flats anglers love flies. In fact, most flies are crafted to catch fishermen rather than bonefish. A review of bonefish literature reveals hundreds of fly patterns created or concocted by myriad fly tiers to throw at *Albula vulpes*. Flies come in an amazing variety of sizes, weights, forms, and colors, and all have likely caught a fish or two. Most guides will tell you, however, that 99 percent of their fishing is done with no more than two or three tried-and-true patterns. And presentation far outweighs the importance of the fly—in almost all cases.

The size and weight of the fly are the most critical elements in pattern choice. The lead-eyed size 1 Clouser cast to a mudding Keys bonefish in 4 feet (or more) of water is totally out of place when facing a Bahamas bone in inches of water among the mangrove shoots. The loud kerplunk of the big weighted fly will send the shallow fish fleeing in terror. Presentations to shallow crawlers and tailers need a fly that lands as quietly as a mouse peeing on a blotter—a great description offered by author/angler Len Wright in Dick Brown's *Bonefish Fly Patterns*. Conversely, a small unweighted "tailing fish" pattern cast to the mudders will end up hovering in the water column, unseen by the bone digging in the bottom. Hence, the well-prepared angler carries flies of different sizes and weights to match the water depths where the fish will be found.

Keys patterns are usually large—tied on size 1 or 2 hooks. At Andros, especially in the

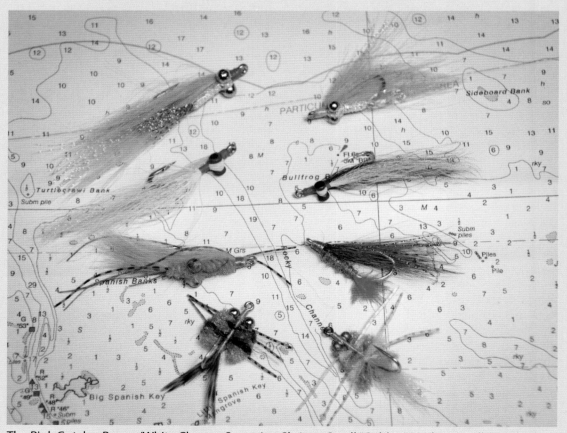

The Pink Gotcha, Brown/White Clouser, Snapping Shrimp, Small "Golden" Merkin, Small Standard Merkin, Mantis Shrimp, Chartreuse Clouser, and Red-Headed Gotcha (clockwise from top tight) are recommended bonefish flies.

Bights and on the West Side, size 2s and 4s are the order of the day and the guides there like heavily dressed flies. But travel to the Joulter Cays northeast of the big island (or Abaco or Exuma), and smaller, lighter flies such as size 6s are preferred. Belize has a reputation for very small flies, with size 8s, and even tiny 10s, being put to use. Mexico (and Christmas Island) seem to be in between, where size 4s and 6s are most popular. The deep-water flats of Hawaii call for Keys sizes.

Shape or form is the second criterion. Bonefish feed primarily on small shrimp, crabs, minnows, and sea worms. Good patterns emulate the different shapes: a longer, sleeker form for shrimp imitations compared to the wide body of crabs. Rubber bands tied on small hooks do a fine job of representing worms, and traditional Clousers or Gummy Minnows imitate tiny baitfish. An overwhelming percentage of patterns—tied in the form of the original Nasty Charlie or the Gotcha—are thought to emulate shrimp. More-imitative shrimp representations such as Ververka's Mantis Shrimp and similar patterns have also become highly popular in recent years. On the crab front, any number of wide- or round-body forms, usually with some kind of protruding legs, are readily taken by hungry bonefish. As noted previously, scaled-down Merkins on size 2, 4, and 6 hooks are an excellent choice for bones.

The use of lively-looking materials is a critical part of successful shape and form. Trout anglers discovered years ago that highly imitative flies, like molded plastic bugs, were damn near worthless on the water. The bugs lacked life. Less-imitative patterns using materials that breathed, pulsed, and shimmered far outfished the less-lively flies. The same is true with bonefish flies. Stuff that looks alive in the water— some natural furs, craft fur, marabou, hen and rooster hackles, and various rubber legs—turns on the bonies. If it looks alive when stripped or twitched, bonefish are likely to eat it.

Color is the last factor. A plebian brown/white Clouser has been a go-to Keys pattern for decades. Not fancy, and not good at catching anglers, bonefish still love it. The more colorful Gotcha, in both its original pink and more recent red or orange versions, may well be *the* universal bonefish fly. The colors are shrimp-like, and the thread underbody glowing through the diamond flash body must look appetizing. Dick Brown opined (in his book *Bonefish Fly Patterns*) that the reflective nature of the body makes the fly stealthier in the water and more imitative of natural prey than the fly appears when dry and in hand. All-white patterns can be useful and represent glass minnows, sea worms, or highly translucent small shrimp.

Orange is an underrated color. Hawaiian guides like orange flies as imitating local forms of mantis shrimp. Chico Fernandez's original Bonefish Special pattern featured a bright orange tail tag to look like the orange egg sacs of some shrimp. I have tied "orange heart" versions of Greg's Flats Fly and used them successfully on spooky Andros fish. And my first trophy Keys bone ate Captain Bergmann's bright orange Clouser—the "Navel."

There exists a general assumption that all flies tied with bead chain or lead eyes will "flip over" to ride with the hook point up. It is a rude surprise to discover this is not always true. Smaller bead chains often will not flip over a fly, and even some lead-eyed patterns will ride hook point down. Many variables determine if a fly will ride point up: overall size, weight of the eyes, placement of the eyes, and the materials used to tie the fly. Another major factor is the knot used to affix the fly to the leader tippet. Some patterns flip only if tied on with a loop knot. In contrast, I have a crab pattern, tied on a jig hook with a 60-degree eye, that flips and rides straight only with a clinch knot at a 45-degree angle on the hook eye itself. Test your patterns and use different knots to determine which combinations actually will turn over the fly to achieve the usually desired hook-point-up attitude.

In my opinion, five patterns should be in every bonefisher's fly box: Gotchas, Clousers, a small Merkin, an unweighted snapping shrimp (for tailers), and a Mantis Shrimp pattern. I suspect 98 percent of the world's bonefish will eat these flies. All the other patterns are for those unusual circumstances—or locations—where the fish are locked onto to something else. Carry these in a variety of sizes and weights scaled to the location and conditions (more important than color differences) and you will be armed for action.

Interview with CAPTAIN RICHARD BLACK: Chasing Bonefish

Captain Richard Black's family has been in the Keys since the 1890s, when his great-grandfather homesteaded Clive Key deep in Florida Bay. Richard grew up in the islands, learning to fly fish at 7 years old, getting his first skiff at 8, and catching his first fly-rod bonefish on Islamorada's famous (and difficult) Shell Key flat at 10. Since then he has explored the length of the Keys, and Florida Bay, as a deeply curious angler and later a guide. He secured his Coast Guard license at 17 and became a guide at 18. Twelve years and thousands of days later on the water, he's earned an excellent reputation especially in pursuit of bonefish, putting his clients on trophy fish topping 15 pounds. Other Keys guides give Richard the ultimate accolade: "He's a very fishy guy."

Are Keys bonefish coming back?
Yes. There are lots of fish around, mostly 2- to 6-pounders. Big ones are still here—just harder to find and harder to fool. But the fishery is different than it used to be, say, 15 years ago. Compared to the historical fishing—before water-quality disasters and freezes—the fish don't tail as much and mud much deeper. I find that the average depth for finding bones is about 3 feet and I often fish as deep as 6 feet. That's different from the past. Plus, there are now more bigger fish in the Lower and Middle Keys than before when Islamorada and the Upper Keys were the only reliable places for big bones.

Why do you like bonefish?
They're the most aggressive fish on the flats. Make a good presentation, show them the fly, and they're likely to eat. Since happy bones will charge flies, bones are easier for a beginner than Florida Bay redfish. Reds get down in the grass, requiring very precise casts—tough for beginners. Bones see the fly from feet away

and come running. As Steve Huff said years ago, bones are honest fish. Do it right and the fish eats the fly.

What skills do you want anglers to bring to the bow?
First, an ability to listen, to be willing to take instructions. For example, deeper bones are harder to see and beginners will have a hard time picking them up. I can talk an angler into the fish if they're willing to listen. Second, a willingness to work on becoming a good fisherman. There's a difference between being a good caster and a good angler. Good anglers are able to adapt to different situations and feed fish. If someone new doesn't have the experience to adapt, their ability to listen is going to enable them to be successful—and learn for the future.

How does one become a "better fisherman"?
In the case of bonefishing, I suggest rookies catch their first on a spinning rod. Watching a bonefish react to a shrimp or jig is valuable; learning from watching the bone eat bait is transferable to fly fishing.

Obviously fly casting is important. What skills are needed to catch fish?
An angler who can give me a quick, reasonably accurate 30-foot cast is going to be able to catch Keys bones. The success rate will be very high if the angler can add more precision and land the weighted fly softly. Practice is important too. Don't waste your first day, or two, of a fishing trip working off the rust if you haven't touched a fly rod for months.

What about flies?
I almost hate to strip away mystery from fly selection. I use one pattern—in different weights and sizes for different conditions. The fly is a generic shrimpy/crabby fly close to a

Captain Richard Black with a Keys bonefish. (Courtesy of Brooke Black)

small Merkin crab or a Kwan or toadfish. As you know, most Keys guides rely on one go-to fly. Showing the fly to the bonefish, quickly, is so much more important than pattern.

How do you want flies presented to bonefish?
For the most part, I like aggressive presentations. Get the fly 4 to 5 feet in front of the fish. For deeper fish, mudders, throw even closer. Situations can be different, especially on a few heavily fished flats, or on calm days, but that's part of the adapting needed to be a good angler.

Quick, accurate casts require the angler to see the fish. Any tips for spotting the elusive gray ghost?
Seeing fish is a learned behavior. Beginners can see the fish but don't know they're seeing the fish. And fish spotting has gotten more difficult as Keys bones have retreated to deeper waters. It helps to look for fish like you read—left to right. Listening to the guide is important too. Many folks hear "50 feet, 11 o'clock" and lock onto one spot. It's better to look at a "zone," not a precise spot, and pick up movement. When the angler cannot pick up the fish, it's "fishing by Braille." Point the rod and listen to the guide tell you left/right or up/down with the tip and get you looking in the right location.

What is standard bonefish tackle in your skiff?
I like a standard 8-weight rod. But find one that you can use with a true weight line. So many new lines are 2 or 3 weights heavy [e.g., an "8" is really a 10], making for less-than-soft presentations. Any reel with 150 yards of backing, or more, and a decent drag will get the job done. ◼

The Frankee Belle, Horror, Nasty Charlie, Snapping Shrimp, Gotcha, Tasty Toad, Clouser, Borski Slider, and Kwan (clockwise from top center) represent the evolution of bonefish flies from the 1950s to the present.

The bone's general willingness to eat flies makes it an ideal species for newcomers, and sharing the magic of the flats with a newbie is always a joy, especially a girlfriend who you later convince to become your bride. Starting in the Keys can be tough—the bones use deeper, mostly dark grass-covered flats and can be very difficult to see. In contrast, Bahamas bones are more plentiful, readily use much shallower waters, and cruise over light-colored marl bottoms, where they can stand out like a sore thumb. So, I talked my now-spouse Jeannette into joining our annual Andros expedition. She was excited to see the Bahamas and try for this mysterious fish about which she had heard so much. What she didn't know was that I had an engagement ring buried in

my pocket. And one other fact needs to be disclosed. Prospective marriage had stumbled on an odd issue: I very much wanted a new bird dog (my other ol' girl had passed), and Jeannette was a firm no.

Back on the flats, Jeannette managed her first bonefish on her first day fighting wind and rain—a 2-pound schoolie out of a nice bunch by Gibson Cay. Next day she got her first "classic" bone:

OCT. 19, MOSTLY SUNNY, 80, WIND SE 10. Back in a complex of small bays, Capt. Patterson [Bowleg], aka PB, poled us toward a shoreline lined with low mangroves and ragged cabbage palms. Pale green water gave way to crystal shallows over a marl bottom and some waking fish could be seen. Jeannette was up and a meandering happy bone oozed in from 10/11 o'clock. A first cast was short and seemed to spook the fish, but it settled, came back into range, Jeannette dropped the RHG close, and the fish was on it instantly. A good one surged away and Jeannette cleared line like a veteran. Mr. Bone warped off running a big circle around the boat with line ripping audibly through the water. It headed for the tangled mangrove roots; Jeannette clamped down and stopped it, creating a big ruckus in the water. A spirited fish, it was back and forth, then PB had it—a solid bright silver five-pounder and a new bonefish angler was born. ●

That evening I enticed her to watch a Middle Bight sunset from a coral point at the west end of the Mangrove Cay Club property. Chilled champagne and flowers were waiting there, and I was sure she would figure what was coming. Nope—she thought I was just being romantic. In the meantime, our group was back at the club bar (with stern instructions to stay away from the point) waiting to see what would happen. As a pretty orange sun dipped into the water, I pulled out the ring, popped the question, and got a prompt "Yes!" We strolled back to the club, and when the gang saw she was wearing the ring, shouted congratulations followed instantly by "So you agreed to get the dog???" Everyone laughed hard. And we got the dog.

Jeannette releases her first good bonefish in Andros Island's North Bight.

Pursuing bonefish remains as enchanting today as it was the first time I tried. A friend refers to bones as the "gateway drug of flats fishing." The late Lefty Kreh, who caught damn near everything in the salt on a fly rod, told people that if he had one day left to fish, it would be on the bow of a skiff looking for bones. There's no quibbling from this addict.

Tarpon

A confession is in order: I'm obsessed with tarpon. *Megalops atlanticus* offers everything that makes fly fishing great. The entire enterprise is a visual feast: Tarpon are hunted in a stunning aquatic environment of aqua, blue, and emerald waters; the big fish are seen laid up or swimming in clear waters, with visible flies presented to individual tarpon or specific groups; tarpon bites can be epic gulping grabs or the most subtle sips, usually no more than 40 to 60 feet from the angler standing on the bow; hookups are followed by great foamy leaps that defy gravity—straight-ups, backflips, cartwheels, greyhounds, and vibrating missile launches.

Great sounds are part of the mix. Rolling poons sigh, leapers rattle gills like castanets, and jumpers sound like belly-flopping Sumo wrestlers. Angling skills are necessary, as the fish are not easy to feed. Precision casts delivered into stiff breezes and from the bow of a rocking skiff are part of the repertoire. And it happens with adrenaline coursing in your veins, courtesy of 5- to 6-foot-long finned submarines bearing down on you.

The fish must be enticed to bite and the hook set in an armored mouth. Then all hell breaks loose with a very unhappy, large creature determined to rid itself of the hook and make tracks for the next zip code. Fly line on the deck becomes a hissing snake looking to wrap around something, anything. Clearing it and getting the line on the reel lets you catch a breath before getting down to serious business—battling the big brute. Lots of pressure is needed, cramping often-unused muscles; too little and you'll do nothing but "walk the dog" for a wearying hour, with the tarpon invariably chafing through the bite tippet.

Bringing the fish close to the boat sets up the critical end game. Big ones always dive under the boat, and you must instantly plunge the rod deep and walk it around the bow; too slow and a pricey graphite rod explodes as it

Tarpon up close reveal subtle colors not seen by casual observers.

A big Keys oceanside tarpon demonstrates the high-flying skills that excite anglers.

slams the gunwale. Survive that, a couple of close jumps where line stretch is minimal, and the tarpon is "caught" as the leader touches the rod tip. You admire the big bright silver scales, a sea-green back flecked with gold, purple coruscations on the gill plates, and a big black-and-gold eye challenges. No one ever asks, "Why tarpon?"

Early flats fly anglers didn't try to challenge the silver king. Split-cane fly rods, salmon reels, and delicate catgut leaders were not up to the task. The post-WWII introduction of fiberglass rods and nylon monofilament changed that, and a few anglers and guides in the Keys and Miami were willing to try. They were severely handicapped by the fly-fishing rules of the day limiting terminal tackle to leader tippets testing no more than 12 pounds. Early and great Keys guide George Hommell recounted his efforts with J. Lee Cuddy to catch a big fly-rod tarpon on this gear. Apparently, Cuddy spent an entire spring hooking fish—and losing them all—until they got very lucky and hooked one of about 40 pounds in the "moustache" (the middle of the upper lip) that kept the fragile 12-pound leader out of the abrasive mouth.

By the '50s the rules were modified to allow the bite, or shock, tippet—a short trace of heavier mono that could stand up to the tarpon's sandpaper lips and mouth—referred to as "Fly Heavy." Cuddy took advantage of the new rules to catch, on a custom-made Paul Young split-cane fly rod (likely the first fly rod built specifically for saltwater fly fishing), the first world record Fly Heavy tarpon. Now the game was joined and improvements in rods, reels, lines, leaders, and knots came rapidly. Those innovators are legends within the tarpon community: Stu Apte, Flip Pallot, John Emery, Norm Duncan, and Chico Fernandez. The latter four were young south Florida fishing buddies; I got to know Duncan years ago via Captain Bus. Apte and Hommell both penned autobiographies, with tales of pioneering days chasing virgin tarpon populations.

Tarpon were plentiful. The late Captain Bill Curtis told the authors of *Tideline*, "Back in the 50s and 60s, there were 20 times more fish than we have here today. I can remember seeing a school of tarpon that stretched an eighth of a mile wide, maybe a quarter mile long, as they funneled along this point. We hooked an 80-pounder at the head, fought the fish nearly 30 minutes, and watched the whole time as the rest of the school flooded by the boat. Hell, all you had to do was get your line in the water and

Putting the "down and dirty" move on a big poon is a proven fish-fighting tactic; too little pressure merely "walks the dog."

it would've been impossible for a tarpon not to have eaten your fly." And the original anglers are unanimous that feeding these unpressured tarpon was easy. Pitch out a big fly—most were tied on 4/0 and 5/0 hooks—and the lead fish would swim 15 feet off her track to eat it. Then the problems started. Those numbers no longer exist, although tarpon populations remain solid.

An objective comparison of tarpon-catching statistics, though, reveals that maybe those good old days weren't quite as good as our selective angling memories recall. The Gold Cup Tarpon Tournament was initiated in 1964 as an all-tackle affair in which tarpon could be caught on fly, plug-casting, or spinning outfits. In the first cup, the largest tarpon was 96.5 pounds, caught by Ted Williams, and George

Hommell and his angler Don Hawley released the most fish—seven. Today it takes 125 to 150 pounds of tarpon to win the big-fish award and seven releases is a good number—for one day. In fact, results from the June 2019 Don Hawley Invitational Tarpon Fly Fishing Tournament in the Keys indicate these may be the real good old days: Winners Captain Dustin Huff and Thane Morgan caught 27 tarpon in five days. They landed a remarkable 10 poons on day one, a mere 8 on day two, and only 9 others on the last three days of angling. I started keeping close track over 20 years ago and have seen no substantial overall drop in Middle Keys oceanside tarpon numbers.

Behaviors have changed as the fish have been chased out of many spots, especially around Key West, by excessive boat and recreation use; tarpon don't mix well with cruise ships, jet skis, cigarette boats, parasails, and water slides. In fact, one of the interesting features of the 1974 Key West "Tarpon" video (referred to by my sons as "the hippies and stoners go fishing") is the absolute absence of other boats and watercraft on the tarpon runs of the area. That level of blessed solitude is long gone in many areas of the Keys.

Fish movements also change over time in response to unknown factors. In the last decade, tarpon numbers in the Lower Keys dipped for a few years and then rebounded, with the fish returning to many traditional haunts. Some longtime guides blamed sedimentation kicked up by cruise ships churning their way in and out of Key West Harbor. Where the numbers have not rebounded, intense fishing pressure is a suspected culprit. One famous locale, discovered and fished by the likes of Apte and Hommell, now gets pounded relentlessly. The last time I fished it we counted 16 other skiffs doing the same. Tarpon get tired of an overhead parade of boats and move elsewhere.

Unknown factors have affected a lower Middle Keys backcountry area. Tarpon would roll in from the Gulf in late February and show up along a series of remote banks. Fishing could be excellent for these fresh migrants. The poons would then filter south, likely heading for Bahia Honda, but stopping en route to hang out at any number of basins and coves. About five years ago, the fish stopped showing up on the remote banks and the number of tarpon working south dropped significantly. Fishing pressure does not seem to be a culprit. Environmental factors are suspected, as some of the same Gulf banks used to host big numbers of bluefish, jacks, and pompano in January and February. These fish haven't appeared either, prompting serious worry.

Florida Bay tarpon fishing has also had its ups and downs, but anecdotally numbers have been up in the last few years. This has occurred, especially along the outside edges of the Bay and waters off Cape Sable, despite the water-quality problems that have decimated some parts of the inner Bay.

Among anglers there is much speculation about tarpon populations. It seems there may be subpopulations in the Keys. I have thought that there could be four such broad groups: (1)

A horde of ocean-migrating tarpon swim into view, causing wobbly knees and sweaty palms.

fish that come in from the deep Gulf of Mexico to the Marquesas, west of Key West, and other areas near Key West; (2) a second group that swims south from the Gulf into the broad backcountry in and around the Contents west to Jewfish Basin; (3) another subpopulation that appears early each year off Cape Sable and works into Florida Bay and other points south; and (4) the major group of Atlantic Ocean fish, a chunk of which stages in Miami's deep Government Cut in January and February and swims south and west along the ocean side of the Keys. Scientists aren't so sure, and some of them are convinced there is simply one population that simply moves around in response to factors such as water temperature, water quality, availability of prey, and disturbance. For example, BTT's science director, Dr. Aaron Adams, offered to me one hypothesis for fewer Lower Keys tarpon: Warmer winters may allow tarpon in the Charlotte Harbor region, in southwest Florida, to remain there rather than being driven by cold water south to the Keys.

Any local movements in and around the Keys and south Florida are also part of larger migration patterns that are being discovered by BTT's tarpon acoustic-tagging program. Initiated in 2016, the project takes advantage of the latest tagging technology. Previously, only sizable satellite tags, costing about $3,000 each, were available. The big tags, about a foot long, could be attached only to big tarpon of 100 pounds or more. Older battery technology enabled the tags to operate for a few weeks, then the tag would pop off, float to the surface, and broadcast its results to a satellite. A new acoustic tag is the size of a pinkie finger with batteries giving it a five-year operation span and costs about $500. The tags can be surgically inserted in tarpon as small as 20 pounds (smaller models are available to be used in bonefish, even freshwater trout) in a boatside procedure that takes about five minutes.

Each tag has a unique electronic signature emitted in a series of pings. When a tagged fish swims by a small receiver placed on the bottom, the receiver reads the ping and records when it swam by and registers which tag it was. Receivers have a range of up to 500 yards. BTT has placed 110 receivers (and replaced a

Paul Turcke bows to a leaping Cape Sable tarpon.

A BTT tagging crew gets ready to tag tarpon No. 15918—part of BTT's tarpon acoustic-tagging program.

batch destroyed by Hurricane Irma), but identical receivers are used by many other fisheries research entities. As a result, there are presently approximately 5,000 receivers along the Gulf of Mexico, throughout the Keys, and along the Atlantic coast to Chesapeake Bay. The other researchers report recorded tarpon pings to BTT, and BTT reports the pings from groupers, sharks, or other species recorded on BTT's receivers—scientific cooperation at its best. Receivers are physically downloaded approximately every four to six months.

Nearly 200 tarpon now carry the tags and over half of the tagged tarpon have been detected. And the detections are providing fascinating results. Within the Keys, three years of data reveal that the mean arrival date for the spring migrants is April 20 and when water temperatures reach 79 degrees. The same fish begin to depart approximately June 7, when water temps top 82.5 degrees. Most return at the end of the year, often following, and

feeding on, big schools of mullet along Florida's Atlantic coast.

The migrants enjoy the winter and early spring in the Keys then head north for a summer sojourn to the mouth of Chesapeake Bay. We think the tarpon like dining there on oil-rich menhaden. But not all tarpon are long-distance migrators. Some are homebodies, wandering around the Keys and no farther north than the Shark River issuing from the Everglades. Others prefer Florida's coasts, swimming back and forth from Tampa to Cape Canaveral. When the fish are in south Florida, the receiver networks are recording about 15,000 pings each month (and this level of data collection is expected to continue in the next three to five years), telling us much about our tarpon and answering anglers' questions about subpopulations and specific movements, and giving us much better estimates of total tarpon numbers in southeastern US waters. BTT plans to expand the effort to track

The odd-looking tarpon leptocephalus will transform into miniature tarpon. (Courtesy of Dr. Jon Shenker)

tarpon from Louisiana through Texas and into Mexico.

Learning more about the adult fish is important. Figuring out the tarpon life cycle and what must be conserved to ensure a steady stream of new fish is critical. Reproduction failure is a great threat to all fisheries, particularly species like tarpon that don't mature sexually for a number of years. Much like bonefish, how and where tarpon spawned and how and where juveniles grew up was unknown. No one was interested in serious research on a fish that wasn't eaten and didn't support a traditional commercial fishery. That has now changed thanks to cooperative efforts among BTT, the Florida Wildlife Commission (FWC), Florida Atlantic University, and the Florida Institute of Technology.

Scientists have pulled back the curtain on tarpon reproduction. Females mature at about 10 years, when the fish are roughly 4½ feet in length or 55 to 60 pounds. Males mature a little earlier and smaller. Tarpon congregate in places like the Keys or southwest Florida's Boca Grande Pass. On or around full and new moons in late May and June, fish venture offshore as far as 100 miles out. Gulf of Mexico tarpon go that far to get beyond the edge of the continental shelf and reach waters approximately 1,000 feet deep. Keys tarpon don't go that far (100 miles would put them high and dry in Havana) but get out into Gulf Stream depths. Offshore fishing captains report giant

schools of tarpon in blue water in late May and June near the full and new moons. Tarpon anglers also know that the inshore fish will almost disappear for a couple of days at the same time.

Once in the depths, the tarpon will dive down to 400 feet, which likely squeezes the eggs to facilitate release—just like the bonefish. *Megalops atlanticus* is also a broadcast spawner like bonefish. Large groups of tarpon will congregate offshore, females expel their eggs, and the males release clouds of sperm-laden milt

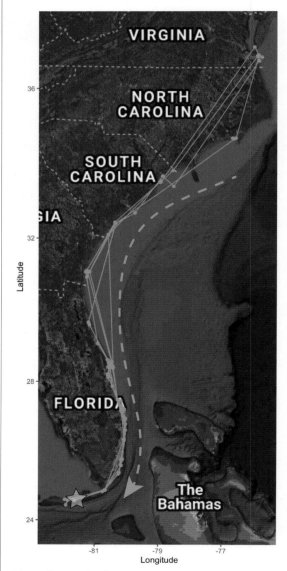

Lines depict the four-year movement of Lower Keys tarpon tagged in May 2016. (Courtesy of Dr. Lucas Griffin)

to fertilize the eggs. When done, these adults head back inshore. Within 24 to 36 hours the fertilized eggs hatch and little eel-like, transparent leptocephali emerge (sound familiar?).

For a month or more this odd little critter feeds on plankton-like stuff growing to 3 or 4 inches while swimming feebly toward shore. There, the lepto seeks estuaries where fresh and salt waters mix. About this time, the "eel" morphs into a true juvenile tarpon—a miniature 1½-inch-long dead ringer for mom and dad. The little poons keep pushing inshore to find protected backwaters, bays, coves, and creeks deep within mangrove jungles. Stagnant oxygen-depleted waters are preferred. Little tarpon can roll and breathe air with their rudimentary lung, enabling them to survive in waters that would suffocate other fish—especially predators. The oxygen-poor, still waters also harbor millions of mosquito larvae, providing a banquet for the baby poons.

As the little tarpon grow, their diet expands to little shrimp, baitfish, crabs, and such. The fish also begin to venture out of the protected backwaters. It takes about two years for the fast-growing fish to reach approximately 5 pounds and swim out to more-open waters. For another year or so the small tarpon are still creatures of the mangroves and protected waters, often living in schools with their peers. At approximately 5 years old and about 30 to 40 pounds, the young tarpon join the open-water migratory grownups. There the fish may live until 55 years old (or more) and reach the staggering size of 300 pounds in rare instances. An average Keys "big" tarpon—approximately 60 to 70 pounds—is likely a 10- to 15-year-old fish.

This dependence on estuaries and protected mangrove backwaters puts juvenile tarpon at risk in Florida. With the state's population growing by leaps and bounds, coastal development chewing up vital mangroves, and water mismanagement killing key estuaries, the warning flags are flying. The precarious state of juvenile tarpon habitat in Florida shines a light on a structural, legal issue on how we manage not only tarpon but all fish and wildlife.

States exercise primacy over the regulation of fish and wildlife in the USA. The states "own" the fish and wildlife on behalf of the people and are to administer the taking of fish and wildlife for public benefit. This is radically different from the European system, where fish and wildlife are considered part of the privately owned land and the landowner controls the taking. This is an outgrowth of the royal ownership systems that sprung up in medieval Europe, where the crown owned the land and the game—and death to any commoner or peasant who ventured onto the crown lands to take a deer, bird, or fish home for dinner. America's founders wanted nothing to do with such systems and vested ownership of fish and wildlife in our sovereigns: the people. Fish and wildlife agencies came into being 140 years ago to manage these resources on behalf of the sovereigns. It is a form of "public trust."

Early conservation leaders such as Teddy Roosevelt founded groups like the Boone & Crockett Club to insist that market hunting be banned, sustainable limits be imposed on how many fish or animals could be taken, and anglers and hunters use methods consistent with fair-chase principles. License requirements were established and the proceeds from the license sales used to fund the fish and wildlife agencies that conserve and manage these resources. Today this is the North American Wildlife Conservation Model for managing fish and wildlife and remains the cornerstone for our state and federal wildlife entities.

Such management focuses heavily on when, how, and how many fish or animals may be taken, the assumption being that Mother Nature will provide the fish and wildlife. In some circumstances, agencies engage in supplementing populations or specific habitat management efforts to increase popular species (e.g., stocking trout or pheasants, creating duck ponds, planting food plots for deer). State fish and wildlife agencies lack, however, more comprehensive habitat conservation authority, especially regarding private lands. Broader environmental rules, which can provide habitat conservation benefits, are most often within the jurisdiction of "environmental" agencies— state Departments of Environmental Conservation or Environmental Protection.

Florida fits this mold, with fish and wildlife authority committed to the FWC. Environmental regulation is the purview of the Florida Department of Environmental Protection (FDEP). Mangrove conservation, so critical for

young tarpon, is regulated by FDEP. It may be time to amend the North American Wildlife Conservation Model and get fish and wildlife agencies more actively engaged in habitat issues. Diminishing habitat, a function of growing human populations and concomitant development, is today's limiting factor on most fish and wildlife numbers—not market hunting or excessive recreational fishing harvest (commercial fishing is another issue but today has limited impact on flats species). Within the Keys' flats fisheries, bonefish and tarpon are already catch-and-release. Other than improving catch-and-release practices to ensure reduced ancillary mortality, traditional regulations targeting fishing means, methods, and bag limits aren't going to do much to benefit these two species. Instead, better water quality and protection of mangrove tarpon nurseries are more critical, and this kind of authority is vested in FDEP rather than FWC. Ensuring that these agencies work together on habitat conservation and restoration makes sense in the 21st century.

Florida's Keys are the highest-profile destination for chasing tarpon. The 150-mile-long chain of islands is not, however, the only place to catch the big fish. Tarpon angling's roots are in fact elsewhere in the Sunshine State: The first rod-and-reel poons were chased and caught in southwest Florida waters near Fort Myers, Boca Grande Pass, and Sanibel Island. Fly fishing for *Megalops atlanticus*—the smaller members of

the tribe—was also born in the same waters in the late 1800s (see A. W. Dimock's *Book of Tarpon*), even though the serious, focused pursuit of big tarpon with a fly rod began in the Keys following World War II.

Texas's waters at Port Aransas (on the Gulf Coast) became a major tarpon destination early in the 20th century. By the 1930s it was famous, and consistent with the angling ethos of that era, big fish were caught in large numbers, killed, hung up for the hero photo, and

An angler battles a leaping Keys oceanside tarpon and ultimately brings it boatside for close-up admiration.

Tarpon nursery waters are found deep in the mangroves, where tannic-stained waters provide protection and millions of mosquito larvae to eat. (Courtesy of Dr. Aaron Adams)

dumped at night. Following WWII, the Aransas fishery began to slide precipitously and was gone by the early '60s. Suspected culprits are overfishing and environmental degradation that followed heavy industrialization of the area.

Cuba would have been the first major international destination for American tarpon anglers. Pioneering guys like *Field & Stream* fishing editor A. J. McClane and baseball great Ted Williams chased tarpon in Cuba in the '50s. Politics intervened, however, as Fidel Castro's seizure of power and subsequent alliance with the Soviet Union slammed shut that door for decades. More-recent visitors have enjoyed spectacular angling for fish in locations long off-limits to Cubans. Castro set up large "parks" to create security zones for him and his cronies, and no-entry rules were enforced zealously by heavily armed Cuban

security forces. The result was vast swaths of almost completely undeveloped, untouched habitat teeming with tarpon (and bonefish and permit). Plus, the resident fish hadn't seen people, boats (the Castro regimes have this thing about their citizens getting into boats), or anglers—for a long time. My friend Rick Hirsch, with dozens of trips to Cuba under his belt, tells me fishing there is akin to the fishing the Keys in the '50s—the 1850s!

Costa Rica stepped in to fill this breach in the late 1960s. Casa Mar Lodge was opened on the Rio Colorado—a jungle river that issues from large Lake Nicaragua (infamous for its freshwater bull sharks) and empties into the Caribbean. The river, and its turbulent mouth, hosted legions of big tarpon in its dark waters. Most of the fishing was done in rickety johnboats casting sinking lines to unseen but plentiful poons. A good angler could catch more big tarpon in a week or two than in an entire season in the clear-water Keys' fishery. Casa Mar attracted a parade of high-profile saltwater fly rodders, including Lefty Kreh, Del Brown, Dan Blanton, Flip Pallot, and Kay Brodney. All I know of the fishery is secondhand from Captain Bergmann. Young Bus visited the lodge in the '70s with his father, caught his first tarpon, rubbed elbows with Kreh and company, and got put on the path to becoming a Keys flats guide. By the '80s, however, political unrest and other factors put Casa Mar on a downward spiral from which it never recovered.

Back in Florida, fly fishing for tarpon off southwest Florida exploded in recent years. Angling there occurs in deeper waters compared to the Keys, along the sandy Gulf of Mexico beaches. Larger boats are commonly used, and the deeper waters (often 10 to 15 feet deep) prompt more reliance on electric trolling motors than push poles. Tarpon "Grand Central Station" is Boca Grande Pass, a relatively narrow, deep (45 to 50 feet) pass connecting Charlotte Harbor to the Gulf. Big poons stack up like cordwood in the pass and get hammered by a packed fleet of boats dropping jigs and live baits. It often looks like bumper cars on the water. Tarpon move in and out of the pass to cruise adjacent waters.

Outside Boca Grande Pass are some beautiful, relatively shallow sandbars and flats that look like perfect spots to intercept cruising tarpon. I asked my Pine Island–based guide why we didn't stake out there. Rather than answering immediately, he offered, "Let me show you." With that he fired up the outboard and began to cruise the area, instantly pointing out numbers of monstrous hammerhead and broad-shouldered bull sharks. After I finished gasping, he explained, "You can hook tarpon on the sand, but they beeline for the deep water and get nailed by these sharks. It ain't no place for a fly rod." I didn't argue. Bill Bishop's book, *High Rollers*, is the bible for the southwest Florida fly-rod tarpon fishery.

Florida's east coast is also part of the contemporary tarpon game. Recall that many of the spring tarpon we see in the Keys migrate up the Atlantic coast as far north as Chesapeake Bay. These migrants can be found off the eastern beaches, in places such as Cape Canaveral and Vero Beach, in late spring/early summer. The silver kings will pause en route to gorge on balls of baitfish often found along the surf line. Millions of small glass minnows (aka majuga) will pack up in dark balls that get preyed upon by hungry poons. In fact, the tarpon often herd the minnows toward the beach and then go to town on the small baitfish. Clued-in local anglers can be found in small boats searching for packs of feeding tarpon just outside the surf line on calm summer dawns. Trolling motors are commonly used, as poling can be difficult in the deeper waters while waves roll into the beach. The boat eases up to the feeding, slurping tarpon and baitfish-imitation flies are pitched into the melee. When the sun gets higher—and brighter and hotter—the feeding ceases until that evening, or the next morning.

A few intrepid souls fish off the beach rather than on the bow. With slick conditions and calm surf, the tarpon can move in hard to the shoreline, well within casting range of beach-bound anglers, offering a chance for the rare and unusual—a fly-rod-caught tarpon while wading. The biggest-capacity fly reels are essential so they can be loaded with hundreds of yards of gel-spun backing. David Olson, an aficionado of this extreme form of tarpon fishing, has had fly-hooked big poons take 500 yards of line and keep going. But landing big fish is not impossible. David has gotten a number of bona fide 100-pounders while wading central Florida's gentle Atlantic summer surf.

Back in the Keys, catching tarpon is far more challenging than "back in the day." The heavily pressured fish are evidently wise to the way of anglers. And it doesn't help that the average migratory poon is a teenager that has seen and rejected flies for nearly a decade. The 1940s-era big-band leader Glenn Miller must have known tarpon. His classic "In the Mood" describes precisely what may be the key ingredient for successful tarpon angling: The fish must be in a willing state, or frustration is the order of the day (sounds eerily like my former love life). Bonefish are usually willing and permit rarely. Tarpon play it in the middle, blowing hot or cold mostly for reasons that defy human comprehension. Lockjaw is an all-too-common experience, especially while chasing Keys ocean swimmers:

Lockjawed tarpon frequently snub even well-presented flies (note the fly line on the right side).

MAY 1, CRAIG KEY, MOSTLY SUNNY, 80, WIND ESE 15. LJMFers! [You can decode it after Lock Jawed.] Found the tarpon today but they were buttoned up tight. About 500 tarpon swam by us on the afternoon ebb tide and moved over grass—generally a good combo for action. But not today. Most of the fish were squirrelly, wouldn't track, and got all out of sorts nearing the skiff. Albert poled his brains out and Mac and I had a hundred good shots throwing Toads and the Mouse in multiple sizes and colors as well as the rabbit strip worm, earning maybe two looks. Definitely not in the mood. ●

Two natural disasters, Hurricane Irma in 2017 and the coronavirus pandemic in 2020, unwittingly (and unfortunately) provided compelling evidence for the "heavily pressured tarpon are hard to fool with a fly" hypothesis. For at least two months after Irma, virtually no one ventured onto the Keys flats. The smaller resident tarpon went unmolested. When anglers

got back onto the water, there was amazement about how friendly the fish had become. Prior to the big storm it was possible to take one or two small tarpon from the pack before the activity shut them down. After the hurricane-imposed layoff, the fish simply stayed happy for a long time and looked upon flies as long-missed delicacies.

Much the same occurred during the pandemic. Visitors were barred from the Keys at the beginning of the annual big tarpon migration, and fishing pressure declined 90 percent or more. Non-angling boat traffic dropped like a rock. Local anglers discovered quickly that tarpon were hanging around backcountry banks and basins in numbers not seen in decades, laying up high or swimming about happily. Diminished boat traffic, and angling numbers, made the Keys look like the 1950s and the tarpon responded in kind. Similarly, ocean-migrating tarpon weren't being run over by boats and were not running a gauntlet of flats skiffs and fly-flinging anglers. The fish were mostly swimming high and slow and really ready to eat well-presented flies. LJMFers were in short supply.

Reversion to normal conditions, however, prompted a rebound in heavy fishing pressure and the return of traditionally finicky Keys tarpon. But even under these conditions, actively feeding tarpon are not too difficult to feed. In fact, if you simply want to catch a poon, drifting live mullet or crabs in Keys bridge channels is almost guaranteed to get you hooked up. The fish stack up in the channels and dine on the baitfish and crabs carried in and out on strong tidal currents. Plus, the bulk of feeding occurs at night or during low-light conditions of early morning or evening. Poons have those big eyes for a reason. Fly anglers are almost always trying to catch them the hard way— when the fish are not eating and focused on reproduction. Typical fly fishing, while the big April–June migration is under way, entails staking out on the ocean side of the Keys, waiting for strings and schools of tarpon to swim by as they cruise from one big channel to the next. It's all part of the big pre-spawning aggregation culminating in those offshore spawning jaunts. In addition, the ocean cruising occurs in broad daylight and in clear water 4 to 8 feet deep. Rarely are these fish seen feeding. So, it should be no surprise that anglers can present lots of flies to these particular tarpon and get relatively few bites.

Fly fishers need luck or hope for "hatches." Saltwater flats anglers have stolen the term from the trout world where actual aquatic insects emerge (hatch), prompting trout to gobble up the bugs or our artificial flies to imitate them. Palolo worms emerging from coral banks and sponges are the only thing in Keys waters that qualifies remotely as a "hatch." And when the little reddish worms swim up to race en masse offshore for their spawning rituals, the tarpon eat the hell out of them. Firing out a worm fly into the feeding melee and swinging it in a hard-running current or swimming it with a two-handed strip usually earns plenty of grabs. But worm hatches can be hard to intercept. Evening falling tides after a full or new moon in late May to mid-June are supposed to be prime time.

Palolos, unfortunately, often don't get the message—they emerge when they want to emerge. During the season, we embark on

A departing school of non-biting tarpon flip their tails at Captain Collins and his anglers.

The mysterious 3-inch-long palolo worm hatches on special Keys evenings, creating tarpon feeding frenzies that provide great opportunities for prepared anglers.

evening "worm patrols" when the tides and moon are right in search of the little buggers, finding them on maybe one evening in four. The biggest emergences are usually found around the big bridges, with Bahia Honda being the most reliable. And because of this, it is reliably packed with boats on prospective evenings. When the stars line up, thousands upon thousands of worms swim out of the sponges and corals, shimmying out to sea, and thousands of tarpon roll up to eat them. It can be one of angling's great wild experiences.

Finding a worm hatch, though, is no guarantee of angling success. Sometimes there are too few worms, other times too many. Sometimes the fish don't show up. My favorite setup is finding swimming worms in modest numbers spread out over a good-sized area as opposed to being concentrated in a hard-flowing channel. Tarpon will hunt the little swimmers, and getting a worm pattern within 10 feet usually gets an accelerating surface gulp. Fish can be widely scattered, and a lot of patience is needed to get maybe a dozen good shots in an evening. An orange sun is often setting, waters are calm and slick, and quiet prevails. Worm-slurping tarpon are visible and audible. It might be the prettiest tarpon fishing there is.

Shrimp "hatches" are another great opportunity for fly anglers. These feeding events, however, are not hatches, or emergences, per se. Rather, patches of floating, dying grass can deoxygenate the water, also turning it a sickly brown/orange, which forces the critters below the surface—shrimp, little crabs, small baitfish—to surface, gasping for air. Little shrimp are the most obvious, as they can be seen leaping, hence the term "shrimp hatch." Tarpon of all sizes key on these spots to bust or slurp the stricken bait. A common event throughout the Keys' backcountry from July through October, the hatches create good fishing for 5- to 25-pound tarpon. Often enough the big ones home in to provide spectacular opportunities, as the fish are eating greedily and will chase down flies:

JULY 18, MOSTLY SUNNY, 90, WIND SLICK CALM TO SE 5. Capt. Rich [Keating] and I set out for the backcountry at 7 a.m. in search of poons. Found a good pod of rollers off one of the little mangrove keys and quickly got a pair of 10-lbers on #1 shrimp flies. Ran E to check another spot and cut the engine to watch and listen. To our pleasant surprise some shrimp were popping in the deeper water, eliciting noisy grabs by good-sized fish. Stowed the 8-weight and grabbed a 10 with a bigger Mouse pattern on the 50 lb. bite tippet. Watched patiently and then a poon took a shrimp off the top 45 feet away at 10 o'clock. Made a quick cast and midway through the first long slow strip the tarpon rose to garbage the fly. The fish turned, the hook sunk into its tongue, and Mr. Poon surged away to the SW in a series of ooh-inspiring greyhounding leaps and cartwheels. Steady pressure finally got it close, three good boatside leaps impressed us some more, then Rich grabbed the 50-pounder, plucked out the fly, and released a fine summer morning poon. ●

A rarer event is the "guppy hatch" which, at least around Marathon, is associated with majuga, aka glass minnows. Late summer and early fall produce large concentrations of the small, translucent, 2- to 3-inch minnows. The little guys will school or ball up near shore and gently ripple the surface under calm conditions. A combination of warm water and too many fish in a small space produces plenty of dead minnows floating on the surface or drifting suspended, ringing the dinner bell for a variety of fish. Small tarpon seem to know exactly where this is happening and home in for a surfeit of majuga. The poons are surprisingly picky and good small minnow imitations are de rigueur; expensive gummy minnow flies are among the best. Fishing starts just after first light and lasts two to three hours—more than enough time to wear out your arm casting to and fighting a dozen energetic tarpon. Small fish in the 5- to 20-pound class dominate, although heftier 50- to 60-pounders will crash the party too.

Then there are the few and far between epic days when the ocean tarpon get in the mood and decide to chew on flies—days cherished deeply and remembered in great detail for decades. May 1, 2002, was a day for the ages. In fact, outside of one or two wild worm hatches, it produced more bites and jumps—in two hours—than I ever saw before or since. It was

Captain Albert demonstrates that not all summer shrimp-eaters are small; this one is about 30 pounds.

so extraordinary that I deliberately left it out of *Seasons on the Flats* (my first book published in 2012), fearing that readers would think it total BS:

MAY 1, BAHIA HONDA, MOSTLY SUNNY, 85, WIND 10–15 SE. Morning in the backcountry was a bust—one lone tarpon without a shot. Capt. Bus declared it was time to check the ocean side, so Bud Hodson and I sat down for the boat ride. Ran under the old rusting RR bridge at Bahia Honda (hoping a loose girder wouldn't fall on us) and Bus wheeled the Mirage east toward the sandy runs off the beach. Ahead in the clear green water we saw a big dark patch that resolved into a profusion of eyeballs, dorsals, and tails. A giant school of hundreds of tarpon was in a big counterclockwise pirouette oozing slowly the "wrong way"—east. Bus got us inside the fish, and I was up first. Clamped down on butterflies to finally make a good cast, got an instant bite, and hookup. One big jump and the tarpon was gone. Bud got on the bow, fired in the fly, earning another immediate hookup

and jump. Decided not to lose the school by fighting and chasing a fish, so the goal was bites and jumps. The tarpon were aggressive and if you pulled the fly away from one, another would charge over to eat. It was giddy, exhilarating angling with big poons acting like farm pond bluegills. Two hours later we were still with the school a couple of miles to the east. The tally was 18 fed, 12 jumped, and two landed (a couple of 50-lbers we couldn't break off!). We were running out of steam, especially poor Bus. Then a big hammerhead shark roared in, blowing up the school and sparing us the need to hook anymore. An ecstatic, exhausted trio headed for the boat ramp. A spectacular, unforgettable day. ●

And one I would love to repeat, but probably never will.

Moody fish are common in fresh and salt. I'm struck by the resemblance of ocean tarpon to Alaska red salmon or Atlantic salmon. Reds, or sockeyes, are notoriously fickle when it comes to eating flies. Tens of millions storm into the Bristol Bay river systems early each summer. The sleek blue/silver fish pack into

Tarpon often swim in a circular "daisy chain," and a well-presented fly often earns a hookup.

pools and runs and are impossible to miss. An angler can show a fly to hundreds on every cast and spend hours doing this without a bite. Suddenly a raven croaks, a small cloud covers the sun, or a breeze ripples the water. Sockeyes now grab the fly aggressively, and for an hour or two, fishing's a bonanza. But it shuts down as abruptly as it started—and no one has a clue why. Atlantic salmon can do the same, rewarding only the most persistent fishers.

Why the tarpon will eat one day and not the next defies explanation. Three seasons ago I experienced back-to-back days that put these mysteries on full display. On May 12 fishing near home on the Atlantic side, I got on a solid afternoon push of tarpon, seeing 300-plus poons in about two and a half hours. A worm fly struck out but, on a hunch, I tried a 1/0 Olive Toad and the fish wanted it. Fed six and landed four fishing solo—which is always a trip, especially when fighting and chasing a hooked tarpon. Returned the following day brimming with optimism:

MAY 13, CLEAR, 85, WIND 10–15 E. What a difference a day makes. Weather was the same, tide was the same, only 45 minutes later. Back to the same spot and tarpon appeared on schedule, but numbers were down a bit. Showed the Olive Toad to a bunch of the swimmers—like yesterday—but now they treated it like a radioactive object, ducking and turning away. Other flies got spurned too. There's never any figuring out these fish. ●

If there's an answer, it's a simple one: Fish a lot and hope to be on the water when the tarpon are in the mood.

Compared to ocean cruisers, backcountry tarpon—those found in Florida Bay or Gulf of Mexico waters north and west of the Keys—have a reputation as easier to feed. I'm not so sure, as many an excellent presentation to such fish has gotten nothing but abject refusals. One Gulf-side haunt owns me. Tarpon appear there predictably in March and April and if the light is OK, spotting the fish isn't difficult. Most lie facing a trickling current that runs east or west depending on the tide. Some tarpon will swim into the basin from outside, rolling occasionally and pushing a surface wake if it's on the calm side. Captain Bergmann knows it well and has one client who always catches fish here. The place is Kryptonite for me, and 10 years have passed since I last caught one here—and I've tried a lot in the interim. Maybe it's gotten into my head and I'm sending bad vibes down the line.

Laid-up tarpon, the equivalent of tailing bonefish, are a substantial part of the early season (mid- February to mid-April) back-country fishery for poons. As noted above, the big fish will float motionless near the surface or down a couple of feet. Those on top stand out distinctly, with dorsal fins and tails sticking above the surface; when you see 3 feet or more between the dorsal and the tail, the anxiety/excitement meter ratchets up. Deeper fish present an outline with the apparent color a function of the fish's depth: high fish tend to browns, a little farther down I see a combo of gray and green, deep tarpon—4 or 5 feet down—tend to turquoise. Murkier waters near the Everglades create "pink tails"—laid-up big tarpon with definitely pinkish tails. Don't ask me why.

Stalking these lurking battlewagons is a heart-pounding, sweaty-palms affair. You know you're going to get only one, maybe two casts. The presentations must be stealthy and precise—with a big fly rod while your knees quake. A fly landing too close guarantees a spook and the big boil of a departing fish—after all, tarpon don't eat stuff that falls from the sky. Too far away and the fish doesn't see it or is too lazy to swim a few feet to eat the tiny morsel. If there's some current, it gets used to drift the fly close to the fish, but the fly placement has to be exact to make that happen. The reward for doing it right is awesome. The fly is gently bumped or wiggled in the tarpon's face, you see the tail make a subtle stroke, and the previously still tarpon eases ahead and eats the fly. Sometimes the take is a big gulp and the fly disappears into the dark hole of the great mouth; other times the jaws crack open an inch or two and the fly is sipped in—like a spring creek brown trout daintily taking a tiny dry fly. Either way, it's game on. The fly goes down the hatch, the line comes tight, and the tarpon goes instantly nuts. Longtime tarpon chasers are nearly unanimous that laid-up poons are the pinnacle of the sport:

Keys backcountry tarpon like to lay up in the early spring, especially when it is calm and warm.

APRIL 2, CLEAR, 85, WIND WSW 10 AND DROPPING. Working a Florida Bay channel for rollers, spotted movement and color 50 yards below me. A fish moved up on the bank edge and I thought "shark." Another look showed tarpon gray/green and the fish stopped to lay up in the slow current. Carefully repositioned the skiff to cinch up 75 feet upcurrent. A first ranging cast was a tad short. The second was on the $ and the Olive Mouse swung perfectly in front of the big tarpon. Saw the mouth open, close, came tight, and the fish shook its head in confusion. Then game on. Off it went jumping across the channel and I unclipped the anchor to follow. Disaster loomed—the line caught on an old lobster trap buoy. Got on my belly on the bow, laid down the rod, held the line to work it free while the tarpon was jumping a hundred yards away (fishing solo can be such a pain). Breathed and another problem—big wads of weeds (Lion's Mane) that I couldn't shake free. Somehow the leader held, managed to gain line on the fish, finally got the weeds off, and down to business. Pulling it close earned me jumps #7 and #8— the last a wallowing, head-shaking, gill-rattling affair. Admired the broad green back and deep girthy body of a triple-digit poon then broke it off. As good as it gets. ●

Weather is a huge factor contributing to success, or lack thereof. Tarpon are fair-weather fish compared to bones and perms. Poons really like nice, stable weather, not too hot, not too cold, and a bit of wind—but not too much. They're the Goldilocks of the flats. Slick, calm days on the ocean will reveal a lot of tarpon, but approaching and feeding the fish is very difficult. You'll pray for a bit of breeze.

Backcountry tarpon, especially the early season fish, are an exception, being very partial to beautiful calm days and exhibiting a willingness to bite. In February when the wind dies away, a bright sun shines, and the thermometer reaches 80, poons will appear almost magically in any number of Florida Bay and Gulf-side basins to lay up or cruise around:

FEB. 14, CLEAR, 80–85, CALM TO A HINT OF SE. A Valentine's Day tarpon for Jeannette. A perfect day meant a long boat ride to a favorite Gulf haunt was in order. Got there

Prime early season tarpon days are hot, humid, and still.

about 10, cut the motor far out, and dug out the binocs. The view was impressive: a few rolling tarpon and tails and dorsals galore marking laid-up fish. We crept in and went to work with multiple shots at swimmers and laid-up fish. But no one wanted to cooperate and bite. The current slacked, more fish floated up, and I moved us carefully to the other side of the basin with Jeannette up front. A trio oozed in from 12/1 o'clock and she put the 1/0 Chartreuse Toad about 45 feet from the boat and in the tarpon track. Fish #2 lined up nicely and eyed the fluttering fly. Jeannette bumped it once to draw attention, a second to draw the fish closer, and a third bump earned the gulp. She stripped the hook home and Mr. Poon was up and off, making the new Riptide hum. A real acrobat, the 90-pounder jumped itself out, clearing the water eight times. Great show. That took the starch out and I got the leader. Asked Jeannette if that was an OK Valentine's Day present—she said yes, but still expected roses when we got home! ●

A day later a cold front blew in and the tarpon vanished. Longtime observers are convinced the tarpon are relatively nearby in deeper parts of the Gulf of Mexico, appearing overnight in inshore waters when it gets calm and toasty and disappearing just as quickly when Keys winter returns.

Earnest ocean cruising begins in mid-April, and these fish are the real Goldilocks. The fish pour on nice days—sun, 80, and east to southeast wind around 10. If it starts to blow hard, say 20+, the fish will still swim for a day or two but if the wind does not relent, a big shutdown occurs. An angler who can stand up in the boat and deliver a fly when it's blowing 20 or more can feed plenty of tarpon during these windows. But by day three of heavy wind, the poons hole up in the big bridge channels, terrorizing mullet and crabs.

Any reference to Goldilocks and tarpon triggers memories of the unique, unusual gold tarpon that periodically visits the Middle Keys each spring. The tarpon is a bona fide golden yellow, matching the color of sargassum seaweed but much brighter. Each year in Florida, reports of pale-colored or piebald-marked fish filter in. But this girl, now an 80- to 90-pounder, is pure gold throughout. She made her first appearance for me on April 29, 2011, swimming near Long Key. Captain Bus and I spotted the odd color, and had no idea what it was until she swam into range. I got a shot, but the fish wasn't interested. I christened her "Moby Tarpon," figuring a rare fish like this is akin to Melville's great white whale. Bus prefers "Goldmember," which always gets a laugh.

Five years later she reappeared—on back-to-back days. April 28 found Bus, Paul Turcke, and me bobbing near Long Key when a tarpon eight-pack appeared to our east. The bright spot of color was unmistakable in the clear green water, and here she came amid her pals. Paul got a great shot, showed her the fly, but alas no interest. The next day I was 20 miles west near Marathon sharing a skiff with Captain Ponzoa and Bud Hodson, and "Moby" showed up again among a bigger group of fish. She ignored Bud's well-presented fly.

The fact that the fish returns to the Middle Keys with some regularity indicates we may be fishing to some of the same tarpon each year. No wonder they're hard to fool. It also has implications for the overall tarpon population. If we're encountering the same fish every year,

the population may be smaller than we think (or want). However, if we get a different mix of tarpon each spring, the more-mixed population may be larger. This is one of the mysteries the acoustic-tagging program is designed to solve. Time will tell. In the meantime, I'm hoping there's an "Ahab" out there ready to catch the tarpon of a lifetime. The release photo will be one in a million.

Back to the weather. Multiple days of meteorological crud can even drive the spring tarpon offshore. In 2012, poons had appeared on schedule and were swimming happily up and down the Middle Keys through April 26. Rotten weather blew in on the 27th with heavy dark gray clouds, black squall lines, drenching rain, and stiff winds. And stayed that way for five days. A few tarpon were seen on the 28th—when we weren't hiding under a bridge dodging a squall—but numbers dwindled fast and then it was too bad to even go out. The tarpon simply disappeared. One of the bait guides cruised under the Bahia Honda bridge and his fish finder came up empty—on May 1. Normally thousands of tarpon congregate then under the bridge. The weather broke on

A flats angler's dream: a big school of May oceanside poons cruises into casting range.

Moby/Goldie appears yet again—this time in a bigger school of poons. (Courtesy of Dr. Neal Rogers)

May 2, but the tarpon remained absent. On May 4 tarpon reappeared inshore, and fishing resumed on May 5. There's no denying the big fish are weather sensitive.

Keys summer tarpon are early morning fish, best when it's calm. The boat is prepped the night before and you turn in early. The alarm goes off in the predawn dark, you fish around for the off button, then sit up and listen intently. Clashing, rustling palm fronds mean wind—back to sleep. Silence beckons you out of bed and you pad to the kitchen and coffee machine

to wake up, excited by the prospect of rolling, feeding poons as an orange sun peeks over the horizon. Daytime heat, and more likely the high bright sun, shut down the tarpon usually by 10 a.m.—a reminder that tarpon have those big eyes (Megalops) because they are dominantly nighttime or low-light feeders.

Nighttime fishing—spring and summer—can be very effective but has its drawbacks. First, all the visual thrills that make tarpon on the fly so special are lacking. Second, most nighttime action is under the big bridges.

Hooked tarpon shred fly lines, cut off backing on barnacle-encrusted pilings, or get eaten by monster bull and hammerhead sharks that are even more proficient nighttime predators.

The annual early spring appearance of big pelagic bulls and hammers is a sure sign that the tarpon migration is about to commence. They shadow the tarpon, waiting for the fish to make a mistake before racing to dispatch a big poon in a maelstrom of foam and blood. We all cringe and lament the loss of a favorite gamefish, but the sharks are doing no more than acting like the apex predators they are.

Tarpon get edgy when sharks are around and, in some cases, anglers feel the same. Two springs ago I was anchored on a clear-water oceanside tarpon run when a relatively young 8-foot-long hammerhead cruised into view. It saw the skiff and glided over for a closer look, swimming around the boat two rod lengths away. By the bow, the shark rolled up angling the unique T-bar head in my direction, and I came eye to eye with the curious fish. Mr. Hammer swam off but returned 20 minutes later for a repeat performance. I know the shark was checking me out—likely out of curiosity but maybe hunger as well.

Danger is not associated, usually, with flats fishing. Weather events like gusty black squall lines, crackling lightning, and evil-looking waterspouts command respect and can put the imprudent at risk.

Big sharks are a threat to the tarpon, but anglers don't expect to find themselves one rung down the predatory ladder. However, there's always an exception to every rule (before proceeding it's necessary to note that Captain Albert's skiff is tippy and he has installed a narrow U-shaped grab bar on the bow):

MAY 6, MOSTLY CLOUDY, 85, WIND NW 5–10. We waited at the low tide end of the channel and a small flutterball of tarpon (8 to 10) fish eased in from the E. Albert had to point the bow N into the current/breeze with the pack 45 feet behind us at 6/7 o'clock. A backcast down the portside got the fly there; tightened up and used the current to swing it into the fish. The fly didn't go far, saw a flash of silver, and the line snapped tight. A very big girl launched straight up showing plenty of girth . . . 20 grunting/groaning minutes later had her wallowing on the surface just in front of the skiff; the leader was well inside the rod guides. Started to break her off when a monster bull shark blossomed underneath the tarpon. The tarpon jumped, the bull shark's ugly blunt head came out of the water a la Jaws, and the tarpon fell back on the bull, creating a seething vortex of brown, silver, and green/white foam almost under my feet. Ms. Poon righted herself, darted right, then dived back under the boat. My rod followed, slamming the gunwale. I jumped to the right edge of

Captain Rich and Don Wright hide from a Keys storm under an Overseas Highway bridge.

the bow and broke off the tarpon. An enraged shark tried to dive after the fish but slammed into the boat, tipping it steeply. Felt myself going overboard, desperately grabbed back, and barely got the bar to stay aboard. The tarpon escaped; the frustrated bull whooshed around the boat then raced off. A shaky angler and guide shuddered at the thought of going into the water with that shark. ●

Moody, edgy, sensitive tarpon have changed fishing for the big beasts. Angling tactics have grown increasingly sophisticated over the decades, with a pronounced trend toward lighter rods, lighter leaders, and smaller flies. Thirty-five years ago, standard tarpon fly rods were bona fide war clubs. Fenwick, Scientific Anglers, and Shakespeare jumped into the tarpon rod business, producing the "Tarpon Tamer" (the FF9012), the "Great Equalizer," and the "Tarpon Ugly Stik," respectively. The Ugly Stik was a thick white fiberglass model capable of deadlifting a marine battery—when

they figured how to keep the tip-top guide on the rod. The Equalizer was also a beast reputedly able to deadlift 12 pounds. Casting them was not a pleasure but all were tough, most of the time. Captain Bergmann's first 1979 guide trip to the Marquesas had Norman Duncan on the bow, who broke one of the Shakespeare rods on a big fish.

Stu Apte and Fenwick came up with a unique rod featuring a 4-foot-long insert: the FF116. When a fish was hooked, the insert was shoved up the butt section of the rod through an opening at the base of the reel seat. It stiffened the rod substantially to allow real pressure to be put on the tarpon, particularly with the rod's butt section. Without the stiffening insert, the rod was more flexible and cast better. Graphite, which appeared on the scene in the '70s, was a big improvement. Lighter and stiffer, the rods cast well, but the early models had thin walls and many blew up when fighting a big poon. The standard rod was also a 12-weight, and a short cork grip on the rod butt—about a foot above the regular grip—was a common feature. Separating your hands was supposed to provide more leverage when pulling on a hooked tarpon. Extra cork grips disappeared about 15 years ago, and rods began to get lighter. More 11- and then 10-weights appeared in flats boat gunwale rod racks. My standard tarpon rig became a 10-weight in about 2006; the lighter rods are easier to throw, and lighter fly lines land with less disturbance—important when pursuing spooky fish.

A big factor in the switch to lighter rods is changing attitudes about what constitutes a "caught" tarpon. Sixty years ago, many tarpon were gaffed, taken to the dock for a hanging hero shot, and discarded. When catch-and-release started to take hold, it was necessary to grab the tarpon by the lower jaw and remove the fly for the fish to be considered "caught." Later this evolved into the "guide grabs the leader" rule or "getting the leader into the tip guide" is a caught fish. Both of these conventions are still reflected in the big three Keys tarpon fly-fishing tournaments: the Gold Cup, Hawley, and Golden Fly. All require "release" fish to be "caught" by the guide grabbing the

leader or getting the leader to the rod tip followed by breaking off the tarpon. "Weight fish" have to be controlled boatside and measured so the estimated weight can be calculated.

A significant cadre of anglers and guides has settled on a "catch" consisting of getting the leader to the rod tip. Two good reasons underpin this call. First, the average tarpon can be "caught" in this way in about 10 to15 minutes; once the leader touches the rod, it's easy to crank down the drag, point the rod straight at the tarpon, and break it off (the preferably de-barbed hook will simply fall out). It often takes twice as long to tire the fish sufficiently to physically grab it for the break-off. Second, the more-tired fish are exposed to predation by the big bulls and hammers, and exhausted, disoriented tarpon are easy prey. So, what does this have to do with the rod? Controlling a boatside tarpon is easier with the heavier, stiffer sticks. Captain Scott Collins, who has won all three of the tarpon tournaments multiple times, wants his anglers to be fishing 12-weights—in the tournaments—for that reason. But for non-tournament angling, he's happy to have his anglers throwing a 10. Getting close to a

Big sharks sometimes attack hooked tarpon. The results aren't pretty.

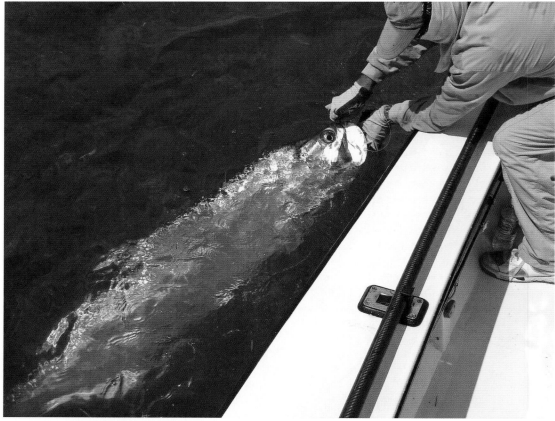

Captain Albert releasing a big fall tarpon subdued on a 12-weight rig.

hooked tarpon, via the outboard or the boat pole, and popping it off reduces or eliminates the need for the heavy 12s.

These considerations and warier tarpon have also changed leaders. The traditional tarpon leader was constructed in three sections: butt, class tippet, and bite, or shock, tippet. The butt was commonly 50 or 60-pound-test nylon mono; the class tippet, 12 or 16-pound hard mono and a minimum of 15 inches; and the bite tippet, 80- or 100-pound-test mono and a maximum of 12 inches. The lengths are prescribed by the International Game Fish Association (IGFA) rules. An improved blood knot (invented by Apte) and a Bimini twist (brought to the flats by Bill Curtis or Norman Duncan) connected the butt to the class. Another Bimini and a Huffnagle (legendary guide Steve Huff's knot) secured the bite tippet to the class. The Bimini connections at both ends of the class created knots about 2 inches long. The fly was tied on with a Homer Rhode loop knot. Since the old mono was stiff, curly stuff, the leaders were painstakingly stretched and stored with flies attached in old stretcher boxes.

Most modern leaders are far simpler. The three-part construction remains, but the knots are either Apte improved blood knots or the Slim Beauty (which is a half Apte and a figure-eight jam knot). Both are easy to tie in the boat and are very small knots less visible to sharp-eyed poons. And as new monos and fluoro-carbon are easier to stretch straight, stretcher boxes are largely a thing of the past. In addition, class tippets are often 20-pound-test Mason hard mono, and there is less need for the cushioning effect of a springy Bimini twist that was more important when using 16-pound or 12-pound-test class line. Plenty of veteran guides still use Biminis and Huffnagles, especially when fishing tournaments that require the use of 12- or 16-pound class tippets.

Bite tippets have shrunk in diameter over three decades. In the '80s, I recall 80-pound test as the standard. By the late '90s we were down to 60-pound test and fluorocarbon was displacing mono. The fluoro is supposedly less visible but more importantly it has greater abrasion resistance—a crucial factor in landing tarpon. In the last few years, I find myself fishing frequently with 40-pound bite tippets, particularly in late May and June on ocean swimmers. As summer approaches, the ocean side of the Keys gets clearer and calmer. The lighter tippet seems to get more bites even if the fish chew through it more frequently. I want the bites and will take the break-offs.

The advent of clear and clear-tip fly lines has also enhanced the ability to fish in stealth mode. Clear lines can be a royal pain to use, as it can be very difficult to pinpoint your fly and its relationship to a tarpon. But a number of very skilled anglers swear by them and are convinced the stealth benefits outweigh the difficult features. Most guides I know hate these lines because they must be able to tell a client the precise location of the fly to talk the client through feeding the tarpon. I use clear lines sparingly but always keep one rigged and ready because there are times when it becomes a necessary tool to fool edgy poons.

Clear-line controversies highlight a crucial skill for successful tarpon chasers—knowing the precise relationship of the fly to the fish.

Tarpon have a much greater propensity to bite when they find a fly at particular angles. Common knowledge recognizes that a fly that "attacks" a fish by coming toward its eye or face usually earns a spook and hardly ever a bite. Conversely, a presentation too far away won't draw much interest, as lazy poons don't swim out of their way for a tiny snack. Veteran guides have watched thousands of tarpon eat flies, and they can watch a fly in relationship to a tarpon and predict accurately a coming bite when the presentation angle and movement is right. Good anglers have developed the same skill, knowing exactly where to put a fly to increase the odds of an eat. In fact, many times it helps to fish a more-visible fly pattern (more visible to the angler) to secure that absolutely precise presentation rather than trying to calculate the location of the unseen fly.

With moving fish, flowing currents, and moving boats, the tarpon/fly relationship is highly fluid and can change in an instant. Being acutely aware of these situations can yield repeated optimal presentations and is a crucial difference between catching the big guys and returning to the dock muttering "They just wouldn't bite today":

Jim's first fly-rod tarpon goes airborne—note the prime calm early season conditions.

MARCH 2, FLORIDA BAY, MOSTLY SUNNY, 80, SLICK CALM. Jim Carter scored his first big fly-rod poon when fish and fly lined up right. A few fish were cruising a basin and positioned him to throw to a three-pack sliding in from 10 o'clock. He acknowledged seeing two and got a 1/0 Olive Bug in the zone. Two of the tarpon shied away and Jim was about to recast when I cried "Leave it." I could see the fly positioned perfectly for fish #3—that Jim couldn't see—and when the tarpon neared the Bug told him to bump it; he did, and the fish slurped it in. A long first run, four jumps, and 20 minutes later I had the leader for him, providing a great look at a solid 80-pounder. High fives exchanged for fly-rod poon #1. ●

Flies have also gotten more diminutive and stealthier. As noted previously, standard 1960s tarpon flies sported big 4/0 or 5/0 hooks. Twenty years ago, Andy Mill led the charge toward smaller flies by winning the tarpon tournaments using a 1/0 Toad. That achievement opened a lot of eyes and flies began shrinking fast. Open a contemporary tarpon fly box and it will be dominated by 1/0 or smaller patterns, especially if the angler plies the Keys' ocean side. Deep in Florida Bay and the Glades, and in murkier waters, big dark patterns like a Black or Purple Mouse dominate. But the clear trend is toward relatively little flies. Too many of us have watched hefty tarpon sipping in little seahorses, guppies, 3-inch worms, baby squid, and tiny crabs to doubt the efficacy of small patterns. Last spring, I tried an experimental swimming crab fly—less than 1 inch in diameter—and caught big tarpon on it. Developments like this have me harkening back to old-fashioned trout fly wisdom. Tarpon flies come in all forms, colors, and sizes—as do trout flies.

Old-time trout guys in patched chest waders advise that size then form are the most important fly factors for selective trout; color is least. It seems tarpon fly development is moving in exactly that direction. However, and there's always a *however* in tarpon fishing, some days color makes all the difference. Captain Collins put me on a bunch of fresh, early season tarpon that steadfastly refused four differently colored Toads and Bugs until color number five did the trick; three relatively quick bites followed.

No discussion of flies and presentations can be complete without recounting the coming of the worm fly 15 years ago. New ways to use the patterns revolutionized fishing for Keys ocean-swimming tarpon. Worm flies have been around for a long time but had almost always been fished in conjunction with the infrequent palolo worm emergences. Stu Apte recognized the importance of the worms and attributed the success of his original orange/red tarpon fly to its color scheme that emulated the palolos. But specific worm flies were reserved for palolo emergences to be cast and swung in the current to worm-eating poons. A few folks used them during non-hatch periods, but no one I'm aware of used worm patterns as a regular go-to pattern. It changed in 2006.

That year, Ralph MacDonald and I were fishing our regular early May days with Captain Ponzoa. Tarpon had been picky, but we had gotten a couple of fish on Mouse patterns. Albert thought the action should have been better given numbers of fish, OK tides, and good presentations. On the morning of May 5, we were on station getting shots at a couple of good schools. My best efforts with the Black Mouse were fruitless. In fact, the tarpon would see the fly and shy from it. The good captain told me to put away the big rod and pull out a 10-weight—with a red rabbit strip worm fly attached. Mac and I questioned our good guide's choice, as we were weeks ahead of the predicted palolo hatches. Albert explained his reasoning: Tarpon come to the Keys every year, and every year they key in on worm hatches. The fish would likely remember the worms, and since the big Mouse patterns were causing them to duck, we should try something smaller.

Couldn't argue with the logic, so I grabbed the rig, stripped out line, and got ready. A small pack of tarpon swam into range; I put the fly in front of them and used the current to let the fly swing slowly to the fish. I was amazed that a poon eased up, gently sipped in the little 3-inch worm, and it was off to the races. Albert leadered the 60-pounder, and he had pretty much convinced me. Later on, Mac tried

Keys tarpon flies have evolved over 60 years from classics like Apte's Tarpon Fly and the Cockroach (below) to Toads (middle), and a host of other fly-box-filling patterns (top).

Choosing Tarpon Flies

Fly selection, for hard-to-feed tarpon, always confronts the unpleasant reality of dock tarpon: those creatures, parked under the marina fish-cleaning table, greedily devouring scraps and offal dumped into the water. Why are these scavengers so utterly picky when it comes to eating flies? Especially when the otherwise magnificent fish are also prone to acting like catfish and eating a dead mullet plunked on the bottom or munching on dolphin (mahi) carcasses scattered under a bridge. Tarpon plainly have extraordinarily catholic tastes, so if they eat damn near everything, why are they so hard to fool with a fly?

Choosing a fly from among the multiplicity of patterns doesn't make it easier. The array of shapes, sizes, and colors can fill dozens of fly boxes, and most can catch anglers. Some catch fish—sometimes. The bulk of tarpon fly patterns fall into the "attractor" category compared to more "imitative" types. Among the latter, only four reflect genuine efforts to imitate specific tarpon prey: palolo worms, baitfish, shrimp, and some crab-type flies. The worms are used extensively in the Keys' oceanside tarpon fishery, and the imitative baitfish flies get used everywhere, especially when the fish are targeting prey such as silvery pilchards. The shrimp and crab imitations can be fine choices in the clear-water parts of the Keys' backcountry spots as well as the ocean.

Far more common are great classic flies that don't look like any particular prey: Stu Apte's patterns, the decades-old Cockroach,

A few of the "fusion" flies (combination of elements from Mouse, Toad, and classic tarpon fly patterns) I like for tarpon: Mouse Toads (left) and Bugs (right).

Recommended tarpon flies, among hundreds of patterns, are the Cockroach, Chartreuse Toad, Olive Toad, Black/Purple Puglisi Baitfish (left from top); Andy Mill Shrimp, Palolo worm, unweighted Kwan for small tarpon (center from top); Purple Mouse, Olive Mouse, and Olive/White Puglisi Baitfish (right from top).

Gary Merriman's Toads, the Mouse, traditional oceanside flies such as the Lemon Drop or White Lightning, and hundreds of variations. The Toad, with a crab-shaped head and trailing marabou or rabbit strip, might look to a poon like a swimming crab with a trailing claw. The Mouse's big deer-hair head profile and long hackles could trigger "mullet" in a tarpon's brain. But the colors are certainly not "natural" to human eyes. The very effective Chartreuse Toad and the Purple Mouse look like nothing I've ever seen swimming around in tarpon waters.

Conventional wisdom posits that successful anglers employ large, dark flies—such as a 2/0 (or bigger) Black Snake or Black Mouse—in

Florida Bay or the Gulf of Mexico where water is off-color or stained. In contrast, oceanside anglers typically prefer smaller (1/0), lighter-colored (chartreuse, lemon, peach) flies or a palolo worm pattern. Clearer Bay/Gulf waters traditionally call for a 1/0 or 2/0 Toad, a 1/0 or 2/0 Mouse, or any other classic pattern. In all venues, fly colors can run the spectrum from black to white including greens, grizzly/brown, olives, pinks, rust, and purples.

I like unnamed "fusion" flies, which are hand-concocted mixes of the elements from various patterns. My "bug" flies have deer hair heads (like the Mouse), trimmed more like a Toad head; a marabou collar; and splayed hackles like the traditional Apte flies. Lately,

I've added rubber legs to Toad patterns, incorporating this feature from the Merkin—a famous permit crab pattern. In my mind, each of these elements can be attractive and putting them together should make them irresistible to big old tarpon.

Any saltwater fly shop, or catalog, will offer a dizzying choice of patterns for big tarpon (over 35 pounds). My experience is to keep it simple, and I'm convinced that five pattern types, in different sizes and colors, will cover 98 percent of fishing for big tarpon in the Keys and elsewhere: the Toad, the Mouse, a Puglisi baitfish, a shrimp, and a palolo worm. Throw in one or more classic-type patterns featuring splayed streamer feathers and you will be armed and ready. If pressed hard to carry only the minimal number of flies, I'd vote for a 1/0 Chartreuse Toad, a 2/0 Purple Mouse, a pair of 1/0 Puglisi Baitfish (one olive/white and one black/purple), a 1/0 Andy Mill Shrimp, and a 1/0 reddish worm (about 3 inches long and your choice of rabbit strip, fur, foam, EP brush, or marabou for the body). If you're classically inclined (like old-time trout anglers who want to fish traditional Catskill-style dry flies), throw in a Cockroach and a White Lightning.

When the quarry is baby or junior tarpon (less than 25 pounds), particularly in the Keys, two patterns do the heavy lifting for me: the Kwan and the Gurgler. The bonefish Kwan pattern looks like a small Toad with the crabby head, a collar of hackle or crystal chenille, a tan craft tail barred vertically with a brown or olive marker pen, and a sprig or two of flash. But as small tarpon love to smack small shrimp scooting around the surface, the weighted eyes of the bonefish Kwan get replaced with black plastic eyes. Stripped near the surface in an erratic, darting manner, small tarpon will utterly smoke this fly.

And if great acrobatic, sloshing bites are more important than actually hooking and catching the juniors, try a Gurgler. The foam head and lip keep the fly on the surface and can drive the fish crazy, eliciting highly entertaining eats. However, a majority of the small tarpon seem to miss the fly or don't get hooked solidly. In my book, the wild bites are absolutely worth it. Tan or white, usually on a lighter size 1 hook, are all you need. These patterns also work well in the Everglades on snook, and occasionally redfish will whomp on them too.

Small tarpon in the fall, in the Keys, also require some kind of glass minnow imitation. The fish will lock onto balls of the small (1 to 2 inches long) silver/translucent minnows and eat nothing else. Gummy minnow patterns or other white/silver patterns—tied small—get the job done on these selective little poons.

In all circumstances, however, presentation is almost always more important than the fly. Well-presented bugs elicit bites; poorly presented flies, even if dead ringers for what the tarpon might be eating, do not.

One last note, please don't hire a guide and reject his fly pattern recommendation, offering, "I want to use _____ because this book said it was a killer." You fish with a guide to tap their extensive professional experience, including which fly to use and when. Rely on that experience and knowledge. ▪

the Mouse, without success, and changed to the worm; he fed two, landing one. Maybe Albert was on to something. Any doubts were swept away the next day, and we were sold on the worm:

MAY 6, CLEAR, 85, WIND SE 10–15.
Spectacular—a bona fide RED LETTER DAY. Seven poons to the boat and five more in the air all on 10-weights and the new worm fly. Albert had explained to Capt. Rich what we were doing, and he chided Albert about using his good clients as guinea pigs for new techniques. When Rich got the after-action report, he got busy digging out his worm flies for the next day. . . . There were two extra cool tarpon. Mac hooked up near shore where a pair of oblivious snorkelers were swimming about. His tarpon raced in and vaulted up about 15 feet from the woman, who levitated out the water heading for shore. Later we felt bad getting a laugh at her expense. I got to throw at a 20-fish daisy chain circling slowly near shore in crystal clear water. The first couple of throws, and regular retrieves, got nothing. Albert told me to twitch it instead. Next cast a couple of twitches interested a poon and two more closed the deal. The fish opened up, surged forward, and inhaled the worm. A simply great bite. Some clown on a jet ski almost ran over my backing but we waved him off at the last instant and got the 75-lber. A really classic tarpon on a 10-weight. ●

In the beginning, five Marathon guides were in on the secret: Albert, Rich, Bus, Scott, and Karl Wagner. Ocean tarpon suddenly weren't so frustrating. As good as the worm fly was, however, it was not absolutely surefire. It took Wagner and a longtime New England client to add the next killing wrinkle. The client came down every year and frequently fished wearing a conical Chinese straw hat. They were fishing the worm, and the hat-wearing client, familiar with the fast two-handed retrieve used for Nantucket false albacore and bonito, suggested it would be a good way to swim the worm when there was little current. So, they tucked their fly rods under their arms and experimented with the two-hand retrieve. The results were eye-popping. Tarpon loved it, and Wagner passed the word to the other guys.

A year later, Captain Scott and Dr. David Dalu from South Carolina secured a spot in the Hawley Tournament. The event came on the back side of terrible weather, and tarpon had vanished. A monster set of worm hatches went unmolested. Fortunately, things turned around, and on day one of the Hawley, Scott and Dave put the worm fly and two-hand to work, along with precision boat setting and casting, and scored six caught tarpon. They went on to win—the first time first entrants had ever won. The two kept up the winning streak in 2008, using the same technique, capturing another Hawley as well as the Golden Fly tourney. They initially didn't have a slot in the 2008 Gold Cup—the oldest, most prestigious, and most competitive of the three tarpon tournaments—but an opening occurred the day before the Cup began and Scott and Dave squeezed in. The pair proceeded to notch another win, using the Worm/two-hand, to set two records: Until then no first-timers had ever won the Gold Cup, and their victory earned them an unprecedented, and unmatched, sweep of all three competitions in a single season. When asked how they did it, the answers were vague and generic, so the secret remained safe.

At the same time, the two-handed technique acquired a politically incorrect name: the Chinaman—derived from the conical straw hat. Some clients, though, couldn't keep a secret. An article or internet posting or two appeared referencing the mysterious "Chinaman"; some called it a fly, others a technique, but no real details leaked out. Success begets scrutiny, however, and before too long Scott and Dave's competitors began to figure out what they were doing. Slowly the cat got out of the bag.

Within a couple of years, in-the-know Keys guides and anglers were working on their worm patterns and employing the two-hand retrieve. Not long thereafter, articles, videos, and internet postings appeared describing the fly and retrieve. None that I'm aware of, however, provided any details about the origins.[1]

---

[1] Monte Burke's book *The Lords of the Fly* credits Scott and Dave for "the realization that palolo worm patterns can work on tarpon all year 'round" (Burke, 2020, p. 252).

The pattern and the retrieve are not panaceas. Casts still need to be on target, the presentation angles good, and the retrieve matched to the speed of the swimming fish. It really helps when the tarpon are in the mood to bite:

MAY 25, MIDDLE KEYS, CLOUDY, WIND ENE 15 THEN 20+. Capt. Alex Zapata and I braved the elements to find chewing tarpon while trying not to sink. When we set up the wind was tolerable, but a squall line raced through blowing like hell on the back side. Standing in the pitching skiff was a chore but the tarpon didn't care. We had each caught a poon when a nice pack appeared in the pitching waves. Got the worm fly in there, started the retrieve when a big wave hit us. I started to go overboard, grabbed the poling platform (I was in the stern), dropping the rod but staying in the boat. Picked up the rod to find myself attached to a tarpon displeased that its worm snack came with a sharp hook. One jump later it was gone but Alex congratulated me on developing a new retrieve for the fly. ●

As effective as the palolo pattern can be, many are the days when even the most adept angler will strike out. But day in and day out, the worm/two-hand is a relatively high-percentage game for ocean swimmers. Captain Albert worries every spring that the tarpon are going to wise up and start refusing the worm, but so far, so good.

Nuances are an important part of chasing poons. Newcomers wonder why their guide staked out at a specific spot that looks no different to the untrained eye than a dozen other nearby locations. Chances are that a combination of tide, current, and bottom type are in play. Experience teaches that certain spots not only attract the fish but also render them more willing to bite. The presence of current is a major factor. Tarpon like current—it brings them food, and something about moving water is to their liking. In the Middle Keys there

Palolo worm flies come in a variety of forms and colors but all are fished best using the two-handed retrieve (demonstrated by Ralph MacDonald).

are long stretches where swimming ocean fish can be intercepted, but the more-limited spots with good current are where you'll find boats and waiting anglers. One small area has a specifically focused current. Fish 50 yards east of it and the fish will snub your best presentations. Set up on the edge of the little current and the tarpon suddenly become cooperative. And when the current slacks, lockjaw sets in. Learning the nuances of such spots takes years and is why a good guide is the only real option for anglers who can't be on the water day after day, season after season.

Tides move around a lot of water, and the tarpon follow suit. These daily changes are on full display along ocean runs. Tarpon will run almost at bonefish depths, scrubbing bars and points when the tide is flooding in. In contrast, the ebb can prompt them to swim hundreds of yards farther out.

Tide stages and switching currents are also critical in the backcountry, and I can think immediately of three backcountry banks where the fishing is different on each tide and related current. One is a falling current location with tarpon nosing into the flow to lie on the rippled, "downstream" lip of a shallow coral bank. When the current slacks, and turns to run the other way, the tarpon vanish. Another is a little basin cupped by a small grassy flat. Some fish like it on an incoming current, but slack is the prime time. Get there with the current trickling out and it looks dead. The current stops and instantly tarpon float up from 10-foot depths to cruise around happily for the 30 to 45 minutes of real slack. A third bar is the opposite: Only when the current is flowing in on a flood tide do tarpon start swimming along its edge. The angle of the bar in relation to the sun makes for tricky visibility. In the morning, it's no good, as the fish cruise in directly from the sun and hit the boat. Late afternoon, the sun is too low to spot the incoming tarpon. Only a relatively short midday window works well and only when that window coincides with the right tide/current. Catch each spot at the prime time and feeding a tarpon or two is a good bet.

Bottom type is also crucial. Sand bottoms are fun because the tarpon are so visible. Strings of brown- or green-backed fish can

Tarpon can be hard to feed on the bright sand.

be spotted 100 yards away and tracked all the way to the boat. But they can be very hard to feed over bright sand with bright sunshine. It's wonderful for tarpon watching, not so good for catching. Fish swimming over grass bite more readily, and I guess it's something about security from predators, or tarpon as predators like to feel that they're sneaking up on their prey. Who knows? Setting up on a grass bottom 50 feet off the edge of sand can be a great tactic. The fish are easy to see on the sand, but you show them your fly over the grass. Hard mottled coral bottoms with sea fans, gorgonians, and sponges can also be really good; something about those bottoms makes tarpon quite happy. Add a good current and guides will fight for the spot.

Years ago, the late Ben Taylor, a fine Keys guide, wrote a very informative book, *Flyfisher's Guide to the Florida Keys*. He explained at length that he could not provide charts or explanations where X marked the spot for fine fishing. The variables of season, weather, tide, tide stage, and current change so frequently and so strongly affect each and every spot in the Keys that it is impossible to put those Xs on a chart without a laundry list of caveats. He was right. A given location can be good when the variables line up, but the critical element is to appreciate the variables and begin applying them to the spots you fish. Careful observation will reveal the fish use patterns, then you mark it in your log book or charts for the next time out. And just when you have an area figured out, along comes a major hurricane literally rearranging the underwater landscape, scrambling everything you know. Learning these nuances and the interactions within the wonderful flats environment is endlessly challenging—and fascinating. Only dedicated flats anglers (and maybe a few ecologists) get to tap into this knowledge, adding an extra dimension that takes our sport beyond mere fishing.

Being in the right place at the right time and in possession of the right equipment puts an angler 50 or 60 feet from the tarpon of his or her dreams. However, that last 50 feet belongs to the angler. Perform and you'll catch fish. Come to the bow unprepared and a whole lot of frustration is in store. The long hours of waiting for tarpon to swim by or show up gets filled with lots of conversation, much of

it unsuitable for family publications! There has, however, been a distillation of the primary mistakes that stand between anglers, particularly beginners, and their tarpon. Seven stood out and became the "seven deadly sins." Every tarpon angler has committed each of these sins multiple times; good anglers repent and promise to sin no more.

The first is number one on everyone's list: failure to develop and practice casting skills before you get on the bow. Among the most deflating words a guide can hear is a newcomer picking up a big tarpon rig commenting, "Gee, this is a lot heavier than I expected." A casting lesson is coming—while tarpon are swimming. Just as bad is a guide poling hard to put his angler on happy tarpon and have cast after cast fail to put the fly on target. If conditions are tough, like stiff winds or rough waters, that's understandable. When conditions are good and the angler just cannot make the chip-shot cast, that's hell. A crisp 45-foot cast without a lot of false casting is good enough to get the job done on many occasions and is more than within reach of anyone with ordinary physical skills—if they practice.

Casting deficiencies are guides' greatest complaint. And most of the guides are real pros with the rod and provide expert teaching. Most, however, want to use time in the boat to chase fish. Guides try their best to be encouraging, and the old days of the angler being on the wrong end of a profanity-laden tirade are gone. However, even when trying to be helpful, guides will reveal their real thoughts about casting skills or lack thereof. Nearly 25 years of sharing a skiff with Captain Bus has revealed a definite hierarchy of casts. On rare occasions the cast will earn a "You're dazzling me." Remember the good feeling because you aren't likely to hear it again for quite a while. Next in line is "Great cast" followed by "Good cast." As the quality of the cast and presentation begins to slide, you hear "You're in the game" or "Play it." A forlorn-sounding "Live with it" means you don't stand a real chance for a bite, but recasting will only spook the tarpon. A suppressed, barely audible groan means you hit rock bottom. There is one other special, softly delivered comment reserved for poor casts to laid-up tarpon: "They don't eat with that end." I've heard them all.

Being a reasonably proficient caster also allows an angler to get the most out of a guide. A fish may be spotted laid up or swimming in a direction requiring a major effort on the pole to give the angler a difficult 60-foot upwind throw. If the guide knows the client is capable of making the presentation, he will pole like hell to set up the shot. However, if the angler doesn't possess that capability, the guide isn't going to chase the fish. Better casting skills translate into more opportunities and more fish caught.

A serious golfer, receiving an invitation to play Pebble Beach, would not show up cold. He or she would hit the practice tee and work to bring their best game to a great course. Taking the bow on a Keys tarpon run in May, with a topflight guide on the stern, is the Pebble Beach or Augusta of fly fishing. It deserves your best game, so practice, practice, practice before you arrive.

The second sin afflicts those who come to the salt from freshwater fly fishing: the dreaded trout set. Presentations to trout involve lots of slack line to let the fly drift as if it were free. So, when a fish eats that little fly, the rod is snapped up to pull out the slack and put the tiny wire hook in the soft flesh of the trout's mouth. Tarpon presentations involve tight line straight to the fish, and a good strike has to drive a sizable hook into the porcelain mouth of Mr. Poon. Lifting the rod either pulls the fly up and out of the tarpon's upturned mouth or exerts about an ounce of pressure on the hook point, woefully insufficient to drive it home. It took me a while to repent this sin.

Tarpon are suction feeders, opening their trapdoor lower jaw and flaring their gills to suck in the prey along with a lot of water. Only after the mouth closes is it time to set the hook—otherwise the fly and hook are simply pulled out. Standard instruction is to keep the rod pointed at the tarpon and keep stripping until the line comes tight, letting the angler feel the fish's weight. Then holding the line tight and seating the hook with a jabbing strip or simply pulling back and low on the rod should set the hook.

The suction take is very efficient for the tarpon, but can result in some heartbreak for the angler. During a worm hatch last June, a tarpon was hanging in the current 45 feet

directly below the boat, gobbling swimming worms. I swung the worm fly down to the fish, letting the fly hang enticingly in the current. Three times Mr. Poon tried to eat the fluttering fake, but as the fly was tethered to a tight line and leader, the tarpon couldn't suck it in. It was pretty entertaining to watch the fish open up and flare its gills while the faux worm remained hanging in the current. The fish looked mystified. Tarpon that stick their head out of the water to take a fly can also be difficult to hook. The big head pushes water that in turn pushes away the fly. The lower jaw often hits the leader, bouncing the fly out of range. A big foamy boil, limp fly line, and cursing angler are the usual result.

Good casting is a crucial skill: JJ Reynal throws a good loop to a school of tarpon from Captain Keating's skiff.

Hooking tarpon, even when done right, is a low-odds proposition because of that armored mouth. On average only 60 percent of tarpon that eat a fly actually get hooked, and maybe a few more than half of the hooked fish get landed. The other half are "jumped"—the fish is stuck briefly, often long enough to get a jump or two before the hook comes free. These low odds are simply part of the game and stymie even the finest anglers. Expert angler Andy Mill suffered a 0 for 16 streak on fed tarpon while filming the "Chasing Silver" videos 15 years ago. Streaks like this are all too common:

MAY 1, LONG KEY, CLEAR, 75–80, WIND ENE 15. Finally got into ocean swimmers late in the afternoon. Set up on dark grass about 50 feet off the edge of a lighter coral/sand bottom and could see the strings of tarpon coming in. A variety of Toad patterns/colors were no go until we switched to a brown/purple version. It got almost instant results. A single saw it, elevated, ate it but came straight at me and couldn't get tight. Threw to another four-pack, got another take, a quick stick, one big jump, and the hook flew free. Then a long string showed swimming under a white foam line kicked up by the wind. Put the fly on line and enticed the big lead fish to eat it. Drove home the hook and the tarpon went nuts with great boatside jumps before racing out to sea. Finally, it settled down and began pumping and reeling to gain back line. Making progress the line slacked—reeled it up to find the tarpon had eaten the fly so deeply it chafed through the 20-pound class tippet. We weren't quite done, and a nice pack gave us a last shot. A really big poon lined up on the Toad, lit up, ate, and turned flashing silver. I prayed for a good corner of the mouth hookup. Jabbed the hook home and the big girl crashed up and raced off. For the first few minutes this fish was in complete control and I was just hanging on. With that the tarpon came up in a classic, lateral, arched back, gaping mouth leap, and the hook pulled. Arg! Zero for four hurt. Bus the counselor tried to console a bruised angler. ●

Sin number three is so insidious that you will spend your entire angling career fighting it: failure to properly manage or tend your fly line. Standard veteran procedure is to strip about 60 feet of fly line off the reel and stack it neatly on the bow or in the cockpit. Marking your fly line at 50 or 60 feet (Sharpies work well) makes great sense—you know precisely how much line to pull off the reel. Too much line, which will never be cast, is an invitation for disaster. Stacking neatly means the line will not tangle when it needs to run out through the rod guides on a long cast or when a hooked fish takes off. Line thrown haphazardly in the boat is guaranteed to come up in a big knot with dire results. And this line has to be checked and rechecked incessantly. I've become convinced that pubic hair is a secret ingredient in fly lines, as the lines curl up tight when you're not looking. And fly lines in flats skiffs are maliciously alive and will tangle up the minute you're distracted. Don't try to kick a fly line out of the way—you'll just roll and twist it with more-dire results. Tending line also means keeping the line and rod on the same side of the boat; otherwise the rod goes one way, the line the other, and finds itself under the boat's hull. You get the perfect shot at 50 feet and the fly crashes to a halt 25 feet away.

Line tending is a shared effort. If there are two anglers in a skiff, the one not fishing has

A rampaging tarpon jumps free—an all-too-common occurrence.

The fruits of good line management: An angler clears the line as the hooked fish races off.

one primary job: Tend the line! Keep it away from rod butts, reels, feet, coolers, etc. I learned this lesson the hard way:

APRIL 30, SUN AND CLOUDS, 80, WIND E 10. Bus had Bud and me looking for "pink tails" in Florida Bay; laid-up tarpon in off-color water where the tails glow a bona fide pink. Bud was up and had made a couple of unsuccessful throws when Bus pivoted the boat to set up a 60-foot cast to 11 o'clock. Bud delivered the Chartreuse Toad, bumped the fly, and the tarpon accelerated forward to eat it. He stuck it good and Mr. Tarpon headed for Flamingo at warp eight. Suddenly the line snapped super tight, I felt pressure on my right foot, and the leader broke. Adios fish. Looked down to see the fly line around my foot. I had been watching the fish and not doing my job. And there was no hole in the boat to crawl into. ●

And there is a final aspect of line tending. When a hooked tarpon bolts for the horizon, loose line hisses up off the deck. The angler's job is to feed it up to the guides and then onto the fly reel. Looking hard at the line helps get this done. But the instant the line is on the reel, the handle will start whirling at some serious RPM. Putting your hand or fingers in there puts them at serious peril. Grabbing for the handle during a tarpon's opening run busts fingers, bloodies knuckles, and breaks leaders.

Sin number four is a product of pure awe. Everything has finally gone right, and a big tarpon is doing its best Polaris missile imitation. The angler freezes at this spectacular sight and 100 pounds of airborne fish falls hard on a stretched-tight 16- or 20-pound-test leader—good-bye fish. You must bow to the silver king, creating some slack in the line to avoid breakage. When a tarpon launches, the fly rod must be shoved in the direction of the fish while the angler bows at the waist in the same line. Failure to show obeisance results in failure.

Feet are the focus of the fifth sin. Black marks from the wrong footwear are a bitch to clean from nice, white fiberglass decks. Wear

Rick Hirsch bows to the silver king—failure to bow lets the tarpon fall on and break the 12- to 20-pound-test class tippet.

non-marking boat shoes or sneakers on a flats boat. And beware of "happy feet." A surprising number of fishers simply can't stand still on the bow of the boat, likely from excitement or balance issues. Work on correcting both, especially balance as the years mount. It seems to be the first flats fishing skill to diminish, and balance exercises before you go fishing can be invaluable. I've often wished I could curl my toes into the bow deck for better purchase, but failing that, practicing plain old balance is the next best alternative. Walking around on the bow also changes the balance of a skiff, and it's all too easy to pitch off the guide or friend working on the poling platform. Excited clients have been known to walk off the bow. Others move their feet while casting, tangling or stepping on the fly line and dumping vital casts. Lastly, dancing around on the bow sends out unwanted vibrations that spook sensitive flats fish. Save your dance moves for onshore.

Sin number six should be obvious but isn't: showing up to fish in the bag or with a bad hangover. This can be a real issue in the Keys, especially in Key West. The siren song of Duval Street, demon rum, and mojitos can be hard to resist. And trying to balance on the bow of a rocking boat (see above) can be impossible when simply standing up is a chore. Fighting the bright tropical sun to spot fish is also impossible when the light sears your blood-shot eyes. Successful flats angling requires concentration and good hand-eye coordination. You ain't going to have either when saturated with booze.

Number seven is a catchall: failure to bring or wear the right clothing and gear. Jeannette and I were at a Bahamas bonefish lodge finishing breakfast when a new guest walked in. Fresh from up north, a pasty complexion was on full display with his thin cotton T-shirt, little gym shorts, and flip-flops. No hat covered a bald head, and there was no sign of sunglasses. Jeannette commented that the boats would be ready to go in 15 minutes, so he better go change into his fishing clothes. He responded,

Happy rolling tarpon are a beautiful sight, surpassed only by a very unhappy one on the end of an angler's line.

Interview with CAPTAIN ALBERT PONZOA: Targeting Tarpon

Captain Albert Ponzoa has been guiding anglers in pursuit of bonefish, tarpon, and permit for three decades. His specialty is tarpon, and the big poons brought to his boat number in the thousands. We sat down with Albert to ask about chasing tarpon—big and small— in the Keys.

What do you want your clients to appreciate about tarpon fishing in the Keys?
They're very difficult to catch on the fly, as they don't like to eat in broad daylight. Success requires everything to line up—tarpon need to be present, presentations must be good, the fly has to stick and stay stuck, line cleared, jumps bowed to, and plenty of pressure. You can see 2,000 tarpon in a day and not get a bite. But they bite just often enough, and are so spectacular when hooked, that it's worth the wait.

Which of the Keys tarpon fisheries do you like?
All of them! We have three distinct ways to catch poons—big fish in the Bay and Gulf backcountry in February to April, big ocean migrants in April to June, and mostly smaller backcountry fish (5 to 40 pounds) in the summer and fall.

Can you describe each one?
Sure. The Bay and Gulf big tarpon are mostly laid up or move slowly in ones, twos, or threes. Water isn't clear compared to the ocean, and tarpon are harder to see. Fish can be seen rolling and diving deep, often requiring a sinking line to get the fly down. Bigger, darker flies are used, and most presentations get the fly within 10 feet, or less, of the fish. Usually the biggest tarpon of the year are early season Bay/ Gulf fish. Ocean fish are constantly on the move, frequently in big schools or strings, in clear water. You don't cast at the fish but lead them by throwing the fly to where the tarpon

will be. We use smaller, lighter-colored flies in the Atlantic. The average ocean migrator is about 70 pounds, but the schools/strings have plenty of aggressive 40- to 60-pounders that make up a lot of the catch. Summer and fall find us looking, mostly in the early morning, for smaller rolling tarpon. The fishing starts at dawn and is done by 9 a.m. or so, unless it's cloudy or overcast. These tarpon are eating shrimp or glass minnows, and getting the fly right to them quickly gets the bites. As you know, when we get into October some much bigger fish can be found as well. I'm sure lots of people disbelieve tarpon like that 140-pound monster we got a few falls back.

Is tackle the same for each season?
Yes and no. I believe a good 10-weight rod and good large-arbor reel lets you handle just about any tarpon you'll hook in the Keys. Floating lines are pretty standard except when dredging for deep divers out back. There some kind of intermediate line is needed. Success with ocean fish can sometimes be improved using a clear line, and the clear lines are almost necessary when it gets calm and clear in late May or June. The increasing sensitivity of tarpon also means longer leaders. I have most of my clients rigged with 12- to 15-foot-long leaders. Throwing a good loop turns over these leaders just fine. If you want to land a big tarpon, get your hands on it, you'll have a bigger margin of error with a 12-weight rod. It should also let you land a good fish quicker. But most of the tarpon "caught" on my boat are leadered and broken off. For that, a 10-weight is more than enough. The smaller tarpon are fished best with an 8-weight rig and floating line.

Any advice on flies?
For fishing outback, I like a dark fly that will suspend like a big Mouse. The deer hair head makes it cast like throwing a parakeet, but the tarpon like it. Diving poons require a sinking big, dark fly. Black is my choice. On the ocean, a good palolo worm imitation or a smallish light-colored Toad are solid choices. Two flies cover the bases for the smaller summer/fall poons: a Gurgler, fished at first light, and then an unweighted tan or chartreuse Kwan when it gets lighter.

How do you like to present flies to tarpon?
Angles are key. I like flies presented from 45 to 90 degrees—the closer to 90 the better. Moving the fly slowly across the tarpon's face, at these angles, is the best. I've never liked the traditional head-on shot. The tarpon's window is maybe 1 foot wide, and only the most precise casts get the fly in that narrow zone. ◼

"These are my fishing clothes." In a motherly manner she asked about sunscreen. "Oh," he said, "I think my partner has some and I'll put it on later. I want to get some sun." This poor guy (who was a complete newbie) was inviting sunstroke and serious sunburn, so we told the lodge manager. Thirty minutes later the new guy was decked out with out-of-the-package long pants, long-sleeved shirt, wading shoes, hat, polarized sunglasses, and a fresh tube of SPF 50 sunscreen from the lodge store. And in case you doubt, this is an absolutely true story.

Sunscreen application is a small item worth noting. Put it on in the morning before setting out. This ensures you cover all the right spots and are able to wash the palms of your hands to remove all of the leftover stuff. Smearing on sunscreen in the boat allows you to only wipe your hands, which doesn't clean off all of the cream or lotion. Residual sunscreen gets into your fly-rod grips and before too long they are a slippery mess. Bahamian guides are notorious for complaining that sunscreen-soaked palms transfer the stuff to flies, spooking bonefish with their sensitive noses.

At the other end of the gear spectrum are the equipment junkies who want to bring everything into the tight confines of a flats boat. Storage space is minimal on the typical 16- or 18-foot skiff, and damn near nonexistent if you make space for a pair of electric trolling motor batteries. Six rods are the max that can be stored efficiently in the gunwale racks—more than that and inevitable tangles become a big headache.

I take three rigged-and-ready rods for a usual day chasing ocean tarpon: a 10-weight, an 11 if it blows up a bit, and a 10 with clear or clear-tip line. If we're running into the backcountry where the water can be murky or deeper, the clear-line rig stays home and a sinking line 11-weight takes its place. When fishing with a guide, one waterproof kit bag comes along with rain gear, leader material, binoculars, small camera, hook file, and a few other odds and ends. Duck blind bags are great because they're smaller than the typical big hard-sided square models marketed to anglers; the big ones often don't fit well into small hatches. Throw in a fly box (if it doesn't fit in the bag) and you're ready for most everything. Guides carry all the needed safety stuff, and most of us with flats skiffs dedicate one compartment to those necessaries: life jackets, first-aid kid, fire extinguisher, flares, Q-beam light, small tool kit, extra spark plugs, waterproof charts, duct tape, etc.

When too much gear clutters a boat, it gets in the way, gets wet, and always snags loose fly line at the most inopportune moments. Like a Boy Scout be prepared but not over-prepared.

Lots of stuff in life fails to meet expectations. A famous place is smaller and less impressive in person; a famous hero turns out to be a jerk. Fly fishing for tarpon exceeds expectations: huge, cool-looking silver fish; clear green waters; a willingness to eat bits of feather, fur, and foam; and those jumps. And you have to earn them with diligence and skill.

Diligence characterizes successful tarpon anglers. Catching the big fish is a hard game, and it's all too easy to get broken down by poor weather, AWOL fish, or a bunch of them exhibiting lockjaw. Successful anglers simply hang in there, stay focused, and keep making good casts. It pays off:

APRIL 28, LOWER KEYS, CLOUDY, 80, WIND SE 20+. A long, rotten, fishless day was rescued with a pair of tarpon in the last 30 minutes. I told Capt. Bus he was the "tarpon proctologist" for pulling it out at the end. At 4 p.m., after struggling to find spots to fish, without sinking in the rough, windy conditions, Bus set us up on a channel edge with a hard-ebbing tide. He hoped fish would come down the edge, hit the boat, and give us a chance. A couple of fish did show but weren't visible until about 15 feet from the boat—no shots there. Finally, the dropping water let us see a fish or two about 30 feet away. Enough time for an ugly "hatchet cast." A single showed dimly, Bus and I both cast into the murky water, the fish appeared to eat, we both stripped, and his line came tight. Minutes later we got the fish—a 70-lber. Back on station, another obscure fish form came in; I hatcheted the fly into the zone and hooked up. We got this one too, about 60, and quit promptly figuring we'd used up all our luck. ●

Money can catch you most great saltwater trophy fish. Charter the right boat for a bunch of days, the mates prepare the rigs and bait, the captain runs the boat, baits are trolled, a fish rises up, and a mate hooks it and hands the pool-cue rod and winch-like reel to the sport. The boat largely fights the fish, with the chair-bound, harnessed fisher pumping and cranking away. Been there. Walk the docks at famous marlin marinas and you will hear stories of a big fish hooked up, the boat backing down on it rapidly, and the marlin gaffed before it knew it was in trouble.

Fly fishing for tarpon has no shortcuts, monetary or otherwise. The best fly-fishing guide in the world can only put you 30 to 90 feet from a tarpon. The guide may have rigged the outfit, but the angler owns that last crucial gap. A good cast is required, the hook must be set manually, the line cleared by the angler, jumps bowed to, and the rod and single-action fly reel handled right. Exactly why it remains the best fly-fishing game in the world.

Permit

Dressed in flats garb (lightweight long pants, vented pastel shirt, sunglasses around the neck), an angler enters the soothingly appointed paneled office then stretches out on a gently reclined couch. The doctor, wearing brown tweeds and an elegant bowtie below a Van Dyke moustache and beard, sits next to the couch. Pince-nez spectacles balance on his nose. He picks up a notepad, unscrews his fountain pen, and asks quietly, "So you vant to talk about ze permit?" A visit to a shrink might be a good idea before picking up the pursuit of the exasperating permit. However, maybe the permit should see a psychiatrist—the fish are crazy enough to need therapy.

Permit are by far the most difficult flats fish to catch on a fly. They will eat the hell out of small, live blue crabs, but when fakes are involved the fish turn infinitely wary. Steve Huff terms them "dishonest" fish. Repeated quality presentations can be made without any reward for the angler. Then after dozens of good shots and casts, one of the black-tailed devils will pounce and grab a fly like it hasn't eaten in a month. Permit anglers must be psychologically prepared to catch nothing.

Catching them on a fly is also real recent history. Into the '60s, only a handful had been

Say *ahhh* . . . Mr. Perm shows off his crushers, which it uses to pulverize and eat hard-shelled crabs.

caught this way and most of them by tarpon anglers pitching a buggy-looking fly, like the Cockroach, at an errant perm that happened to swim by. Veteran Keys guide Nat Ragland cooked up the first fly designed for permit—the Puff, short for Puff the Magic Dragon. Heavily weighted, and sporting big doll eyes, the fly sank like a rock and induced a few perms to take it. Steve Huff and Harry Spear worked on an epoxy fly to make it sink, and the Mother of Epoxy, aka MOE, behaved the same and fooled a few fish as well.

Huff and angler Del Brown revolutionized fly fishing for permit in the 1980s by concocting the Merkin and the "hit 'em on the head" presentation. The Merkin roughly imitates a crab with its body of crinkly yarn, rubber legs, and rear hackles looking vaguely like claws. It too features heavy metal eyes and sinks fast, apparently appearing, to the permit, to be a panicked crab diving for the bottom and safety. Brown went on to catch over 500 perms—mostly with Huff, a few with Bus Bergmann and others,

and later with Huff's son Dustin—until he was into his 80s and no longer able to fish.

The fly's name is unique. As noted, it is tied with crinkly brown yarn fibers and trimmed into a rough triangle. Merkin is a medieval term. When a lady of the night of that era was determined to be carrying disease or lice in private parts, local authorities would order her nether region be shaved. Apparently, this was to warn potential clients to take their business elsewhere. Enterprising women decided to fool clients and the authorities by having the local barber make up a pubic wig called a "merkin." Put these facts together and the fly was named. Fly-fishing suppliers started stocking the flies for sale under the given name. It seems, however, there were some blue noses in the business because "Merkin" was dropped soon thereafter and the fly remarketed as "Del Brown's Permit Fly." Whatever it's called, it works, sometimes.

Permit are not a "starter" fish like bonies. Numbers of bonefish and tarpon are usually

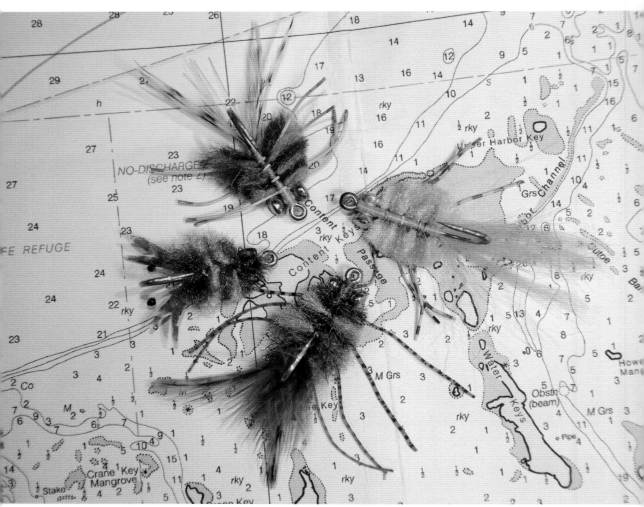

Traditional Merkin and three variations (clockwise from top) are all versions of the famous Merkin fly.

caught before the first inklings of permit dementia creep into an angler's brain—should I try now for the Holy Grail, the perm? Succumbing to these thoughts subjects one to the most excruciating form of flats fishing masochism. The "dues-paying" stage can be long, and much frustration and heartbreak precedes the coveted first permit. My friend and fishing partner Joe Kelley suffered through a seemingly endless set of travails—in one tough day:

JULY 15, MARATHON, MOSTLY SUNNY, 85, WIND ESE 10. Midday found us on the pancake flat that proved to be full of hungry permit. Joe presented the crab to a mudding tailer, got the take, and jerked up the rod—the dreaded trout set. A boil of mud and turtle grass marked the spooked fish. No meltdown though. He fed another, but the hook simply didn't stick. Joe retrieved the crusher-mashed fly and Capt. Albert hurriedly tied on a fresh fly. Joe got back up, threw to another sickle tail, Mr. Perm pounced, and Joe's strip got the line tight—hookup! He cleared the hissing line onto the reel, and the battle began. A nervous guy clamped down on his nerves and was doing it all right. Many anxious minutes later, Albert prepared to tail the fish. The rod was hooped up and Joe's first was only a few feet away when the rod snapped straight, and 15 pounds of fish sank from sight. At the end of the limp line and leader was a curly pigtail where the fly had been—a pulled knot. ●

Ultimately, the story had a happy ending—two years later—when Joe exorcised the demons and got his first permit: a fine 15-pounder on a Gulf-side flat with Captain Albert back on the stern.

The occasional permit beginner gets outrageously lucky. Albert possesses the absolute best, and oddest, first permit tale. He had aboard a rookie permit angler suffering a bad case of buck fever when he got a shot. A fine permit was tailing at 10 o'clock about 60 feet out, the Captain directed "Cast now," and the fly line went airborne. The nervous angler lost control of the line and the fly crashed into the water on the backcast at 4 o'clock—where an unseen perm jumped on the fly. Fifteen minutes later the fish was in the net. The guy should have bought a lottery ticket the minute they were back on shore.

A little luck during lunch is always welcome too:

MARCH 13, BIG PINE BACKCOUNTRY, CLEAR, 65–70, WIND NW 15–20. A surprise lunchtime permit on a cool windy day. The record cold (in 2010) and prolonged "winter" continued to show its teeth with yet another front blowing in overnight. Needed the fleece jacket while running. Fortunately, the bright sunshine warmed the water a bit and we found critters. Got four decent shots at permit, including a big one with an odd red bloody tail, with the usual dismal results. Getting hungry we made plans for lunch and Bus nodded toward a semi-protected point where he had taken a lunchtime perm years ago. I offered, "Why not?" Bus dropped the anchor and we dug out sandwiches and Gatorade. Kept the rod and crab fly ready just in case. While munching away glanced periodically at the flat edge and halfway through my sub a pair of black tails came cruising in. Scrambled to pick up the rod and made a hurried cast to 1 o'clock. The left perm saw the fly, darted ahead, and opened up to gulp it in. A long deliberate run to the NE followed and lot of backing hissed off the reel. Bus pulled anchor and we gave chase. Mr. Perm did his relentless pulling act and four or five times it was near the boat only to run off again. Unusually it stayed up top and never went deep to try to rub out the fly. The fancy folding net got unclipped and the good Capt. had a handsome 15-lber, with lots of yellow on the belly, in the meshes. ●

The lunchtime perm: a nice 15-pounder that ate a "realistic" crab fly.

Luck was essential in the years following the 2010 cold snap. It seemed to wreak havoc on the Keys' permit population. That spring it was common to find permit sporting bright red, bleeding tails, apparently some kind of fin disease triggered by the exposure to 40- to 50-degree waters. Barracudas and sharks likely made short order of these ailing perms. In the following years, finding permit became ever more difficult and numbers diminished. Before 2010, a day on the permit flats with good tides would often serve up 15 to 20 or more legitimate shots. Quality fishing. After the cold, it was a struggle to get five shots, which makes catching a perm damn near impossible.

An evident population rebound began in 2018:

JAN. 11, MOSTLY CLEAR, 75, WIND ESE 0–5. Joined Capt. Rich to head for the Contents, planning to look for cudas and sharks. Got to one of the long banks and it was full of floating permit. Multiple schools and packs were visible up and down the 500-yard-long bank, showing spiky black fins and tails poking out of the slick water surface. Cool stuff. And the most perms we've seen on one flat in years. Even though we knew the odds of getting near the fish, and getting a bite, were low, we had to try. We made our throws, realized that most of the fish were 5- to 10-pounders (the next generation of fish we've been waiting for since 2010), and got the number of bites we expected—0. ●

The growing interest in permit and questions about the overall health of the population, its life cycle, and what should be done to conserve these magnificent fish prompted BTT to get heavily into the permit research business. A variety of studies and tagging programs are producing lots of fascinating data, shedding light on the fish and enabling better regulations to conserve perms.

Permit, *Trachinotus falcatus*, are not really flats fish. Compare the deep moon-shaped body to the sleek torpedo form of the bonefish and you can see why. Perms will get up on deeper flats but particularly love the edges of bars and banks along deep channels and cuts. The fish can swim onto these edges from the deeper water in search of crabs and vamoose immediately back to the depths if danger threatens, or the tide drops. Offshore reefs and wrecks, in 15 to 90 feet of water, are optimal habitat. Shoals of permit can be found on such spots. Which begged the question—are these deep-water perms the same as those found on the flats? The short answer is yes, but what percentage of the offshore fish use the flats is not yet known, though should be soon.

The permit life cycle is not a dark mystery compared to bonefish and tarpon. Starting in April, schools of permit assemble on selected offshore reef locations on the Atlantic side as well as wrecks on both the Atlantic and Gulf of Mexico sides of the Keys. These fish engage in broadcast, open-water spawning, and fertilized permit eggs hatch quickly into larval permit. Different from bones and tarpon, the larva stage lasts only two to three weeks, followed by the emergence of bona fide little permit less than an inch long. Adult permit will continue to congregate on these reefs and wrecks and spawn into July. Then a percentage of the fish—now unknown—will return to the flats.

The freshly emerged little 1- to 2-inch fish make their way inshore to hang out along sandy beaches. Lots of small permit can be taken netting along these shorelines, in marked contrast to our inability to locate young bonefish. Young permit grow rapidly and in approximately three years will reach 20 inches in length and be sexually mature. After 5 years, and about 25 inches to the fork, growth slows down considerably. At 10 years old, the average fish is about 29 inches. Permit are thought to live up to 30 years and can reach 60 pounds. A typical 15-pound perm is 6 or 7 years old.

BTT has implanted acoustic tags in over 150 permit, emulating the tarpon tagging effort. Nearly 100 of the tagged fish have been recorded on the receivers throughout the Keys and almost half a million acoustic detections, or "pings," have been recorded. Receiver returns demonstrate that permit move readily back and forth between the reef and wrecks and the flats, with most of the offshore movement concentrated in April through July. The April migration was a surprise, as previous limited research indicated permit not moving out until May. Florida regulations mirrored the

May dates by prohibiting the catch and keep of permit in the Keys' "Special Permit Zone" (SPZ) from May through July. When the new data was presented to the state, the SPZ harvest closure was immediately expanded to include April.

Tag results also demonstrate that flats permit exhibit strong "site fidelity"—that is, the fish are homebodies, preferring to use only a handful of flats within a mile or two diameter circle (much like bonefish). This finding contradicts years of angler/guide speculation about permit populations. Common wisdom, years ago, was there was a single population of inshore perms that shuttled back and forth—mostly east to west—between the Content Keys in the east and the Marquesas in the west. When fish could not be found at one location, the guides were sure they were at the other. That bit of anecdotal knowledge has bitten the dust.

Site fidelity also has implications for anglers and conservation strategies. It indicates that specific flats are used by only a limited number of the homebody fish. So, if these fish are chased away by fishing pressure or environmental problems, the flats they use may remain vacant. Additionally, repeatedly fishing a set of flats—and chasing the same small population of permit over and over—may educate these fish and make them even more difficult to catch. The prospect of "more difficult" permit is mind-boggling and disheartening!

Permit vulnerability in spawning aggregations is another conservation concern. Even though the SPZ rules prohibit the retention of permit caught in April through July, catch-and-release fishing is permitted. The problems arise from suspected high mortality rates for permit caught and released on offshore sites. Catching the fish there isn't too difficult. As noted, perms can be suckers for small, live blue crabs and reef/wreck permit are complete fools when they encounter a swimming crab—even if pinned on a bright yellow jig. Many boats run to the spawning sites in the spring months and pitch crabs, and hooking dozens of permit is not out of the question. What happens next causes concern. The same reef/wrecks crawl with sharks very adept at running down and chomping hooked permit. In fact, when the sharks are thick a majority of hooked permit may be taken by the toothy predators.

And after one perm makes it to the boat, gets hoisted for the hero pic, and released, it too might get munched. This may be catch-and-release on paper, but reality appears to be significant hook-and-kill.

All bona fide catch-and-release fishing involves incidental mortality. Even when done right, about 3 to 5 percent of caught and released fish die shortly thereafter. Mortality rates in this range have been found to be sustainable and are accepted by fisheries managers from Alaska to Florida. Unfortunately, the first round of specific studies (conducted in 2018 and 2019) on Florida Keys reef/wreck sites show that almost 40 percent of hooked permit are eaten by sharks. There is likely additional mortality from the sharks taking some portion of the 60 percent that get released. In any event, mortality rates beyond 20 percent are considered unsustainable, so something needs to be done to further conserve Keys permit.

Tarpon confront similar mortality issues in selected fisheries. Concentrations of poons in deep-water channels attract many predators—humans and sharks. Big bulls and hammerheads shadow the tarpon and home in rapidly on hooked, struggling fish. Tarpon are particularly vulnerable at boatside in these deeper-water environments, and any number get cut to pieces. No one knows the actual mortality rates in these ostensibly catch-and-release tarpon fisheries and whether or not the numbers of tarpon deaths are significant, substantial, or acceptable.

Fly patterns and tactics for permit continue to evolve. The Merkin remains an effective pattern, but legions of more-realistic crab imitations have followed. My first perm fell to a modified Merkin, the second to an interesting crab "tied" (in reality, glued) onto a jig hook. That pattern is in version 5.0 as it continues to be tweaked. In the Yucatan, new spawning shrimp patterns—featuring plenty of highly visible bright orange colors—got developed. These too are stripped aggressively, imitating fleeing shrimp. And permit apparently like it. A couple of Lower Keys guides have adopted the pattern and technique with a modicum of success.

Of course, weather affects the pursuit of permit. The fish tolerate a wider range of water temperatures than bonefish and like a lot more

Interview with CAPTAIN JUSTIN REA: Pursuing Permit

Justin Rea is a veteran Lower Keys guide who has developed a reputation as a permit ace. He entered the fishing guide ranks out West but ventured to the Keys 20 years ago, fell in love with the flats, and became a flats guide in 2001. Justin is in high demand, especially for permit, and has lived up to that reputation by winning four times the Del Brown Permit Tournament in Key West and finishing second three times. He and his wife, Loren, also founded and run the Cuda Bowl—a fun tournament targeting barracudas on the winter flats.

What do you like about chasing permit?
They're hard to catch, very challenging, and you don't get them every day.

What don't you like about perms?
They're hard to catch, very challenging, and you don't get them every day!

I can't argue with that! What should an angler appreciate about the pursuit of permit?
Good anglers need humility. They need to be ready to be humbled—frequently. And it takes real effort, and some luck, to catch the black-tailed devils.

Has permit fishing changed in recent years?
Yes, and for the better. Fish numbers may be down a bit, but angler attitudes are better and we've learned so much about the permit's habits. This translates into fishing with confidence. If I have a reasonably capable guy for five days, and good weather, we'll likely catch one or more.

What seasons do you prefer?
Permit can be targeted with reasonable chances of success for at least eight or nine months in the Keys. The early season—now January to mid-March—can be good. Brisk winds and clear skies are common—the conditions you want on the flats. Perms largely leave the flats by the end of March and return by late June/July. July is my favorite month. Big tides in the fall, and cooler temps, can make September and October pretty damn good.

Any particular times within those seasons?
The tides leading up to the new or full moon are usually the best.

What about presentations/techniques?
The classic approach is a heavily weighted crab fly dropped just in front of the fish. It still works, particularly in the early season when the fish are on deeper flats digging for crabs. I find myself leaning more and more to lighter flies that land more quietly. Perms seem to be more and more skittish, and lighter, quieter flies work better. The ability to land a fly quietly—heavy or not—is an important skill to master. Later in the year, when winds are down and fish are cruising, not mudding, I like stripping flies such as spawning shrimp patterns. Get the fly moving with long slow strips, see what the fish does, and strip more quickly when the fish locks onto the fly. And be prepared to strip fast. Smaller fish that seem to be only chasing a fly are often eating it and spitting it out instantly before the angler can come tight.

Now I know why I keep missing those chasers. What other techniques do you use to deal with skittish fish?
Once a 10-weight was considered standard, but my guys now use mostly 9s. The bigger stick has its place in the early months with big weighted crabs, but the 9s are more stealthy. Less-weighted flies—crabs and shrimp patterns—are put in play. Paying attention to stealth is a big change over the last few years. Standing lightly and motionless on the bow

lets me pole closer to feeding fish. Longer all-fluorocarbon leaders help too, and use hand-tied leaders that can turn over flies into a breeze. Plus, when there is an opportunity to wade after permit, we're jumping out of the boat. You can get more shots on foot than from the boat.

Good casting is always part of successful permit angling. What casting skills do you want on the bow?
First, speed. The ability to deliver the fly quickly. Often the window to make a good shot is open only for seconds, and delay is a killer. Second, accuracy. The fly needs to be put in the zone or the game is over before it begins. Third, distance. Lots of perms get caught 40 feet from the boat, so speed and accuracy are more important.

Any other critical skills?
Good eyes. The quicker you can see a fish allows you to deliver the fly right away. If I have to tell my angler where the fish is, it's likely too late.

Plenty of anglers lose the first couple of permit they're able to hook. Any advice on fighting the fish?
Plan on one minute per pound! Early in the fight a high rod is key, as the fish will dive for the bottom to try and rub the fly out of their mouth. Permit will go for structure—coral heads, rock ledges, bridges, and such. Be

Captain Justin Rea (Courtesy of Justin Rea)

prepared for that. Hell, we had a big permit off Key West run under a sea turtle. It took some effort to free the line from the flippers and catch that fish. Rookies don't appreciate that perms are also real shifty around the boat. Most will come in close then do a 180-degree change of direction—be prepared. That will happen three, four, five times. Mr. Perm isn't done until he starts to roll up on his side. Trying to horse it before then is a recipe for disaster. ■

Choosing Permit Flies

Face it, whatever fly pattern you present to a permit will be rejected 95 percent of the time—if you're lucky. Successful flies (truly a relative term) generally fall into three categories: crab imitations, shrimp imitations, and buggy, natural-colored tarpon flies.

Crab patterns by far garner the most interest from the fish and anglers, and run the gamut from impressionistic Merkins to highly realistic versions sporting the correct number of legs and claws. And crab flies can be divided into two camps: the patterns—like

Merkins—dropped on the nose of a perm and allowed to dive for the bottom, and the swimming crabs designed to be stripped by the angler.

Merkins are tied in a range of sizes and colors. The classic usually appears on a size 1 hook with sizable lead eyes to make it dive fast. Alternating brown and cream yarn strips are positioned 90 degrees to the hook shank; the yarn is then trimmed to a rough triangle, although some prefer a more ovoid body. A set of splayed cree hackles protrude out the

A weighted realistic crab, Strongarm Crab, unweighted realistic crab, Spawning Shrimp, Olive Merkin, and Goldilocks Merkin (clockwise from bottom left) are recommended permit flies.

back (emulating claws) along with a couple of sprigs of flat pearl Mylar flash. The yarn colors can be varied, with olive hues or a cream/golden-tan combination being popular choices. In some instances, the cree hackles are replaced with a single hank of suitably colored (to match the body) craft fur; I think that looks like the trailing claw of a fleeing, swimming crab.

In the Keys, it seems each permit guide has his own secret weapon fly, usually a far more realistic pattern—some look like they will crawl out of the fly box! I confess to crafting such flies in the endless effort to come up with something the *&%#@+ perms will eat more regularly. But one of my best permit was caught after these "killer" flies struck out; Captain Bus insisted I tie on a classic Merkin, and minutes later we were releasing a fine 20-plus-pounder. The realistic flies are rarely available commercially except from some custom tiers.

Besides the realistic critters, swimming crab flies have burgeoned of late. Fly tier Dave Skok and Key West's Nathaniel Linville cooked up the Strong Arm Crab featuring a prominent trailing claw. The fly is stripped to simulate a fleeing crab, and Linville has caught a lot (by permit standards) of perms this way. I suspect we will see more swimming crab flies before too long

Shrimp flies have become more popular in recent years. Various spawning shrimp imitations, with bright orange features ostensibly designed to look like egg sacs, are now used routinely in Florida, Belize, and Mexico. Peterson's Spawning Shrimp and the Puglisi Spawning Shrimp are readily available commercially. In addition, the bonefish super-fly—the Gotcha—has accounted for plenty of perms, especially in its Red Headed variation. My biggest perm—somewhere north of 35 pounds—scarfed up a size 1 Red Headed Gotcha (RHG), and I recently got a pair of permit in one day on the RHG. Biscayne Bay's Captain Bob Branham has his clients throw, and strip aggressively, a weighted brown epoxy fly with significant success. My guess is the fly looks shrimpy.

Permit are also caught each year, particularly in the Keys, by anglers targeting tarpon. A perm will swim by a skiff staked out for poons, the angler will present a buggy, natural-looking tarpon fly (like the classic Cockroach), and the permit will munch it. I don't know anyone who would choose one of these tarpon patterns when specifically targeting permit, but Mr. Falcatus has been eating such flies for decades and will likely continue to do so.

Bottom line, carry some Merkins, a swimming crab, a spawning shrimp, and a Gotcha, and mooch a super-secret pattern from your guide, and you will be well armed for permit.

wind than tarpon. It's safe to say permit can be found on flats over a longer period of time in the Keys than the other two. Bonefish leave the flats when water temperatures get into the upper 80s. Permit routinely get fished for and caught with water temperatures of 90 or even more. Perms are also among the first flats species to return when winter waters start to warm after a cold snap. Water temps of at least 70 are essential for finding winter/early spring permit. One mid-March outing west of Key West had water temps teetering on the edge of 70, and a few perms were found on 71-degree flats. Late in the afternoon, we got a 74 reading on a big, dark grass flat—the water getting warmed up as the dark bottom absorbed sunlight. The warm spot was alive with cudas, sharks, jacks, and more perms.

Real permit aficionados must learn a special mantra to be repeated over and over: *The wind is my friend, the wind is my friend . . .* Common wisdom in Florida is that the ideal fishing day for flats permit features clear skies (for visibility), 15 to 20 mph winds, and warm-enough waters. Flapping, snapping pant legs and a hat tugged down hard and low are sure signs of permit weather. The stiff winds make the fish happy and they seem to feed with abandon—or as much "abandon" as permit can muster. White foam lines streak across the flats, obscuring the perms from the angler and vice versa. Wind-ruffled waters also mask sounds, as well as enable closer shots, which are invariably more accurate. Captain Bergmann and I once found these very conditions (although the wind was 20 to 25) on back-to-back early season days near Key West. When we closed day two, we calculated 70 total shots for the two days—the most unbelievable concentration of flats perms I've ever seen. Boat handling and casting were a bitch in the gale, but we managed to catch one perm. Years later, I still kick myself for not fishing better and taking advantage of a once-in-a-lifetime opportunity.

Wind and currents, plus the feeding habits of permit, require guides and anglers to be on their toes, ready for immediate action. Tarpon are found laid up or swimming slowly. The boat can be set deliberately, and the angler has time to calibrate the coming cast. Bonefish are usually on a feeding mission, and interception is again relatively deliberate. Deliberative,

however, is a very relative term. Very little on the flats is as deliberate and contemplative as fishing for trout. A trout takes up station by a rock, a downed log, or a cut bank, rising regularly for an hour or more while hatching insects drift by. An angler may spend an hour trying for a single fish, often changing flies half a dozen times in an attempt to fool it. There is time for thought about the presentations, time to wade into a different position, time to lengthen the leader, and time to consider and execute different kinds of casts. Speed is not a prerequisite to success.

While on the bow of a flats skiff, speed is usually very important. The fish are moving, the boat is moving, and the fish are within casting range for only seconds. Casts must be made quickly; too many false casts are death. In fact, the need for speed puts real pressure on the angler (and guide) and is a facet of the flats game that flusters virtually all neophytes (it sure flustered me). Permit put a high premium on quickness. The fish dash about psychotically, darting to and fro, defying prediction. A good breeze and current create situations in which the guide must set the boat quickly, and the angler is provided a casting window of only a few seconds before the relationship of the moving fish and boat change and the little window slams shut. If the cast and presentation can be made now, odds of success jump way up:

AUGUST 30, MIDDLE KEYS, INCREASING CLOUDS, 85, WIND E 20. Albert got us into perms in the afternoon on a small flat. Current was running in hard but 90 degrees to the puffing 20 mph wind. He spotted four or five permit darting about the flat and mudding hard. A pair popped into range a bit behind us at 4 o'clock. Albert had to crab the boat hard to give me a fleeting shot before we lost the angle. Instantly drilled the fly into the zone, one fish saw it, dashed ahead, and tailed on the fly. Set the hook as Albert lost control of the boat and it started blowing toward the fish. Fortunately, the perm took off the other way, lifted the rod, line up over Albert's head, and settled down for the fight. 15 minutes later, and three bolts from boatside, he tailed it for me. About 12 lbs. ●

A Florida Keys guide makes a good release of a perm that wolfed a size 2 Red Headed Gotcha.

Instant control of the cast fly line is a corollary to the speed requirement. Too many fly casters let go of the fly line, especially when shooting a few extra feet. The result is the fly lands and it takes a few precious seconds to locate and grab the loose fly line then strip in the slack to establish control—and get a direct connection to the fly. Permit will often eat a fly immediately—and not get hooked—while the angler is fumbling to find the line with his or her stripping hand. The solution is to shoot fly line through your stripping hand and clamp down on the line, creating control the instant the fly lands.

Finding permit on easier-to-fish slick, calm days isn't too hard. But good luck showing them a fly. There is nothing on the flats more sensitive than a floating pack or school of permit in dead-calm conditions. The visuals are exciting: a picket fence of pointed, spiky black dorsal fins and tail lobes; when the pack moves, the fish push wakes; and when they stop and feed, silver sides flash brightly. Alas, a fly line in the air and the plop of even a softly landed fly creates instant panic and the school explodes like so much shrapnel.

Bonefish and tarpon bites are pretty easy to discern if visibility is good. As noted previously, when a bonie stops on a fly, tips down, and curls, 99 percent of the time it's a solid eat. A tarpon bite, resembling a flushing toilet, is pretty hard to miss. Permit don't play by these rules. Fish will chase flies, tail on them, and appear to eat a fly but the strip-strike comes up empty—just another exasperating feature of the permit game:

MARCH 14, KEY WEST, MOSTLY CLEAR, 75, WIND SE 15. Bus and I were looking hard for perms and after a set of empty flats he declared, "No lunch until we see a permit." Starvation was avoided when we spotted #1— at 1 p.m.! Warmer water and good currents changed our afternoon fortunes, finding fish on a big turtle grass flat and getting half

a dozen good shots. A single crossing the bow saw the crab fly fall three feet ahead of it, raced to the fly, tipped down, and Bus instructed "strip," expecting the line to come tight. Nope and the perm fled. Relocated N, finding half a dozen on a new flat including one fish we thought we fed twice. A single swam in from 1 o'clock (SE); it appeared first as a disembodied black sickle tail. Put the crab on its nose, it tailed down, Bus said, "Try him," but no hookup. Hopped the crab, the perm darted ahead, tailed again, opened its mouth, and quivered—sure signs it ate. Nope. Just another faux eat. #*!*# perms! ●

The utter randomness of permit behavior is similarly exasperating. Dozens of pinpoint presentations yield nary a take, followed by yet another good cast, often on the same flat, that gets wolfed down by a permit acting as if it hadn't eaten in a month.

July in the Keys is an excellent time to chase perms, as the fish return from spawning offshore and the weather is pretty good. I joined Dave Merryfield and Captain Albert on a perfect blue sky, midsummer day to chase the black tails. We found ourselves on the edge of the Gulf of Mexico, poling a big grass and sand flat with clear green waters charging in on a flood tide. Happy permit were home and feeding. I had the first turn and got half a dozen good shots, getting only sneering rejections from the fish. Dave jumped on the bow, and three feeding, mudding permit came into range. Two perfect presentations were simply ignored, but his third throw—not as good as the others—earned

Dave Merryfield hooks a big permit on a wide Gulf of Mexico flat, lands the trophy . . . and makes the photographer envious.

an immediate take. I suffered a serious twinge of jealousy taking pics of Dave battling the big perm and the hero shot!

Fly fishing for permit is obviously not limited to the Keys. Caribbean flats along Honduras, Belize, and Mexico host lots of permit in a variety of flats environments. Fish numbers are higher than in the Keys, and many are smaller, less wary perms. But there are plenty of trophy fish in Central America, and permit are permit (i.e., exasperating) wherever they are found. Angling tactics are much the same, and Keys guides have begun to adopt some of the tactics employed in the Yucatan fisheries. This includes getting out of the boat to wade after the fish and employing lighter flies—crabs and shrimp—that are most effective when stripped to emulate swimming prey.

Interview with GUY FULLHART: Ascension Bay Perms

Guy Fullhart spent 15 years as an owner/operator of the Ascension Bay Bonefish Club in Punta Allen, Mexico. The club was one of the first bonefish and permit lodges opened to fish the beautiful waters of Ascension Bay. He and his Mayan guides spent years developing and perfecting ways to catch permit there—which can be as tricky in Mexico as they are in the Keys. I first met Guy decades ago when he was guiding in Alaska. Years later we reconnected in the Keys, where he also guided for many years, before I learned of his connections to Ascension Bay. He is uniquely qualified to talk about Yucatan permit and the differences, and similarities, between fishing for them and pursuing their Florida cousins.

What's different, compared to the Keys, about challenging permit in the Yucatan?
There are at least three big differences. First, the fishery is genuinely year-round. The fish are always around and do not leave the bay [Ascension Bay]. This part of Mexico is also,

on average, about 6 degrees warmer than the Keys. We don't get the same kind of winter cold fronts that drive the fish into deep water in Florida. Second, tides are minimal and change only once a day versus twice a day in places like the Keys and Bahamas. A given fishing day will likely be a high-tide day or a low-tide day. The guides can pick areas that fish better on high or low water and focus there. Surprisingly, wind speed and direction have more impact on bay water depths than the tide. Third, many of the "flats" are more like permit "ponds"—large areas of waist-deep water among scattered mangrove cays. There aren't many of strip banks and edges that typify Keys permit spots. These "ponds" are big permit feeding zones.

Can you tell us more about the flats?
Sure. Most of Ascension Bay is sandy bottom with some areas of slightly softer marl. Fish are much easier to see over these light-colored bottoms. As you know, the ability to see the

Guy Fullhart shows off his 40th birthday permit from Mexico's Ascension Bay. (Courtesy of Guy Fullhart)

permit and get the fly to them quickly is crucial. It also lets anglers pursue permit on foot.

So, most of the permit action is while wading?
Yes. We pioneered the two guides in the panga technique a long time ago. Perms are so much easier to approach on foot and much easier—in permit terms—to feed when the boat isn't in the game.

Please explain.
When permit are spotted from the boat, one guide and the angler hop overboard and the boat is backed away. This gives the angler a big advantage. Permit are not so spooky and very approachable on foot. The fish stay calm when approached stealthily—and calm perms are easier to cast to and bite so much better. When we adopted this tactic, it upped dramatically the numbers of caught perms.

I would worry about sharks wading waist deep in the Keys. Is that a problem in Mexico?
Not really. Sharks are rare in Ascension Bay—mostly small non-aggressive lemons in limited areas. You don't see sharks daily. As you know, there are a lot of places in the Keys that waist-deep wading would be downright scary.

Some pooh pooh Yucatan perms as little school fish. Is that true?
Yes and no. Ascension Bay functions as a permit nursery, so there are a lot of schools of smaller fish that can be targeted. There are plenty of larger fish available for those up to the added challenge. The average Ascension permit is in the 8- to 12-pound class—just a tad smaller than the Keys. Plus, we used to routinely find, and catch, permit in the 30-pound range at the club [Ascension Bay Bonefish Club]. The little-fish reputation comes from some guides who focus on pet schools of little perms.

How big is the permit population in Ascension?
No one knows for sure, but there are more fish than you now find in Florida. But fishing is fishing. You may go out and get 25 shots and the next day see only one or two perms.

What kind of tackle and rigging do you recommend?
We wanted anglers to hit the water with three rigs: an 8-weight with a lighter fly for shallow fish or calm conditions, a 9-weight with a mid-weight fly—that was the standard rig—and a 10-weight with a heavy fly for windy conditions or deeper water. You might use all three in a given day. Of course, a high-quality reel with a silky-smooth drag with lots of backing was vital to the setup. Long leaders are important. We liked hand-tied 15-footers tapered to 12- or 15-pound-test fluorocarbon tippets. Good hand-tied, tapered leaders turn over.

And flies?
The traditional heavy Merkin is not a regular pattern in the bay. We always liked swimming flies—crabs and shrimp imitations—rather than the heavy "dive for the bottom" patterns. A highly specialized, custom-tied Raghead Crab was the club's go-to fly. But it had to be perfectly symmetrical and tied with lighter lead eyes hidden in the yarn. When shown to perm, the fly had to swim dead perfect—no tilt, no spin. And when the strip stopped, we wanted the fly to glide down. That's when the bites would come.

Any secret flies you want to reveal?
Well, I did use a special baby lobster fly.

Baby lobster??
Yup. The Mexican government allowed the placement of lobster "casitas" in the bay—mini artificial reefs that would attract spiny lobsters. Permit would often hang around looking for a tasty lobster dinner. So, I whipped up a far too complicated fly to imitate a baby lobster. You stripped it to look like a little lobster jetting away. Caught a dozen or so permit on it!

Any other unique features to fishing Ascension Bay?
Cenotes. The bay is littered with cenotes—the Mexican equivalent of the blue holes found in the Bahamas. Some cenotes are blue, but some are black given their depth. Some are fresh water, that bubble up throughout the bay, but others appear to be connected to the reef and pump out lots of salt water. Sometimes the water flow in these saltwater cenotes is so strong that there is a visible hump in the water surface over the opening. Find these conditions and fish—permit and tarpon—will be present, bait will be welling up, and catching is a gimme by permit standards. I've never seen anything like it anywhere else. ■

Non-permit types can inadvertently cause significant embarrassment for committed permit anglers. Nothing is more deadly than the simple question "Did you catch any today?" Ninety-nine percent of the time the answer is "No," truncating the conversation. We need to spread the word that the proper inquiry is "How was your day?" This enables the angler, returning fishless for the umpteenth time, to respond at length about the weather, the sights, how many fish were seen, the number of shots, etc.—all important stuff to the angler while avoiding that soul-killing reply, "But I caught nothing."

In fact, this word should be spread to the friends and families of all flats fishers. Following a day being tormented by lockjawed tarpon, asking "How was your day?" avoids the painful question and opens the door to descriptions of strings of poons, a couple of near eats, maybe a bite or two, and the beautiful jump before the tarpon broke off. Jeannette had a difficult time learning this lesson and bristled when I returned with reports that "we saw 200, had 22 shots, fed three, and jumped one." She then bored in with "But did you catch any??" My head dropped, eyes on my shoes, and I mumbled "No." A reeducation campaign commenced, and I can report that she now appreciates the need to spare the fragile flats angler's ego that dreaded question.

Leopold von Sacher-Masoch must be the secret patron saint of permit fly fishers. Nineteenth-century Austrian psychiatrists relied on Leopold's writings to describe a then-unknown mental disorder: masochism. Defined as seeking pleasure in pain, it sounds like permit fishing to me. No other fish requires a frame of mind that expects rejection and failure while nursing the flickering internal flame of hope that this will be the cast and presentation that entices the elusive bite. Besides that flickering hope, endless perseverance is needed. And even that reminds that the definition of insanity is doing the same thing over and over again while expecting a different result. Sounds like permit fishing too. But comes the day when against all odds, a shining silver, bright-yellow-bellied, black-tailed devil eats the fly and comes to hand, all the pain vanishes in a burst of angling euphoria. That's a memory to be stored in the best vault you've got.

Other Flats Fish

A myopic preoccupation with bonefish, tarpon, and permit is a weak spot within the flats community. There are plenty of very game, very willing fish on the flats, particularly in the Keys, able to run deep into the backing and tax a heavy fly rod. Most of these fish, however, lack cachet and don't earn the successful angler any kudos on the dock or at the bar. These cooperative but too often disdained species are available in the otherwise difficult winter months when scratching up the big three can be damn near impossible. Yet many winter visitors lock onto the quest for the big three, forgoing other excellent high-odds opportunities for angling success. Maybe because I live in the Keys and get plenty of chances to pursue the glamour fish, I have grown fond of the winter chances to target, with a fly rod, other shallow-water fish: barracudas, blacktip sharks, the occasional cobia, pompano, and hordes of bluefish and jack crevalles.

Cudas are underrated. The speed and unadulterated savagery with which they wolf a fly is downright impressive. They wage a spectacular fight on a fly rod, and enticing them to take a fly requires some real angling skills. The silver-and-black toothy marauders have great eyes and can be very hard to fool. Popular wisdom has cudas ready and willing to chase down any shiny, slinky green fly designed to emulate a needlefish.

Getting looks is pretty easy, but convincing a big cuda (15 pounds and more) to close the deal is difficult. The recipe for success involves long casts and a pulsing, speedy two-handed retrieve that accelerates the fly when the fish nears it; never forget that barracudas can run down a fleeing bonefish, so you cannot retrieve a fly too fast. There will be plenty of lightning rushes at the fly followed by a fast swerve away when Mr. Cuda figures out the green thing is a fake. Much like casting to tarpon and permit, perseverance and repeated good presentations will earn a take:

MARCH 19, GULF BACKCOUNTRY, CLEAR, 65, WIND NE 15–20. It remains abnormally cool and bones, perms, and poons were nonexistent on the flats. But late afternoon

An athletic 25-pound blacktip shark that couldn't resist a brightly colored shark fly.

action with cudas—including the memorable "Jo Boo" cuda—saved the day. . . . By 2:00 we hadn't found a single target fish, but a traditional dark grass permit flat held a bunch of barracudas, looking like pointed logs, soaking in some afternoon sun and warmth. Albert and I decided screw the perms and pulled out a cuda rig. Despite a bunch of good presentations, I got only refusals or spooks. Albert suggested prayer might be in order but for some reason I remembered the movie "Major League" and one of the characters invoking "Jo Boo"—a voodoo deity—to help hit the curve ball. So, we laughingly invoked Jo Boo's aid. With that a big cuda appeared about 100 feet out at 9 o'clock facing left. Albert positioned the skiff about 70 feet away, and I launched a long backcast, getting the double-hooked needlefish fly about 10 feet beyond the cuda and a bit in front. Started the two hand, pulled the fly in front of the fish, pulsed the retrieve, and the cuda lunged ahead to grab it. Got tight and the fish went to warp speed heading NE while it executed a set of great greyhounding leaps. The hooks stayed stuck

and a long stubborn fight ensued before Albert grabbed the nearly 30-pounder (carefully!) and we got the hero pic. Wonderful fish. ●

Winter drives a number of species into Keys waters: bluefish, cobia, pompano, and bigger jacks. Cobia are a real prize, as the brown shark-like critters routinely run 15 to 40 pounds. They occasionally wander onto flats edging deeper Gulf of Mexico waters, where the fish will aggressively eat tarpon and crab fly patterns. Some cobia will be found shadowing stingrays or big sharks. We once saw a six-pack of cobia following a monster sawfish in 3 feet of water.

Florida Bay and adjacent Gulf waters also host hordes of bluefish and some concentrations of pompano in the cooler months. Toothy blues will push baitfish onto banks and flats and tear the fleeing prey to pieces in shallow waters. The rampaging blues, usually in the 2- to 6-pound range, will utterly devastate flies and fight very hard on an 8- or 9-weight rig. Fly pattern is immaterial, and we save our poorly tied rejects for the indiscriminate blues.

Barracuda flies are supposed to look like needlefish—and when stripped superfast sometimes fool big sharp-eyed fish like the "Jo Boo" cuda.

Pompano can be found in the same areas, flashing as they feed or skittering on the surface. Little cousins of the permit, the hard-fighting 1- to 4-pound pomps will eat bonefish shrimp patterns. I like to use weighted Gotchas stripped aggressively. However, a confession is in order: If we suspect we'll get into pompano, a spinning rod, small pink jigs, and shrimp find their way into the boat along with plenty of ice in the fish box. Pompano are superb on the plate, and fly-rod purism evaporates when visions of baked pompano in parchment dance in your head.

Jack crevalles are year-round Keys residents but seem more numerous and bigger in the winter and early spring months. They can be caught on the flats and on wrecks 200 feet down in the Atlantic. Most on the flats will be in the 1- to 10-pound class, but every once in a while a 20- to 25-pound bruiser shows up to cramp your arms. Jacks have a permit-like profile and will follow rays, as permit are wont to

Del Brown, aka Mr. Permit, shows off a flats mutton snapper, circa 1990. (Courtesy of Captain Bus Bergmann)

do. Captain Scott Collins and I were after permit one cloudy March day and barely made out a pair of permit-sized fish on a ray. I dropped a crab fly on the ray's back, the line twitched, and I hooked up. A strong fish smoked off, and we were hoping perm. It turned out to be the dreaded "yellow-tailed permit"—a healthy 10-pound jack. Jacks fight as hard as a perm but are the Rodney Dangerfields of the flats.

Packs of jacks also follow big sharks, especially the mean broad-shouldered bulls. Bay and Gulf tarpon basins and banks will feature cruising bull sharks in the late winter/early spring months, as the sharks are looking for tarpon as well. Many a fishless tarpon day has been rescued, in part, by throwing at the husky jacks shadowing a shark.

Sharks are another excellent fly-rod flats quarry, particularly the athletic, handsome blacktips. Blacktips, lemons, and nurse sharks are the common flats species, along with the ubiquitous little bonnetheads. Lemons can grow big—10 feet—and enticed to eat flies, but lack the dash and verve of the blacktips. Nurse sharks are really big catfish.

The blacktips are perfect for the fly rod. The ones on the flats run in the 10- to 60-pound range, with an occasional bigger specimen making an appearance. A 50-pounder on an 11-weight is almost as much fish as a tarpon. Cruising sharks can be enticed to eat brightly colored flies, and after a highly visible hookup, a lot of backing will whir off the reel, punctuated by the odd jump. And the action can be nonstop if the sharks get chummed up and excited:

MARCH 14, FLORIDA BAY, MOSTLY CLEAR, 80, WIND SE 10. Blacktip Bar lived up to its name. Jim Carter and I prepped for sharks and timed our arrival to coincide with the incoming current. Anchored off the stern by the cut in the strip bank with a good current running NW and hung the butterflied bonito and jack carcasses off the bow. Within 15 minutes we had a dozen 10- to 50-pound lit-up blacktips quartering in the scent trail within 75 feet of the bow. Initially they weren't excited enough to chomp the bright orange/

silver flies—until we cheated by rubbing a little fish juice on them. Catching a couple got the remainder fired up and now they would gobble a fly in their face. By the time we caught a dozen of the hot sharks, and used up all our pre-rigged shark flies, another couple of dozen blacktips were racing around the bow. ●

A brief reference to mutton snappers must be made too. Muttons are reef and wreck snappers that can grow up to 30 pounds. They fight hard, are superb table fare, and have a beautiful orange to brick color. Thirty years ago, they could be found occasionally on the flats near Key West, where the fish were a rare prize for flats anglers. Frequently stingrays, trailed by waving brick-red tails, were the usual giveaway, and a well-presented crab fly would yield a hookup. Feeling the hook, a big-shouldered mutton would bulldoze for deep water, and subduing the fish on a fly rod took real angling skill.

This fishery has all but disappeared, as the offshore spawning site for the muttons, the Western Dry Rocks off Key West (also a major permit spawning spot), was discovered in the same time frame. Commercial and recreational fishers descended on the early summer spawning aggregations, catching huge quantities of the fish when they should have been protected instead. By the time regulatory action imposed more-reasonable catch limits (still too large in the eyes of many of us who think the spawning aggregation should be off-limits to any harvest), the mutton population was driven into the ground. Fewer fish translated into virtually no snappers on the flats—a cautionary tale to be heeded by anglers and fishery managers alike.

If "the tug is the drug," there are myriad ways to achieve that goal on the flats. Bonefish, tarpon, and permit have earned big-three status by being handsome, challenging, hard-fighting fish. But it's foolish to overlook the other opportunities out there.

CHAPTER 3 | # The People

The dominant vision of flats angling is a solitary interaction with great fish. You stand on the bow with the guide (or a trusted friend) on the stern, laser focused on a tailing bone or perm, or a big laid-up tarpon. No one else is in sight, and the silence is broken by a softly spoken command from the stern, "Land the fly quietly." Other people and the broader world don't exist.

The reality of fishing the flats, especially in Florida, is a lot of people. For starters, there are guides and fishing partners, both indispensable in their own way. Fishing with friends creates lasting bonds and memories that are as important, if not more, than the fish. And in most locations other people are about, such as spongers in the Bahamas or jet skiers off Key West. Pleasure boaters, commercial fishing boats, kayakers, paddle boarders, and other anglers are all part of the scene.

There is little escape from all these people. Some are sources of angst and conflict; keeping your cool ain't easy when a boatload of drunken partiers runs over the school of happy, rolling tarpon you were about to intercept. We fish in public waters, and there are no private flats. Etiquette is increasingly important as it wanes. All of this activity on the water creates calls for new government regulations to conserve natural resources and reduce user conflicts. Within the United States and a growing population over 330 million people, these issues are not going to go away. Anglers who care about the resource and their sport will have to be engaged if we want a future.

Guides

Guides represent the "fun" side of the equation. Good ones are a unique amalgam of teacher, drill sergeant, scientist, handyman, psychiatrist, and hard-working mule. They're a paradox too: guys (99.9 percent are still male) who love to fish but do so rarely. My Marathon guide friends can go months without getting on the bow or catching a bone, perm, or poon. The pull of the water and enduring fascination with the fish substitutes for "the tug is the drug." In addition, getting their clients into fish—and catching them—is a deep source of personal and professional satisfaction for good guides. Steve Huff, who started guiding out of Marathon in 1968—and is still working the Everglades—offers that helping people achieve a lifelong dream, such as catching a permit or tarpon, is a soul-enriching experience.

The weekend mob descends on a popular Islamorada sandbar (which used to be a great bonefish flat). (Courtesy of Ian Wilson)

Every guide has a different tale about entering the fishing business, but a love of the fish and the outdoors are common threads. Albert Ponzoa was a math teacher who simply couldn't resist the pull of the water and the fish. His son Lucas, studying marine biology in college, may follow suit. Lucas is an absolute fishing fiend, inheriting his father's Zen-like "one with the fishes" capabilities.

Rich Keating was raised fishing and hunting in central Florida. His father was a judge and brother an attorney, but Rich didn't want to follow that well-worn family path. He tried restaurant management and some other venues but succumbed to the siren song of the water—which was great news for his many clients.

Bus Bergmann grew up fishing under his physician father's tutelage, and a previously noted father-son visit to Costa Rica had Bus getting casting lessons there from Lefty Kreh, meeting Del Brown, and capturing his first tarpon. He was already doing some guiding in Alaska and for steelhead on the Babine River, but the saltwater thing got into his blood. In 1979, Bus and his dad were chasing tarpon in Marathon and he appreciated that the Keys "were the major leagues for guides." Next thing

he knew he got a flats skiff, entering the Keys' guide ranks—and is still a member in good standing 40 years later.

The great Stu Apte had a very interesting trajectory into guiding, as spelled out in his fascinating autobiography, *Of Wind and Tides*. Once again, a deep abiding love of the fish was the key. He got hooked on fishing growing up in Miami in the '30s and '40s, when it was a small town. Bicycle or bus rides to Biscayne Bay let young Stu wet a line. Later he became a real Keys devotee, unraveling the ways of bonefish, permit, and tarpon. His other love was aviation, and he ended up a Navy fighter pilot. Following his discharge after the Korean War, Stu started flying DC-6s for Pan Am. When laid off for lack of seniority, he put his Keys knowledge to work, going into the guiding business in his boat *Mom's Worry*—a family nickname he got for lots of scraps and damn near dying when forced to eject from a flaming F9F-5 Panther jet. Many of the anglers' place names in the Middle and Lower Keys were bestowed by Stu back in the '50s.

Six years ago, Captain Apte was working on his latest book, *My Life in Fishing*, when we visited him and his delightful wife, Jeanine.

A younger Stu Apte peers out from a Pan Am cockpit. (Courtesy of Stu Apte)

Captain Alex Zapata is about to release an Upper Keys bonefish.

Stu had me sit down with him at his computer, and we spent a couple of hours poring through his collection of vintage Keys fishing photos dating back to the '50s. I was entranced. My first memory of Stu was watching him and Joe Brooks catch tarpon in grainy black-and-white on *The American Sportsman* TV show in 1964; I was 13 and dreamed desperately of doing the same. To become friends with Stu many years later was like a typical American boy from the '50s and '60s becoming pals with Mickey Mantle.

The newest generation of guides shares the same affinity for the fish and the fishing. Captain Alex Zapata entered the Keys' guide ranks seven years ago. He was born and grew up in Cali, Colombia, coming to Miami as a teenager. Peacock bass in a neighborhood canal turned him into a passionate angler. Originally a musician, playing a mean jazz trombone, he would play gigs at Key West's Green Parrot Bar until the wee hours, sleep for an hour or so, and hit the flats—for three or four days in a row! Ah, the energy of youth. The lure of the flats and the fish hooked him into guiding.

Russian author Ivan Turgenev wrote a famous novel, *Fathers and Sons*. It depicted generational fallout in 19th-century Russia, with fathers and sons going different ways. Among Keys guides, that kind of fallout is belied by a number of guides following their fathers into the guiding business. Harry Snow and Harry Snow Jr. were the first prominent father-son guide duo. Snow Sr. settled in Marathon in the 1930s, working first for the Florida East Coast Railway–Key West Extension (the official name of Henry Flagler's Railroad That Went to Sea). The vicious Labor Day 1935 hurricane obliterated Islamorada and Long Key, ripping up miles of tracks and putting the railroad out of business. Snow's next job was toll collector on the new Overseas Highway but traffic was sparse, so I suspect he had a lot of time on his hands. The solution—become a guide. Working the waters around Marathon in a wooden skiff and using old conventional tackle (revolving spool reels, linen thread line), he found plenty of bonefish, establishing an excellent reputation.

His son Harry Jr. started guiding in the '50s. Building on his father's knowledge, Junior became an ace guide, fishing effectively from Sugarloaf in the Lower Keys up to Long Key between Islamorada and Marathon. Most veteran Keys guides speak highly of him and his encyclopedic knowledge of the fish and the

The Snows—Harry and Harry Jr. of Marathon—were the first father-and-son flats guides in the Keys. (Courtesy of Jerry Wilkinson)

flats. He wasn't a fly-rod guy—there weren't many fly anglers in that era—but developed killer techniques for use with spinning and plug rods. Tipping a jig with a rubber worm or tail and reeling it in front of tarpon was particularly effective. We now realize this was probably the first way to imitate a swimming palolo worm, presaging the technique's resurrection, or rediscovery, using a worm fly and the two-hand strip just a decade ago.

Marathon has produced three other father-son guide duos: the Huffs, the Collinses, and the Cochrans. Steve Huff is widely known and regarded by a lot of his peers as simply the best Keys guide ever—high praise. BTT recently honored him for 50 years of exemplary service as a guide and a contributor to flats conservation. Huff fished out of Marathon for a long time using Hall's Fishing Camp (now the Hammocks Hotel) as his base. Trained as a marine biologist, the water and sense of freedom that came with guiding was an irresistible drug. "When the boat throttle goes down, and the wind hits my face, I'm free," he confessed to a rapt crowd at his induction into BTT's Circle of Honor. His guide career was hardly an instant success. Clients were difficult to come

by, and his second client sent him a how-to book on bonefishing after they fished together! It wasn't long, though, before he became *the* Keys guide, won multiple highly competitive tournaments, and began his long partnership with Del Brown and the quest for permit. He relocated to Chokoloskee on the northwest edge of Everglades National Park, where he still guides a handful of select clients in pursuit of snook and tarpon.

Steve's son Dustin still lives in Marathon and has become a topflight guide, booked solid by a cadre of utterly loyal clients, in his own right. As a kid, Dustin would tag along with his father and the occasional client. Del Brown took a liking to little Dustin, who had a front-row seat in the Huff/Brown development of permit fishing on the fly. There was little doubt that the younger Huff would follow his father into the guide profession. Dustin brings an intense, competitive focus to the game, and, as noted earlier, has won major tarpon and permit tournaments. Athletic skills, a great work ethic, and that competitive edge comes ashore too, as Dustin is an ace golfer, winning the Marathon Country Club's club championship multiple times.

Steve Huff (center) receives his BTT Circle of Honor award flanked by sons (and fine guides) Dustin and Chad. (Courtesy of BTT)

Dustin's brother Chad also recently entered the guide ranks. He decided that chasing fish for a living was preferable to his work as an electrical engineer. Chad guides in the Chokoloskee/Everglades City area near his dad.

Dave Collins was another Marathon guide who worked the area in the '80s and '90s before moving to central Florida. In 1989, I was scheduled to fish with the late Captain Bud Carr of Duck Key. A couple of days before our charter, Bud called to report a back injury that put him on the beach. I asked if he could suggest someone else, and he recommended Dave. We fished together in his 18-foot Maverick Deluxe (the workhorse boat of the day), looking for bones around Long Key. I muffed a few good shots and had one hooked fish pull free.

Fast-forward to 2006 and I'm introduced to Captain Scott Collins, my Marathon neighbor. Lo and behold, Scott responds to my question with "Yes, Dave is my dad." Small world. If you've gotten this far, you know Scott is an accomplished master guide and a good friend to boot. A guy with his fishing pedigree, credentials, and achievements (he has won multiple bonefish and permit tournaments in addition to his sterling set of tarpon victories) could

easily be an insufferable SOB. Not Scotty. He remains a gentleman, a great family man, and a superb guy to fish with.

Like other guides, Scott veered away from a career on the water, trying his hand, successfully, in the computer business. But the Keys, the aqua waters, and those challenging fish were too much to resist. He returned to Marathon and within a few years embarked on his very successful guiding career. In 2017 Scott painstakingly refurbished his father's boat, and he fishes it on rough days that would sink his little Dolphin Super Skiff. It was pretty interesting to join Scott in his dad's boat—nearly 30 years after I fished in it with Dave.

Cal Cochran was Marathon's first serious fly-fishing guide, guiding clients for tarpon in the 1960s. There are photos of Cochran gaffing tarpon for Lefty Kreh in Lefty's 1974 book. I met Cal—the first time—on an airplane to Bozeman, Montana, and spent the flight picking his brain about the good old days and chasing big poons around Marathon. Years later I would bump into him at Marathon's 33rd Street boat ramp. Cal passed away in 2015 at the age of 87. Jim Cochran, Cal's son, entered the flats guiding business in the '80s and '90s.

Captain Scott Collins and some of his well-earned tournament trophies.

Up the road in Duck Key and Islamorada, the Alburys, Brewers, Morets, and Pribyls have kept the father-son thing going. In the Lower Keys, well-known guide Bruce Chard's son BJ recently joined the guiding ranks.

Guide norms in the Keys have evolved substantially in the past 40 years. A gruff, barking drill sergeant style was pretty typical in the early years, likely reflecting the military experiences of most men following World War II. A few took it further, commonly subjecting clients to invective-laden tirades about casting skills or the lack thereof. My Marathon guide friends recall new clients, many years ago,

asking specifically if they would be yelled at during a day on the water.

Such concern was legitimate then. Before one old guide retired, decades ago, he had a new client on board, anxious to catch his first tarpon. The pair ended up in Florida Bay, found a couple of fish early, and the angler gave it his best but didn't make good casts. The guide climbed down from the poling tower, walked to the bow, grabbed the fly rod, reeled it up, and stuck the rod in the rack. The flustered angler asked, "What's going on?" The guide spat back, "This is PhD fly fishing and you're still in kindergarten. Here's a spinning rod." Teaching obviously wasn't this guide's forte, and word is the angler was not a repeat customer.

Going out with guides now on a busman's holiday and putting them on the bow is educational and fun. When the guide as angler makes a mistake, giving him a hard time—humorously—turns the table on the usual direction of criticism. In fact, my friends appreciate the reminder that the bow can be a lonely place when fish appear and a good cast is called for. However, every angler should play guide, at least once, to appreciate fully the skills needed to know where and when to locate fish; handle a boat; spot bones, perms, or poons; and most importantly set up the angler for a good cast.

Poling in bonefish depths with gentle winds can be learned fairly quickly. Expect to push the skiff in circles when you start; all of your untrained instincts will have you overcompensating with the pole on damn near every push. But folks with normal balance and hand-eye coordination should figure it out before too long. Deeper water, more current, and more wind up the ante. A pole placement error in a foot of water is easy to correct. The same error in 4 feet of water is difficult to overcome. The pole cannot be moved underwater at such depth, and it must be pulled up hand over hand and put back—correctly—hand over hand. If the wind is blowing during the correction, the boat weathervanes out of position and more correction is required.

Overcome these issues and the final step looms—setting the boat for a good shot, meaning stopping the boat quietly 40 to 80 feet from the fish and cocking it at the correct angle (dependent on the fish direction, the wind, and accounting for the angler being a righty or a lefty) to provide a cast. Anyone grumping about guide fees, after being poled into excellent shots at tarpon in a strong current or permit on a typical 15 to 20 mph wind day, lacks appreciation for these skills.

Care and feeding of your flats guide are mandatory in the Keys. Established custom has the angler providing lunch on the water for the angler and the guide. More than a few hungry afternoons have occurred when a new client thought the guide served up lunch. Those used to western river drift-boat fishing are surprised, as there the guide is responsible for lunch and

many set up a folding table, complete with red-checkered tablecloth, on a riverside gravel bar, then cover the table with a sumptuous spread. The Keys origin of "the angler is responsible for lunch" is lost in the mists of time but likely arose from the need for the flats guide to be rigging leaders, tying specialized flies, filling the old stretcher boxes with pre-rigged tarpon flies, and gassing the boat before meeting the client. Adding lunch to the mix was simply too much.

Too many anglers take their responsibility lightly, grabbing some soggy, premade sandwich from a convenience store. Or the provider goes Cheap Charley, serving up the same skimpy ham and cheese Wonderbread sandwich for days in a row. I recommend asking the day before what the guide might like and coming up with something good. You expect the guide to work hard for you on the water, and a little reciprocal love goes a long way toward securing the best service. Besides, poling a boat all day burns up a lot of calories—you don't want your guide feeling faint from hunger when a big permit waves its tail upwind from the boat.

Young anglers, frustrated with limited time to fish, often think out loud, "I should be a guide, bag this office gig, work for myself, and be able to fish more." Think again. The work is hard, physical, and long. The hours in the boat with anglers are sandwiched between almost as much prep and after-angling cleanup time. Utter diligence is required. Good Keys guides will be on the water during tarpon season for up to 90 or more consecutive days. Day after day of rising predawn, loading the boat, checking weather and tides to make a fishing plan, picking up the clients, engaging in pleasant banter, launching and running to the fishing grounds, poling for hours, teaching or counseling patiently, running back to the ramp, dropping off the clients, going home to clean the boat, squaring away the fishing gear, tying up new flies and leaders for the next day, spending a little time with family, and off to bed. The pace is exhausting, and good humor must be maintained. Every set of new clients shows up revved for action; good guides can't be Debbie Downer in the face of that excitement.

Veteran guides have a big advantage over their younger counterparts: regular return customers. A cadre of annual returnees makes things much easier for a guide. The experienced clients know what to expect, the guide knows the clients' capabilities and temperaments, and in most cases longtime guide-angler teams become great friends.

In contrast, the beginning guide must take all comers to build a list of regular clients. Stories of ill-prepared clients are legion. Guide and new client converse on the phone and agree where and when to meet the next morning. The guide is at the boat ramp ready to go and watches the shiny new pickup pull in and park. Out steps Mr. Rodeo in pointed, heeled ostrich boots, tight jeans, big belt and buckle, western shirt, and 10-gallon Stetson. The other door opens, disgorging a striking female thinly attired, except for layers of makeup, and stiletto heels "ready" for her day on the flats. The guide swallows hard, looking ahead to a long day. True story.

Most Keys guides strongly prefer that new clients, especially rookies, leave fly rods and reels on shore and use the guide's equipment. Some clients resent the implication that their gear is not up to snuff, but please understand the guide's perspective. He's going to work hard to put the client on fish and get hooked up. Getting hooked up can be so difficult that the guide does not want to risk the fish on unknown gear and, more importantly, unknown knots in backing and leaders. Anglers arrive with weight-forward fly lines spooled backwards on fly reels—casts go straight up, as the thin running line cannot load a saltwater fly rod.

Rich Keating had an incident that puts it in perspective. A new client booked a couple of days, claiming he was experienced and intends to bring his own rods and reels. Rich gently asked a few probing questions about the rigging and was assured the gear and terminal tackle is first rate. Next day on the ocean, here come the tarpon, Captain Keating poles the guy into position, and damn if he doesn't hook up. The good guide heaves a sigh of relief and starts to leisurely climb down from the poling platform to stow the pole and ready the outboard to give chase if necessary. Suddenly the client is screaming, "Start the motor! Start the motor! I'm running out of line!" This surprises Rich, as the tarpon just jumped about 70 feet from the boat. The guy keeps screaming,

and Rich tries to assure him that there's plenty of backing. Rich is floored by the response, "Backing, what's that???" The big Tibor reel contained only a 100-foot-long fly line.

Keys guide numbers have been growing steadily in recent years. Only a handful existed in the '50s and '60s—half a dozen in Islamorada led by Albright and Hommell, maybe two or three in Marathon, and a couple in the Lower Keys, notably Stu Apte. Key West had no committed flats guides until about 1970 when Lefty Kreh badgered the Montgomery brothers—Bob and Gene—to get into the business. Bob moved over to offshore fishing not long thereafter. He's gone now, but I fished with him a few times in the mid-'70s aboard his center-console Blue Runner.

The story today is very different. Islamorada has over 100 flats guides. Key West has at least three dozen, and Marathon, Big Pine, and Sugarloaf contribute another 50 or so. Until recently, virtually all these guides were mainland Florida or Keys residents and almost all worked the Keys year-round. Even these numbers, however, seemed manageable. Numbers seemed to jump about five years ago with an influx of seasonal guides, fishing primarily from February through May. An appreciable number are from Idaho, Montana, and Wyoming, where they row drift boats each summer and fall on the big western trout rivers. A lot of these skiffs disappear abruptly near the end of May, which coincides with the beginning of trout fishing in the Rockies.

Tarpon runs are more crowded. A notable Middle Keys stretch routinely had half a dozen boats from the mid-1990s until about 2015. That spring it was not uncommon to encounter 15 skiffs in the same area. Finding a fishing spot verged on the impossible—if etiquette was to be honored. To our east, another favorite reach has been a "five boat" spot for many years. Usually only three or four of the slots would be occupied by regular guides—everyone knew each other. In 2014–15 finding eight skiffs wedged in the reach became common, fraying the normal etiquette and courtesy. Veteran Keys guides started grumbling, as did longtime clients and local do-it-yourself (DIY) flats anglers.

Guide numbers are not regulated in Florida or the Keys. The primary requirement is a Coast

Interview with CAPTAINS BUS BERGMANN AND RICHARD KEATING: What New Flats Anglers Should Know

Bus Bergmann and Richard Keating are veteran Keys guides with over 70 years of combined experience guiding on the flats. I couldn't think of a better pair to ask about what new flats anglers should know and appreciate before getting on the water in pursuit of bonefish, tarpon, and permit (and other critters).

What do you want new clients to appreciate or know before coming aboard your skiff?

Bus: That the Keys are one of the world's great fishing destinations. It's also considered the major leagues of saltwater fly fishing, so try to bring your best game to the bow.

Rich: Absolutely. Let me add that there are many flats or shallow-water fishing options. Everyone knows about the clear-water tarpon and bones and perms. But too many don't appreciate great opportunities to fish for barracudas, sharks, or run up to the Everglades for redfish and snook. That makes the Keys a completely unique fishery within the US. Even though the fishing can be great, it can be terrible too. There are no guarantees re the fish and variables we can't control like weather, equipment breakdowns, tides, and such.

What can a beginner do to prepare?

Bus: Practice! To be good at anything you must practice your skills, and the more time spent participating, the more you learn and improve. You will get out of the fishing what you put into it.

Rich: Talk with your guide and ask questions. Be honest about your skill level, which will help us put together a good fishing plan. Plus, you can get a handle on some of the basic required gear. Many show up without polarized sunglasses and wonder why they can't see the big tarpon 50 feet away. The right footwear is important too, which includes non-marking soles—hate to spend hours cleaning my skiff to remove those tenacious black marks.

Bus: Amen.

What can you compare it to?

Rich: Anything we try to do takes work, practice, and repetition to succeed. Flats fishing is no different. I had a race car driver get in the boat and become frustrated that he couldn't cast more than 25 feet. I asked if he'd practiced at all, and he answered no. I then asked if he would take a car on the track without practice. "NO" was the answer, and then he got it.

Bus: There are some parallels to golf. No one shoots par or breaks 80 when they start. The same is true on the flats, although I once had a rookie catch a grand slam his first time out. Take casting lessons, acquire the basic skills, become familiar with heavier saltwater fly rods, and practice. It's difficult when someone new comes aboard, picks up a 12-weight fly rod for the first time, and says, "It's heavier than I thought."

Why is preparation and practice important?

Bus: Fishing the Keys flats is a game of chances, and some days you might get only a handful of shots at fish. The prepared angler will be able to convert more shots—put the fly where it can earn a bite—and catch fish. Failure to be able to do that takes you out of the game. Dealing with frustration is a major flats fishing skill, and keeping it under control is easier when you've prepared.

Rich: Complete beginners usually have only one cast—downwind. It means half of the field is out of play, and the fish have a nasty habit of showing up in the quadrant where the most difficult cast is needed to get in the game. More skills, more practice, allows you to play the whole field and get more shots.

Bus: Bill, you remember the day when it was blowing 25 and we got into all those permit? I could only hold the boat bow into the wind, and your shots were all into the gale. In that situation, an angler without a decent into-the-wind cast would have missed out on all those perms.

Rich: Reminds me of a similar experience. Poled hard into a stiff wind to put a guy on a bunch of happy permit, got within range of the fish, and then the angler sat down telling me he wouldn't even try a cast into the breeze. Of course, those were the best shots of the whole day.

Any other advice?

Bus: How many pages do we have?? Seriously, try to make the casting automatic, a function of muscle memory, so you can focus on the fish. Thinking "wait on the backcast" or "don't overthrow" while casting distracts you from the fish. A predatory focus on the bonefish, perm, or poon really pays off. When you can do that, you fish with confidence and enthusiasm, which I always want in my boat. Making your own good luck also puts good mojo in the boat—and I want that too.

Rich: Keep an open mind about the fishing. Don't get locked into one approach to the exclusion of other opportunities. Conditions may force you to try something different. For example, I had a guy who was set on catching a tailing bonefish. But we had very high tides and lots of clouds, making bonefish a very low-odds proposition. I suggested we try for small rolling tarpon. The client wouldn't have it and we passed up what could have been a good day on 5- to 20-pound tarpon to not see a single bonie. Be flexible. ■

Guard license to operate a boat for hire. A "six-pack" license is sufficient for a flats boat, and the license is available to all comers who can pass the required tests. Monroe County (the Keys) regulations also call for guides to hold a county occupational license, but enforcement is nonexistent. And in any event, these licenses are not limited in numbers either. State of Florida fees for a guide-boat fishing license are the same for Florida residents and nonresidents. The result is anyone with a boat and some motivation can quickly get into the guide business in the Keys.

Out West the story is radically different. Fishing guide licenses in Idaho, Montana, and Wyoming are subject to substantially more regulation as well as access limitations. For example, Idaho licenses only seven outfitters to provide fishing guide services on the famous Henry's Fork of the Snake River. In Montana, a fishing guide must obtain a license and work for an outfitter licensed by the Montana Board of Outfitters. Obtaining an outfitter license requires taking a rigorous exam and paying a $1,300 fee. Moreover, Montana Fish, Wildlife & Parks has separate rules requiring additional permits and governing river access. Presently, guide numbers are restricted on the Beaverhead and Big Hole Rivers, with similar restrictions coming soon on the famous Madison River.

Some rivers are also regulated by federal agencies, and separate federal permits, licenses, or concessions contracts must be obtained before any guiding may occur. Most of these permits, licenses, and contracts are also issued in limited numbers; Yellowstone National Park capped the number of fishing guide permits nearly 20 years ago. The upshot is Florida residents are prohibited from guiding in these western states without jumping through a lot of regulatory hoops and paying much higher fees than the residents. And it's worth adding that these strict and costly regulatory regimes out West are supported strongly by affected outfitters, guides, and anglers. Ensuring better-trained guides and limiting numbers of guides/anglers seems to provide a more quality experience.

A British term coined in 1883, "tragedy of the commons," describes these issues. The concept penetrated American consciousness in 1968 following Garrett Hardin's seminal article using that title in the journal *Science*. When a public resource is shared in common, no one individual has a vested interest in ensuring that use is sustainable. Rather, competition among common users creates short-term incentives to maximize personal use of the resource regardless of long-term consequences. The classic case, set forth in 1833 and 155 years later, involved livestock overgrazing common property. Without limits on the number of cows, a far-seeing responsible cow owner who limited his use of the commons would find such restraint offset by someone else with more short-term interests. The resulting free-for-all would eventually damage, if not destroy, the common grazing land.

I encountered the concept and article in 1971 while working for Trout Unlimited. An explosion of canoe rental services on Michigan's Ausable River was inundating the stream (the so-called "aluminum hatch") to the detriment of anglers and a major user conflict had erupted. And, during my 8 years as a federal land and wildlife official,[2] use conflicts and "tragedy of the commons" issues were a daily staple.

In fact, public resource management agencies (fish and wildlife departments and public land management entities) were established long ago to prevent this from occurring by acting as the trustee for all and establishing limits on taking and usage to provide sustainability. Anyone familiar with the agencies, laws, and competing users (all of which are intimately familiar with our open political processes) knows that this is much easier said than done. In fact, the political world has a very hard time saying no to users—of all stripes—risking the tragedy of the commons over and over again.

The power of some users over government agencies has led free-market environmental thinkers to urge modified ownership or regulatory schemes to better emulate the incentives associated with private land and resource ownership. Providing individuals with vested interests in a resource creates incentives to use and manage the resource sustainably over time. Or so the theory goes.

Commercial fishing regulations are dominated by these issues. The fish, especially oceangoing species, are a common resource.

Commercial fishermen face strong short-term pressures and incentives to catch as much as they can when they can—to make boat payments, pay the mortgage, feed the kids, and otherwise meet life's challenges. The overfished state of many species is testament to the consequences of these incentives. Fishery agencies tried first to regulate fishing effort to block unsustainable catch levels. It worked in cases where fish runs are short and physically confined; Alaska's Bristol Bay sockeye salmon fishery is the best example.

In too many other cases, fishing effort limits have failed. Elsewhere in Alaska, fishing effort for halibut became so intense that the season was one day. Even with a one-day season, too many halibut were being caught, resulting in a very controversial new scheme: individual fishing quotas (IFQ). The fishery agencies determined the total allowable catch (to assure sustainability) and divided the total catch into separate IFQs awarded to individual commercial fishermen. If someone got an IFQ of, say, 10 tons, they could catch those fish when they wanted to, and there would be no incentive to exceed the quota—violation would result in termination of the quota and loss of fishing privileges. From the broadest conservation perspective, the scheme has worked. Halibut fishing now appears sustainable. From a user equity perspective, however, the scheme is a political hot potato. Bitter battles are fought over the precise size of the IFQs and who gets them. Others resent enormously that some private interests are given a property interest in a public asset (the fish). Recreational anglers (or charter boat operators) don't get IFQs and instead find themselves subject to short fishing seasons as well as severe limits on how many halibut they may catch each day. IFQs represent an attempt to partially "privatize" a public resource in the name of conservation. It works at one level, not so well at another.

Access to public resources—notably land and waters—is another battleground affected by the tragedy of the commons. Managing access to public lands for hunting is a huge issue, particularly in the western United States. There is no doubt that where access is wide open (national

---

[2] During 1981–1988 I served as Assistant Secretary for Fish, Wildlife & Parks and Deputy Under Secretary within the U.S. Department of the Interior, as well as Chairman of the US/Canada Great Lakes Fishery Commission.

forest lands) and certain hunting licenses/tags are easy to obtain (such as elk tags), the quality of the hunting is diminished in the eyes of many hunters. There is lots of competition in the public woods, and trophy bull elk are few and far between. Some states have adopted this strategy in the name of equity and public access. In contrast, access to private land (including some Indian reservations) is severely restricted and elk herds are managed to produce enormous bulls. Steep prices get paid for access to these private lands and managed elk; the hunting experience is generally a high-quality, solitary experience for trophy animals. In the middle are other states where getting elk tags is difficult, tag numbers are very limited, and the best way for a nonresident to hunt is to hire a guide (as the guides get tags they can provide to clients). This latter approach is an effort to make public hunting a little bit like that offered on private lands at much lower prices—but still not as available or inexpensive as the first, more equitable approach.

The federal land management agencies—especially the National Park Service (NPS) and US Fish and Wildlife Service (FWS)—have adopted fishing and hunting access policies that reflect the "quasi-privatized" concept. Only six fishing guide operations are authorized to provide services on the reach of the Snake River that courses through Grand Teton National Park in Wyoming. The guides must compete for limited numbers of permits and if they win the competition, receive 10-year permits that may be renewed. NPS believes that limited, long-term permits create incentives for the winning guides to be protective of the resource while simultaneously creating a quality angling experience courtesy of limited fishing competition. FWS has similar fishing guide rules on rivers in Alaska as well as hunting guide restrictions. The hunting guides compete for 10-year, renewable permits to guide clients within designated hunting zones in places like Kodiak Island. Within each zone only one or two guides are awarded these prized permits. Again, FWS maintains that this limited entry scheme makes the guides care deeply (and act protectively) about the zones in which they hunt, a limited number of hunters is better for the wildlife, and the hunters enjoy a quality, more solitary experience. As

Assistant Secretary, I oversaw these programs and in later years represented any number of permittees, or those who wanted permits.

So, what does this have to do with flats fishing? There is little doubt that as populations expand and even more people start using the public waters in and around the Keys, these very same regulatory issues will rear up. Already longtime Keys guides wonder out loud why a western guy is able to come here and jump immediately into the guide business when the Keys resident cannot do the same out West. Is the current system fair, or should there be reciprocal treatment? Should there be limits on the number of flats guides, and if yes, how would that work? Can regulatory efforts to benefit resident guides pass legal muster under complex federal Dormant Commerce Clause rules? Those are major questions. And as will be discussed later, the federal agencies referenced above have significant jurisdiction over Keys waters and can be expected to consider in Florida the same issues they have wrestled with in Alaska, Wyoming, and elsewhere. My sense is pretending such contentious matters do not exist, and willfully looking the other way, is not a smart option for committed flats fishers.

Besides these human-created issues, Mother Nature has not been kind to the flats guide industry in recent years. Hurricane Irma slammed the Keys in 2017 and badly hurt the local guides. Many lost homes, and business was slow to rebound in the following year or two. Two years later, Hurricane Dorian obliterated part of Abaco and Grand Bahama Islands in the Bahamas. Homes were blown or washed away, bonefish lodges flattened, and marinas wrecked. It will be years before some areas recover and locals, including the guides, dependent on visiting bonefishers have few if any employment options.

Then came COVID-19 and the worldwide shutdown of travel as well as strict limits on visitors. The Florida Keys closed to visitors, and the police erected roadblocks on the single road (US 1) in and out of the islands to enforce the closure. At the same time, the Bahamas was shut down too and travel to the Out, or Family, Islands (where the bonefish live) prohibited. Flats guides—in both locations—took it in the shorts. On the backside of the pandemic is a great time to support your favorite guide!

Etiquette and Attitudes

More anglers, guided and DIY, create a greater need for courtesy and etiquette just when both appear to be diminishing commodities. The rules when pursuing bones, perms, and laid-up tarpon are pretty simple: If you encounter another boat poling (or using a trolling motor) on a flat or basin, the right thing to do is to go elsewhere. If it's a sizable area, quietly work in behind the other boat (at least a few hundred yards back) and follow it across the flat. Cutting someone off is a no-no and just as bad is motoring onto the flat too close to the other skiff. Either tactic guarantees an unpleasant confrontation.

Staking out or anchoring to wait for migrating ocean tarpon is a little trickier. The fish typically swim a linear path, largely parallel to the shoreline. Boats will wait at intervals along the line to intercept the swimmers. Many particular locations can reasonably accommodate three to a dozen skiffs approximately 250 yards or more apart in a rough line running north to south in the Upper Keys or east to west in the Middle and Lower Keys, as most April/May/June ocean tarpon swim in a southern or western direction. If a boat occupies the first spot, the proper thing to do is tuck in behind it (south or west) at a discreet distance. It gets more complicated if a boat is in the middle of such of run. Getting ahead of it is OK if you get far enough in front. The objective is to be far enough in front that any tarpon you cast to have time to settle down and get happy before encountering the next boat in line. Tucking in behind the other boat, at a respectable distance, is almost always acceptable. When you do pull-in in front or behind another waiting boat, courtesy demands coming in at a right angle to the tarpon's swimming line and doing so slowly and quietly. Racing in on plane isn't kosher.

Each specific tarpon run will have "local rules" or quirks that take some time to learn. Near my home is a nice spot that can easily handle three boats. Venturing out one day, I discovered a skiff I had never seen before poling around in what I thought of as "no-man's-land" somewhere between stakeout spots #2 and #3. I took a wide turn outside of the tarpon line, putted in from way outside toward

#1, and used a trolling motor to ease in slowly about 300 yards ahead of the other boat. I just finished anchoring when the other guy ran up visibly angry and berated me for "cutting him off." I patiently explained this was a three-boat spot—and had been for over 20 years—and he was effectively using #2 and #3. He continued to bitch, and I answered courteously I would be happy to move back if he wanted #1 but he couldn't sit in the middle and claim all three spots. Got a mumbled response, he slid back to #3, and peace reigned. The moral of the story is, when working new spots don't be afraid to ask other boats about the local customs and do your best to fit in politely.

Common sense and the golden rule—do unto others as you would have others do unto you—will keep the peace on the water. Noise spooks fish, so move quietly. If you're ahead of other boats on the tarpon line and you hook up, don't fire up the outboard to give chase unless and until you're far outside of the swimming line. Good, courteous guides will pole a long way after a hooked tarpon in these circumstances.

Eating a "chill pill" is another antidote when confronting clueless or rude behavior. The biggest culprits are non-angling boaters who know absolutely nothing about flats fishing: the ones that run close by at full speed, drop anchor 100 feet in front of you, and send kids splashing over the side, or motor up to you—when you're casting to the first tarpon you've seen all day—to ask "How's the fishing?" Maddening but getting mad doesn't do much good. A little patient educational conversation can be very beneficial. Be prepared, though, for the belligerent numbnut who bellows, "Go fish somewhere else, it's a big ocean!"

Aggressive, discourteous anglers and guides are becoming a new problem. Most of them are newcomers to the Keys. I've had a couple of unpleasant situations with a young guide pulling in to fish 50 feet from me. When I complained the response was, "I'm making a living doing this so bug off." And one of my Keys guide friends—with over 35 years under his belt—was fishing a very public location (submerged lands around Florida are owned by the State of Florida) when some other, much younger guide motored in to claim he "owned the spot" and yelled my friend had to leave. When he didn't, things got ugly fast. This kind of nonsense is a cancer on our sport and must not be tolerated.

Attitudes and behavior on the water are changing—at least it seems that way to me, but maybe I'm just becoming another aging curmudgeon pining for the mythical good ol' days. The original fly-fishing ethic came from the British trout world, with upper-class Victorian gentlemen plying very private waters and fishing per strict private rules: dry flies only, fishing upstream only, and more. Probity and understatement were primary virtues. Fly fishing for trout in the northeastern United States in the pre-WWII era followed many of the same precepts. Major changes began in the '50s with returning GIs swelling the ranks of anglers and new fisheries developing on the Keys flats and along Rocky Mountain trout rivers, largely immune to imported British values.

Fly fishing has become far more democratic and egalitarian but seems to have gone a bit overboard in rejecting the good elements of the old ethos. "Let's rip some lips" is a commonly used phrase to start a fishing outing. Trophy fish are "Toads" or "Hawgs." Manic, nonstop pursuit of fish gets glorified on social media. I consider myself pretty hard core and dearly love the pursuit of fish. But injecting a little quiet respect for the fish back into the equation can't hurt, and a bit more thoughtful contemplation about angling and all that it entails has got to help too. This is not a plea to sit on the bank or your flats skiff reading Izaak Walton or nature poetry. I spent 40 years in a hyper-competitive profession (the law) and a hyper-competitive environment (Washington, DC) and hate to see those attitudes and ethics (or lack thereof) bleed into angling. If it occurs, particularly on a wide scale, angling will lose its recreative powers and cease to be a necessary refuge from the noise, swirl, and in-your-face attitudes encountered in everyday life.

These highly personal considerations color my thoughts about fishing tournaments. I have enormous respect for anglers and guides who have the skills and focus to win the Gold Cup or the March Merkin permit tournament. Non-tournament anglers benefit greatly from the cutting-edge fishing developments spurred by competition in these events. And some of my best friends are tournament anglers and guides. It's just not for me. When the fish gods smile and I'm able to catch a tarpon or two on a given day, after that I'm playing with house money. My next thoughts are about trying a new spot, experimenting with a different presentation or retrieve, and showing the poons a new fly pattern or two. Curiosity gets the better of me, and scratching that itch is more important than catching another fish. In a tournament, boating/releasing the third or fourth fish does not open the door to experimentation. It means back to work to catch numbers five or six and score points. I don't ever want my angling to become a chore.

New technology has also given rise to etiquette issues unknown just a few years back. The advent of the electric trolling motor, especially the fancy remote-control models, creates particular rules of etiquette becoming more important each season. These motors are not completely new in the Keys. In fact, they were briefly popular about 25 years ago, and many guides put a pair of electrics on stern mounts to facilitate chasing tarpon. However, it became apparent that the fish hated the hum of the motors. These older models also lacked reliability and required big, heavy batteries, eating up precious storage space in a small flats skiff. The motors fell quickly out of favor.

Major improvements in the form of quieter operation, remote-control capabilities, and better batteries breathed new life into trolling motors on the flats. Increasing numbers of DIY anglers spurred new demand for the motors. But plenty of veteran guides and anglers don't like or use the electrics, and I understand why: Too many ill-used motors create real problems during tarpon season. Since I do a lot of solo angling, I have little choice but to rely heavily on an electric, and in the process have learned a thing or two about operating them without precipitating WWIII on the flats. Chasing packs or strings of tarpon with the motors is the major problem:

APRIL 27, CLEAR, 85, WIND ESE 5–10. It was a perfect day, prompting Jeannette to announce that I was taking her tarpon fishing. Ran E a bit and set up on run seeing decent numbers of poons but none interested in eating our flies. A flash or two outside to our SE turned into a big wad of happy tarpon oozing to the west. They were too far to intercept without running straight at them with the trolling motor, so I told her they were gone. She insisted, "Give me a try at them." Warned her it wouldn't work but the eventual answer was "Yes, dear." Used the electric to close the gap but when about 150 feet from the slow-moving big round "meatball," the tarpon heard the motor and began to string out and haul ass. A minute later the couple hundred previously happy tarpon were in a long single-file line and swimming away very fast. I shut down the electric motor. ●

We were the only boat in sight, so at least I hadn't screwed up anybody else's shots at these fish.

Too many trolling motor users haven't learned this lesson, causing substantial irritation. A boat that motors after tarpon, while in the middle of a string of skiffs, is destroying opportunities for the boats down the line. Two seasons ago, near Bahia Honda, two guys in a flats boat with out-of-state registration stickers had the #1 spot, and about half a dozen other boats were strung out behind it for nearly a mile. Every pack of tarpon that hit #1 got chased with an electric motor while one of the anglers cast over the backs of the rapidly departing, unhappy poons—"tail whipping," which is also frowned upon in the Keys. Most of the fish boogied out to sea to escape the harassment, killing the opportunities for the others. Another ugly situation was brewing as a result of ignorance about the fish and discourtesy to fellow anglers. If you own a trolling motor, don't use it to chase fish.

An effective tactic is to intercept groups of swimming tarpon *if* you're the last boat in line (or the only boat around). Run a reverse J-shaped course that gets you to a spot 75 to 100 yards from where the fish will be and wait—silently. Nudging the boat a little bit one way or the other when the tarpon are still 50 yards out can be OK. Let the happy fish swim to you for a few good shots, then let them swim off. Warning: Trying this maneuver with other boats behind you screws them royally, and if you try, you're going to hear about it—loudly.

A trolling motor is like any other inanimate tool: How it's used makes all the difference. The big three fish will tolerate the motors as long as the running speeds are very low *and* the speed is kept fairly constant *and* the propeller isn't banging the bottom. Abrupt changes in motor/propeller pitch are pure death and will send the fish scurrying away. Very patient, very slow-speed approaches can put you within 50 or 60 feet of the fish, but patience and more patience is the key to getting a good shot or two. Quality stealthy poling remains the best way to get close, and it's plainly the preferred option. Unfortunately, trying to simultaneously pole and fly fish is a fool's errand (at least for me), so the electrics come into play. Think of them like a gun—used carefully the motors are OK, used wrongly and big trouble is coming your way.

Etiquette within a flats skiff cannot be overlooked. In fact, sharing the close confines of a small boat—for eight hours or more—can create all kinds of friction. Finding a compatible boat partner is often a years-long enterprise. Most are found via a lot of effort and trial and error. Others are pure happenstance. The late Ralph MacDonald and I got thrown together more than 20 years ago by a mutual friend who runs a superb fishing lodge in Alaska. Mac didn't know me, and I barely knew who he was except for a brief conversation during après-tarpon cocktails and dinner. That he was a New York City investment banker and I was (then) a DC lawyer/ex–government guy—professions that speak alien languages—made for a poor match on paper. But it worked. I didn't know NYC bankers could be funny and creative and more addicted to fishing than doing deals. Only God knows what Mac thought of me originally. Our skill sets matched, and we became a team—with our good guide and friend Albert Ponzoa—catching fish for the boat rather than each other. This development was very fortunate during a multiyear stretch when Mac could do no wrong on the bow and caught tarpon with devastating efficiency while I performed at a reduced level. In the midst of this run, Albert christened Mac "The Devastator." I'm glad I didn't get a nickname—"Screw Up" would have been likely.

Mac was also very creative, and we found a funny way to kill time on the flats when the fish weren't moving: writing flats fishing song lyrics set to well-known tunes. We collaborated on "hits" such as "Please Mr. Tarpon," "Steadily Depressing, Mind Messing Fishing for the Permit Blues," and "He Went to Andros," among others. One of my favorites was a solo effort by Brother MacDonald, after I caught a Grand Slam (bone, perm, and tarpon in one day), to be sung to the tune of "O Danny Boy":

> O Billy Boy, the poons, the poons were rolling,
> Throughout the Keys from Vaca to Big Pine.
> The bones and perms were there behind them,
> You caught a Grand Slam, Billy, that was fine.
> But come ye back when wind blows
> from the northwest,
> And the clouds roll in to the block the sky.
> That's when I'll stop and ask my
> green-eyed question,
> You caught a Grand Slam, Billy, why can't I?

Mac and I enjoyed a great run—I miss you, buddy.

How to split time on the bow is the big issue when two anglers join one guide. Curiosity has compelled me to ask guides about the strategies used to achieve equitable and peaceful results. Answers span the gamut from the ridiculous to the sublime. Limiting each angler to a set period of time is common. One bow "Nazi" brought a noisy timer, set it for 20 minutes, and when it went off—come hell or high water—the guard got changed. Trading a number of shots is another method. It works great when fish are plentiful and neither angler spends a long time sitting. Beau Hodson (Bud's son) and I were trading tarpon shots one April day and fish were pouring. We started at three and change, bumping it to five shots because we were like a pair of jack-in-the-boxes bouncing up and down given the numbers of fish. Despite all the action, neither of us could buy a bite. Some loose mix of time, shots, or caught fish dominate.

The bow hog may be the most unwelcome individual. Some guys just have a hard time sitting down and are forever finding annoying ways to extend their time up front. Like handicap hustlers on golf courses, the hogs wear out their welcome in a hurry. One capable angler I know confessed to me his "hog" predilections in turning down a fishing invitation. I appreciated the honesty.

Dealing with disparate angling abilities is more sensitive. Two anglers board a Bahamas bonefish skiff and agree to take 20-minute turns or catching a fish, whichever comes first. The rub is one is a veteran and the other a rookie. The vet takes four turns totaling maybe 45 minutes and catches four bones. His partner spends twice as much time up front, gets shots, but can't close the deal. By afternoon, the disparity has gotten worse and the experienced angler has a dilemma: (a) give up his bow time hoping the other guy will catch at least one, or (b) stick with the 20-minute turns knowing the newcomer will likely catch nothing.

Five years ago, I got a fishing report presenting this problem in living color. A longtime angler was hosting a friend new to the sport and yet to catch a big tarpon. They booked a late-February trip expecting to chase bones, but unseasonably warm, calm weather pushed a big wad of happy tarpon into a Gulf-side basin. The tarpon were willing to eat a reasonably well-presented fly, and the rookie got about 10 shots without a good presentation. The experienced guy then caught two in fairly short order, opting to surrender the bow for the rest of the day. More than 35 good shots later, the new guy hadn't made a good presentation and was without a bite; the guide was staring daggers at the veteran to the effect of "get your ass back up front." In comparable circumstances, I've been happy to opt for (a) above when it was my spouse or one of my offspring. It's harder to go that way when it's one of your peers and you're paying half of the guide tab. Guides recommend a simple solution: Beginners should book solo trips. Rookies need all of the shots they can get to learn the game and increase the odds of catching something.

Skill levels are frequently a function of an angler's motivations for being on the water. Additionally, why one chooses to fish the flats has a huge impact on expectations. My spouse loves the water, the colors, and the interesting critters. She wants to catch fish but has few problems with limited action. Being out there is her primary motivation and it shapes her expectations.

A variety of angler types fish the flats. The collectors revel in the newest rods, reels, fly lines, and associated gadgets. I suspect that the rods and reels represent a vicarious form of angling when actual time on the water is very limited. The casters love to cast more than fish. Fly guys are sure the next pattern is the surefire remedy to fish lockjaw and are happier when a new fly works than when they catch something.

The competitors are just that. Friendly competition is fun but can get out of control in a hurry. Bill Levy and baseball great Ted Williams were friends, fishing rivals, and competitors. They each had a salmon camp on the Miramichi River in New Brunswick, Canada, and kept tabs on each other's fishing exploits. Williams returned from a trip to Cuba and couldn't wait to report he racked up something like 75 bones in one incredible day, closing the report with "Bet you can't top that!" Levy accepted the challenge, flew to the Yucatan, and chartered two boats: one to fish from and the other to scout ahead and locate bonefish muds. Fishing with a heavy fly on a tough 20-pound-test tippet, he derricked the typical 1- to 2-pound bones out of the muds, ending up with 80 or 85 and winning the bet.

There are social anglers who enjoy joining friends in a skiff and save their strongest anticipation for evening cocktails and the chance to listen to the day's fish stories. One pricey lodge had a regular guest who fished halfheartedly for only a couple of days (of six). He spent most of his time taking photos of the guests, the staff, the setting, boats, etc. At home he assembled beautiful photo albums he sent back to the lodge.

The social side of fishing is important to most of us, even if not taken as far as Mr. Photo Album. Guides and clients often become the best of friends. A highlight of our Andros Island visits is après-bonefishing sessions with icy Kalik beers by the dock when the skiffs returned to the lodge. Annual angling conclaves are eagerly anticipated events and over time acquire a regular cast of characters and a cherished shared history. For nearly 25 years, a group of us has assembled each spring in Marathon to spend a week chasing the mighty tarpon. One year it got accidentally christened "Tarpon Camp" and the name stuck. Besides the fishing, the centerpiece of camp became a backyard party that includes the anglers, guides, spouses, significant others, and a variety of Keys friends. Camp participants cannot now imagine a week of fishing without the party.

Regardless of valued camaraderie, fishing matters deeply to flats anglers, and there is no

Captain Apte holds court at our annual Tarpon Camp party in Marathon.

Interview with Captains
SCOTT COLLINS AND DUSTIN HUFF:
What a Regular Flats Angler Can Learn from the Tournament Winners

Scott Collins and Dustin Huff, neighbors and friends in Marathon, are fly-fishing tournament aces. In the Keys, there are seven annual "major" fly-fishing tournaments for tarpon (three), permit (two), and bonefish (two). Scott has been the winning guide 14 times (and is one of only two Keys guides to score a "species tournament slam" winning at least one bonefish, permit, and tarpon "major"); Dustin has notched six victories. Only two guides have ever won the Gold Cup Tarpon Tournament on their first try—Scott and Dustin. Only two guides have ever won the Hawley Tarpon Tournament on their first try—Scott and Dustin. Suffice to say, they know their stuff.

What can regular flats anglers learn from the tournaments?

Scott: Preparation, meticulous preparation. In a tournament, we leave the dock with everything ready to go—all rods rigged, multiple backup leaders ready, flies with sharp hooks. Time wasted on the water rigging gear can cost you a fish, or two, making you lose crucial points.

Dustin: When I started guiding, too many clients showed up unprepared. They might have their gear, but rods were in tubes, leaders unattached to fly lines. Shots at fish were missed while we did in the boat what should have been done on shore. All of my clients now are regulars, and they know the value of being fully ready from the start of the day.

Scott: You never know when your best shots might be at your first stop on the flats. Missing chances is a killer in the tournaments. It always come back to haunt you. Let me add that tournament flats fishing is purely a team sport. The guide is only as good as the angler, and the angler is only as good as the guide.

Anything special about the rods and reels used in the tournaments?

Dustin: Everything should be the same. The regular rods/reels should have identical backups. And the terminal gear—leaders and such—should be the same too. That lets the angler catch a fish, or lose one, pick up a backup rod, and get back in the game without adjusting your casting stroke, or guessing how hard to pull on the next fish.

Scott: One of my winning clients was super anal about having the same rigs. All of his 12s were alike, all of his 10s were alike.

Is the repetition associated with using the exact same equipment important?

Scott: Absolutely. Multiple quality presentations equal more eats and more caught fish. When a string of tarpon swims by, a set of quick, accurate throws ups the odds of a bite.

Dustin: One tarpon in every school or string is willing to bite—you just need to show the fly correctly to that fish.

Scott: Pinpoint presentations are crucial—being off an inch or two is the difference between an eat and a refusal. A fly a couple of inches too far has the retrieve attack the tarpon's eye rather than slide across its face. Familiarity with the same gear—same rod, same reel, same line, same leader length—all leads to precision.

Dustin: The fishing is so technical now that the correct angle of presentation, the correct speed of the retrieve, are essential to getting the tarpon to eat.

Any other advice on good presentations?

Dustin: Don't flock shoot. Pick out a specific fish and target it. Just pitching the fly into the neighborhood rarely gets the job done.

Scott: It also makes sense to usually leave the front fish [in a string] alone. Focus on the middle or back of the pack. Those fish bite better.

Dustin: I agree. Tarpon number 6 in a 10-fish string is swimming along focused on the tail of his buddy in front, the fly appears in the right spot, and the fish grabs it. I think it's thinking, "Damn, my pals passed up this morsel, good for me."

Scott: The lead fish is so much more sensitive and if it spooks, it will take the whole group with it.

Dustin: I also want my anglers throwing clear lines. Yes, it's harder to see the fly, but if you can learn that skill while using the clear line, you won't regret it. Tarpon that will run from a colored line simply swim by the clears.

Scott: My guys don't use the clear lines as much as Dustin's do, but the clear ones are an important part of the angler's arsenal. When the oceanside tarpon runs get that crystal-clear late-season water, it slicks out, and the sun shines, you better break out the clear line.

What weight rods do you like for tarpon?

Scott: For landing tarpon (and scoring points) I want the biggest rod. Especially during the close-to-the-boat-end game. A 12 can maneuver a big fish better than a 10.

Dustin: I want my guys using 12s unless conditions absolutely dictate going lighter. Big fish in the tournaments must be held boatside and a girth strap put around them. That calls for a 12.

Scott: But there are times when you need the light rod. A 10 with a clear line is the ticket for those clear, calm days.

What is the most important personal attribute of successful tournament anglers?

Dustin: Focus—laser-sharp focus. You may watch and wait for hours before you get a shot. The guy still focused, still in the game, makes the presentation and might catch the fish. The guy daydreaming misses the chance.

Scott: Yes, sir. Every winner possesses that combo of focus and preparation.

Dustin: It's one reason that tournament angling is not necessarily enjoyable. Serious focus and competitive commitment enable the angler—and guide—to stay in the game and catch the fish.

Scott: I've often said nothing can ruin a day's fishing like a tournament can! When you catch a fish, it becomes a checkmark and your focus must turn immediately to the next fish. But let me tell you there is almost no other feeling in fishing knowing you just landed what you are pretty sure is the clincher to win. High fives and hugs covered in water, sweat, and tarpon slime is memorable and a big part of why we subject ourselves to the tournament tortures.

Any tips on keeping that focus?

Scott: Continuity in your fishing is a big help. Multiple consecutive days on the water let you appreciate how your guide wants you to fish. You begin to learn the spots and where to focus to see the fish. You also watch the fish behave, which lets you anticipate what they will do, where they'll swim. Your guide learns your skill levels and can adjust accordingly. All of this breeds success, and the prospects of successful fishing makes focus easier to achieve and maintain.

Dustin: Five days in a row should be a minimum! For the reasons Scott outlined and the weather. Catching good weather is important, and the more days committed to fishing gives you a better shot at getting at least a couple of good-weather ones.

Any last comments on the good or bad effects of the tournaments?

Dustin: On the good side, the tournaments make us all work harder to get better at finding and catching fish. My clients and I do a lot of experimenting, especially in pre-tournament fishing. We look for new spots, test new flies, different retrieves. This often pays off with knowledge that benefits directly my non-tournament anglers. On the bad side, the high catch rates in many of the tournaments create unrealistic expectations for regular anglers. The tournaments have the best guides and the best anglers fishing hard—and focused—for multiple days. It's difficult for the guy who comes to the Keys once a year for two or three days to match their success.

Scott: The non-tournament people should recognize how good and how committed the tournament winners are. Unless the regular angler is going to match that commitment—hone their skills, practice diligently, and spend weeks on the water each season—he or she is unlikely to match the tournament guys.

Dustin: Think of it like golf. The casual golfer is not going to break 80 or compete with any professional. The major tournaments in the Keys are like a fly-fishing PGA. ■

doubt the most successful fishers bring a level of focus and intensity to the bow of a boat. Non-anglers have a hard time understanding the commitment and are aghast at incidents that reveal this intensity. Blue skies, bright sun, and clear green waters announced a perfect July morning, and Joe Kelley and I were back with Captain Albert to hunt permit. A first flat was empty, and as Joe stowed the rod, disaster struck: A crab fly (with a bit of barb left) jammed deep into his thumb. Albert tried the snatch technique to remove the hook, but all that did was drain blood from Joe's contorted face. We beelined to the boat ramp, which is close to Marathon's hospital, and arranged a ride to the emergency room for Joe. Once there he reported a two-hour-plus wait. Albert and I figured there was nothing else we could do, so back to the flats—and told Joe to call when done and we'd get him at the ramp. My spouse was appalled.

She later granted me a pardon after hearing Captain Steve Huff tell his tale of a pair of tarpon-fishing clients. A longtime regular client brought a friend, who was desperate to catch his first big poon. The friend flew a red-eye flight from California to Miami and drove straight to Marathon. The boat was launched, and not far into the backcountry, laid-up tarpon were located and the rookie friend hooked a big girl that Huff pegged at 125 pounds. Fearful of breaking off the trophy, the angler was babying the fish, prompting Huff to bark some orders to pull hard on the damn thing. The guy complied. Huff was briefly busy in a hatch, hearing grunting and groaning followed by a loud boat-shaking thud. Startled, he looked up to see the angler face down, out cold on the bow with the fly rod wedged underneath. Huff and client extracted the fly rod, broke off the tarpon, and got on the radio (pre-cellphone days) before racing back to shore, where EMS and the cops were waiting. The unfortunate guy was manhandled off the skiff and EMS tried all the emergency techniques to no avail—he was dead. For the next hour, Huff and client answered questions, then the ambulance, the deceased, and the cops left. The remaining client turned to Captain Huff and asked, "What's the protocol here? Do we go back out?" And they did.

Women often find these obsessive attitudes, and the lack of empathy, disconcerting. But it hasn't stopped a goodly number of distaff anglers from taking the bow to chase the big three species. In fact, a set of Islamorada sisters were on the ground floor of Keys flats fishing. Beulah, Bonnie, and Frankee Laidlaw lived in Islamorada in the 1930s. All were adept, avid fishers. Beulah married early Keys guide Johnny Cass. Bonnie was married to Bill Smith, who is credited with the first purposefully caught fly-rod bonefish in 1939. Smith was also an early flats guide, and when he left the island to serve in WWII, Bonnie took over his guiding business. She was no mere fill-in, though, and kept guiding after her husband returned. She put Joe Brooks on his first fly-rod permit. It's also obvious she knew her stuff: Old photos show her on the long-gone A & B Docks (today the Morada Bay restaurant sits there) with two dozen big bones pinned on the fishing racks. Bonnie also played matchmaker. A young veteran fished with her right after the war and Bonnie introduced him—Jimmie Albright—to sister Frankee. They later married.

Frankee was a flats ace before Albright—Islamorada's most famous founding guide—knew the Keys existed. They were a great

Islamorada's Laidlaw sisters, Beulah, Bonnie, and Frankee (left to right), pioneering Keys anglers and guides, pose for the camera. (Courtesy of Brad Bertelli, Florida Keys History and Discovery Center)

husband-wife fishing team and guided the likes of Joe Brooks and Ted Williams. In 1957, Frankee caught the then world record permit. Later in life she became a well-known horticulturist, contributing articles to publications like the *Bromeliad Society Journal* (bromeliads are flowering subtropical plants).

Other Keys women joined the guiding ranks in subsequent years. Linda Drake worked out of Key West in the '70s and '80s. In the '90s, Ann Molohan guided out of Bud N' Mary's in Islamorada.

As a college kid, I had the good fortune to meet two leading lady anglers: Joan Salvato Wulff and Kay Brodney. Joan is legendary, Kay largely unknown. Little Joanie Salvato (she's all of 5 feet) of Paterson, New Jersey, started winning fly-casting tournaments as a young girl in 1943 and held national casting titles for the next 17 years. She uncorked an unequalled 161-foot cast in a 1960 competition. In the '60s she met and married Lee Wulff—another angling legend. I met the pair in 1972. Sixteen years later I enjoyed a wonderful dinner with them on the banks of New York's Beaverkill River and most recently saw her at Stu Apte's place in the Keys. Joan has caught damn near everything under the sun, and her unparalleled skill with a fly rod as well as gracious demeanor earned her the title "First Lady of Fly Fishing." Almost as important, she has demonstrated that fly casting— even with heavy saltwater rigs—is not a matter of strength but timing.

Kay Brodney, despite incredible fly-fishing achievements, flew under the radar. I met her when a small group of us, including Kay, revitalized the Trout Unlimited chapter in Washington, DC. She had moved to DC in the '60s to take a senior position at the Library of Congress. A humble, self-effacing woman, it took a while to pry out of her information about her exploits with the long rod. In 1956, she won the National Woman's Fly Casting Accuracy Championship. In 1969, fishing with Captain Apte, Kay boated a 137.6-pound tarpon on a 12-pound tippet that was a record fish for many years. Her recounting a bonefish outing to Biscayne Bay with Captain Bill Curtis, as well as her tale of the big poon, fired up my saltwater fly-fishing bug. Between 1974 and 1983, Kay served on the American Museum

Kay Brodney caught this record tarpon with Captain Apte in 1969. (Courtesy of Stu Apte)

of Fly Fishing's Board of Trustees. We lost her in 1994.

Closer to home, my spouse caught her first fly-rod trout in 2003 and was catching bonefish the next season. She then graduated from bones to poons in six years.

Known among our friends as the "Tarpon Queen" because of her high "batting average" on the big fish (no one catches more tarpon with less effort), Jeannette is among the rare beginners who scored a big tarpon on her first try. Her great batting average got better on Mother's Day 2015:

MAY 10, CLEAR, 85, WIND SE 10. The Tarpon Queen, operating in high efficiency mode, strikes again. After breakfast, I was informed that she wanted to go tarpon fishing but didn't want to spend hours on the water. Scratched my head, looked at the tide table, and figured we could intercept some fish about 4 p.m. Got to our spot and anchored the Mirage to give Jeannette a downwind 45-foot throw from the stern. Asked her to make a practice cast or two to get the range and was told "I don't need no stinking practice cast" (been watching

The "Tarpon Queen" (my spouse Jeannette) chases a hooked fish on Captain Albert's skiff.

too many Mel Brooks movies). Five minutes later a six-pack of lazy, happy tarpon glided in behind us, the TQ made one pinpoint cast, and the lead fish—a good 90-lber—eased up and gulped the fly. Game on. . . . When boatside, Jeannette wanted a picture of the fish but was having a hard time lifting the big tarpon to the surface. Gave her the camera, I took the rod, pulled hard, rolled the fish up, heard the Nikon go click, and the 10-weight exploded. At home, I was directed to secure another Mother's Day gift—a replacement rod. ⬤

Younger women in their 20s and 30s are also entering the ranks. Alex Woodsum was introduced to the flats by her father and still fishes with my Marathon friend Captain Albert Ponzoa. She is very adept with a fly rod, managed a Grand Slam on the *Silver Kings* TV program, and has contributed to flats conservation as a former key staffer at BTT.

Young Heather Harkavy, a veteran angler at 23, was introduced into the ranks by her father Jeff, a BTT board member. She began serious angling as a young child and by 17 had snared numerous IGFA world records, many caught

with former Marathon captain and guide Chris Morrison. In addition to her angling passion and skills, she is director of Fish for Change, a youth summer program promoting fly fishing, conservation, cultural immersion, and creative writing. Camps are conducted around the Caribbean at locales including the Bahamas, Honduras, and Mexico.

My 29-year-old daughter Victoria started fishing as a young child, captured her first bonefish as a 10-year-old, and entered the ranks of tarpon catchers in her mid-20s. Her fly fishing, however, was limited to trout until 2019, when she took up the challenge of big tarpon on the fly. Following some casting lessons and diligent practice, she arrived in Marathon ready to become a Tarpon Camper, and like Jeannette (must be something about distaff anglers), scored a good fly-rod fish on her first morning:

APRIL 28, MARATHON, MOSTLY CLEAR, 85, WIND SE 10. Tarpon started swimming about 9 a.m. on the current switch and Victoria showed the fly to a couple of groups without any interest from the fish. Waiting for more westbound tarpon, she noticed bouncing water behind us that turned into an eastbound 10-pack of happy tarpon. The fish proceeded to stop and slid into a slow counterclockwise daisy chain. Capt. Ponzoa poled the skiff to about 45 feet and directed a cast to the left edge of the circling poons. Victoria's first cast and presentation got a hard follow, the second spot-on throw earned a gulping eat, she stripped tight, and a solid 60-lber launched. Fifteen minutes later the silver fish was boatside and broken off. Congrats followed—a handshake from Albert and a proud hug from me. ●

I have always thought women have the skill sets to be successful on the bow: patience, dexterity, a willingness to listen to a guide's instructions (rather than a boyfriend or husband!), and curiosity about the whole flats environment rather than just the targeted fish. Adding young women and their different attitudes to our community is also important if

we want our sport to flourish, and critical to grow support for conservation of the fisheries. A sport with only half of the population willing to participate will not fare well.

People issues can also be entertaining, sometimes bizarre. Anglers of all stripes are a superstitious lot, and fishing is encrusted with rituals and superstitions despite the fact that Western civilization prides itself on attachment to facts and reason. We shake our heads at the Dogon people of Mali. Their shamans, or witch doctors, prescribe a single day each year when fishing is allowed in small sacred Lake Antogo. When the spirits provide their assent, thousands of people descend on the tiny lake in a frenzy of fishing, literally fishing it out in 15 minutes. I heard the story and rolled my eyes—until I remembered my early '60s trout opening days in New Jersey with shoulder-to-shoulder anglers beating the water to a froth at 8 a.m. when the warden blew the "OK to fish" whistle.

Everyone has good luck charms and bad luck omens. Old ratty hats are a common charm.

Heather Harkavy jumps a small tarpon along the mangroves. (Courtesy of Heather Harkavy)

My daughter Victoria puts the heat on her first fly-rod tarpon.

But not everyone comes to cherish an ancient pair of boat sneakers. Sometime in the '70s I acquired a pair of sneakers with a blue half circle on top of the toes, giving them their nickname—"Smileys." They became my flats fishing shoes, getting very little use over a long period when the vicissitudes of work and a young family constrained severely my time on the water. When I started fishing with Captain Bus in the 1990s, the Smileys were going strong, bringing pretty good luck to our tarpon endeavors. Each year Bus would check to see if I still had the shoes, which were in fact falling apart, barely held together with duct tape. The sneaks could no longer be washed—they would have simply fallen apart—and stunk, defying Johnson's Odor Eaters. They died on my feet one fishless day; we conducted a brief onboard memorial service for them, took a photo, and that night, after 30 years of use, pitched them into the trash can. Our luck evaporated and no poons were caught over the next three days!

Old Testament Jonah, him of the whale, gets invoked on flats skiffs. Chip King, the head guide at Tikchik Narrows Lodge in Alaska, and I shared a boat one day. My turns on the bow caused a tarpon drought. Chip would hop up and tarpon would swim immediately into

range. Midday I was given "Jonah" status and told to let Chip bring in the fish.

Rituals are commonplace in the form of eating the correct breakfast, using a specific sequence to rig a rod, starting with a particular fly, or bringing on board a special kind of lucky sandwich (liverwurst in one case if you can believe it). Oft-repeated comments or declarations are part of the mix. MacDonald, channeling his inner "Spartan mother," always started the day admonishing his fellow anglers to "come back with your shield or on it."

Filling up the gas tank should be a ritual for one of our Marathon friends. He forgets with disheartening regularity, and to cover his sins, has told boatmates his outboard suffers from "vapor lock." Late one summer afternoon my phone rang and I hear, "Buddy, I'm broken down a mile north of Bahia Honda. Can you come tow me in?" "Of course" was the answer but I asked pointedly, "Should I bring a can of gas?" "No, no, it's an engine problem," I was assured. So, I hitched up the trailer and down the road I went. I launched at the state park and motored out to find my friend and his client, drifting slowly north on the incoming tide. After securing the tow lines, we putted back to the park ramp. I offered my boat for the next day if the engine couldn't get repaired

"Vapor lock"—we get towed in to the gas dock to fill an empty fuel tank.

overnight. Two days later I ran into my friend at the gas station and asked about the outboard. Sheepishly he confessed to another bout of "vapor lock," but it was a new client and he didn't want the guy to know they had run out of gas. I'm still laughing.

No bananas on board, however, is the Keys granddaddy fishing superstition. One of the flats boat companies even gives away "no bananas" stickers to put on the skiff console. I learned this taboo—and witnessed its "power"—firsthand one fine spring day:

APRIL 29, MOSTLY CLEAR, 80, WIND NW 5. Bus picked up Bud and me and headed down US I. Clipping across the Seven Mile Bridge revealed an exquisite day with a bright yellow sun rising into a clear blue sky and light breeze just ruffling the water. Launched and hit the backcountry in search of poons. But a long morning checking out multiple spots turned up only a couple of fish and no shots. Hoped to change fortunes by having lunch and resuming the hunt. At this time, I pulled out a banana, getting a horrified reaction. Got ragged on, especially by Bud, and jettisoned the evil yellow fruit with great ceremony. And incredibly the tarpon appeared. I jumped a fish then Bud was up. Bus spotted a swimming foursome, poled into position, and predicted the fish would hit the flat edge, skirt a red crab pot buoy, and turn toward us. They did, Bud delivered the green Toad, and got a great bite. He hooked up, played the fish aggressively through four or five jumps, and Bus had the leader. My turn had a pair ooze in from behind us, cast to 8 o'clock, earning flared pectorals and an elevating bite looking straight down its throat. The fish went nuts, jumping and running off 200 yards. Way out there it erupted in a jaw dropping, lateral, arched back, vibrating, mouth gaping leap. Finally ran it down, administered the "coup de grace," and released another fine 80-pounder. Thank the fish gods I'd gotten rid of the banana. Then Bud dug into his bag and produced another banana. S.O.B.! ●

Rituals and superstitions are merely part of the layers of experience creating the rich texture of quality flats angling. We recall the heft and feel of a favorite rod with a well-worn cork grip and a reel sporting a collection of hard-earned dings and nicks. Each new season you anticipate climbing into the guide's truck—with the door latch that doesn't work and dog hair on the seats—and being back in a skiff with your friends, and actually look forward to hearing your pal's favorite joke—for the umpteenth time—while killing time. After a few bright days on the flats, familiar "raccoon eyes" stare at you in the bathroom mirror. Getting off the tropical waters reignites an old internal debate—a crisp, cold beer or the pleasant bite of rum, tonic, and lime? Beyond the fish, you'll find these little things etched in memory.

Public Use and Access

Guide numbers, more and more people on the water, and new forms of crafts and vehicles (e.g., paddleboards and jet skis) all create the need for courtesy and common sense among oftentimes competing users. Some user issues become environmental matters when tangible physical resources are affected adversely. Inevitably user conflicts and adverse impacts on natural resources trigger calls for governmental intervention in the form of management plans, regulations, and restrictions. Anglers are slowly waking up to the need to be engaged on these matters.

Keys waters are filled with increasing numbers of new boaters, jet skis, kayaks, and paddleboards. And a substantial number of these new boaters are damn near clueless about basic safety and navigation markers. Coast Guard statistics indicate nearly 90 percent of Florida boating accidents are a function of operator error in the form of alcohol, inattention, inability to read navigation markers, or unfamiliarity with running a boat. We once encountered a rental boat wandering about that waved us over. The people on board were in search of a well-known sandbar that is well marked on charts—and the operator had an apparent chart in hand. Told them where the bar was and "it should be right there on your chart," the paper was handed to us: an AAA road map. You can't make up this stuff.

Florida has no license requirements for private boating, only a limited educational

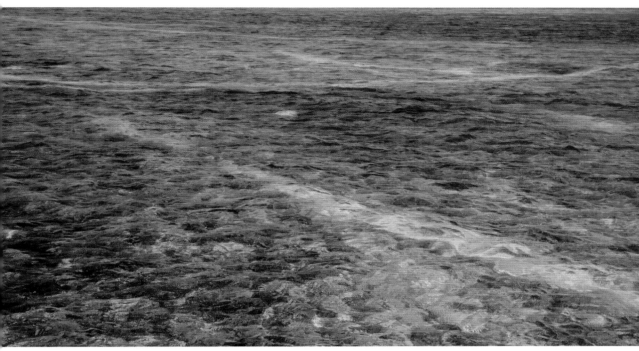

A Middle Keys flat shows prominent propeller scarring caused by errant, ignorant boaters.

mandate for those born after 1987. Most of this free-for-all on the water is a nuisance although safety concerns grow, as it seems many of the nearshore boats are new, big center consoles, sporting three or four huge outboard engines. I've had these boats roar by no more than 75 feet from my staked-out skiff, threatening to swamp us under a big wake. The big boat's sound system is invariably blasting.

The Keys are blessed with a number of sandbars, often exposed at low tide, that are wonderful spots for a boating picnic and a little floating around in clear, warm, shallow waters. Most used to attract a handful of locals who knew precisely where and when to go. Today some of these are mob scenes attracting hundreds of boats, partiers, very loud sound systems, and plenty of booze. Look out toward the Atlantic when crossing Islamorada's Whale Harbor Bridge some spring or summer weekend. Arrests for disorderly conduct and drunkenness are common. Boat traffic to and from these spots can be intense, dangerous, and absolutely ruinous for nearby fishing. Bottom damage, from big boats trying to get shallow, and piles of litter and trash are routine at the most popular locations. Authorities have been slow to react, but a few spots in the Gulf

backcountry, under the joint jurisdiction of the FWS and FWC, have been closed to stop the havoc.

Annoying as this can be, the greater damage from unknowing boaters is inflicted on the flats environment. Flats are interspersed throughout the islands, and rarely can a boat run in a straight line from point to point. If it tries, running aground is guaranteed. When a boat plows into a grass or coral flat, critical habitat for our fish, the bottom gets ripped up and backing off—under full power—causes the propeller to dig up more. Sometimes the boats can get across, under full power, with the propeller leaving a long visible gash. These "prop scars" can be found throughout the Keys, destroying valuable sea-grass beds, killing corals, and creating underwater erosion that exacerbates the original damage:

JUNE 3, MOSTLY SUNNY, 90 DEGREES F, WIND CALM TO 5, SE. Jim Reinertsen was visiting to catch the worm hatch and we were on station by a worm bar at 6:30. A bigger boat appeared about a half mile to the E and on the far side of the bar/bank. It was running fast and straight toward the bar. Turned to Jim and said, "Watch this, bet the guy is going to hit the bar." Jim argued, "No way, there are two big red diamond shoal warning markers and I see a bunch of birds wading on the flat—the guy can't miss that!" He did. Moments later the boat plowed onto the bar at full speed and then compounded the error by pouring on power—I guess to drive across—pushing the boat higher and drier. As the tide ebbed, and the water fell, the boat careened over high and dry. Worms were a no-show and the clueless boater and crew were still there when we left before dark. ⬤

The damage creates pressure for boating closures, including proposals to bar any and all boats from the flats. Everglades National Park is legally obligated to prepare a General Management Plan (GMP) for the park, including Florida Bay. The newest GMP was adopted in 2016 following long controversy. Early versions included activist-inspired proposals to close most of the Bay to all motorboat traffic—including flats skiffs. Keys anglers and guides reacted by pressing the park to act rationally and appreciate that flats skiffs run by knowledgeable people were not the problem and should not be the victims of efforts to get at the bad actors. There was a lot of back and forth, and a reasonable approach was ultimately adopted requiring boaters to pass an online course on navigating in the Bay and acquire a permit demonstrating the test was passed before boating the Bay. A number of flats were designated as "pole and troll zones" where only poling a boat or running with an electric trolling motor is allowed. Motorboat corridors were designated to allow flats skiffs and other small boats to cross the Bay and motor to the edge of the pole and troll areas. Big boats and multiple-engine rigs—which simply cannot operate safely in the very shallow bay—are now prohibited by the GMP. Some hard-core anti-engine and anti-fishing activists weren't pleased, nor were a few of the party boat crowd, but almost everyone else agreed the outcome was a reasonable compromise.

This entire exercise is a peek into the future. Another larger plan is in the offing for the Keys, this time from the federal National Oceanographic and Atmospheric Administration (NOAA). Congress designated the Florida Keys Marine Sanctuary in 1990 and put NOAA in charge. Like Everglades National Park, NOAA must update periodically its Sanctuary Management Plan and started the process a few years ago. The updated plan is likely to be completed in 2022 or shortly thereafter.

Controversy popped up quickly when activists insisted the plan create very large special sanctuary zones that would start offshore on the Atlantic side of the Keys and run miles to the Gulf/Bay side. Within these zones, there would be severe limits on boating and fishing and outright bans of both activities in particular locations. When these restrictive proposals were given serious consideration by a sanctuary advisory committee, all hell broke loose. NOAA and the advisors backed away from the severe restrictions proposal, but the agency is still deep in the midst of its planning effort. A draft management plan was released for public review and comment in 2019, and the political pot has been boiling since the proposed plan was issued. Most careful anglers know that something needs to be done to better conserve the Keys marine environment, including the flats. But some proposed restrictions on minimal impact catch-and-release flats fishing are disproportionate to the limited environmental impacts associated with poling across the flats in a shallow-water skiff. Time will tell if a rational conservation and restoration plan, akin to the Everglades/Florida Bay model, prevails.

But wait, there's more. The hundreds of backcountry islands and little keys that stretch from East Bahia Honda to the Marquesas, on the edge of the Gulf of Mexico, are part of three national wildlife refuges (NWRs): Great Heron NWR, Key Deer NWR, and Key NWR. All are administered, as one unit, by FWS within the US Department of the Interior (which also houses the NPS). Federal law also requires FWS to create Comprehensive Conservation Plans (CCPs) for each refuge unit in America (there are over 500), and the last CCP was finished in 2009. Federal law prescribes that the plans be updated every 15 years, meaning an updated plan is due in 2024.

There are huge numbers of famous, productive bonefish, permit, and tarpon flats within the refuges' boundaries, and access to these areas will likely be affected by any new CCP. And the matter is more complex because of

An Everglades National Park sign denotes a "pole and troll zone"—only poling and electric trolling motors may be used in the zone.

shared jurisdiction over the waters with the State of Florida. Technically, the feds own only the uplands above the mean high-tide line. Florida owns the submerged lands under the backcountry waters between the many islands, but these submerged lands and overlying waters (full of our fish) are within the refuges' boundaries. Rather than a big fight over control of the waters, FWS and the state have an agreement to work together on management of the area. So, the planning process must include the state in a substantive manner.

Had this planning exercise occurred 25 years ago, anti-hunting/anti-fishing radicals would have jumped up and down arguing that as the waters were part of a "refuge," it would be illegal and immoral to allow fishing. Congress stopped this nonsense in 1997, enacting the National Wildlife Refuge System Improvement Act stipulating that fishing and hunting are legitimate activities in refuges and that these activities constitute "priority public uses" within the units (provisions that I helped draft). Hence, continued fishing within Keys refuge waters is assured. However, access to those waters could be an open issue. Just like the Florida Bay GMP and the NOAA Sanctuary Plan, someone will press hard for severe fishing restrictions or substantial closures in the Lower Keys backcountry.

Consideration and debate regarding use and access issues are invariably contentious, loud, and as clear as mud. Interests pressing for severe access restrictions usually do so in the name of environmental or resource protection. Unfortunately, oftentimes those reasons are a smoke screen for other objectives. Many user interests don't like other users and the real issues are clashes over competing uses—not conservation of the environment or natural resources. These intense fights are about what is the "right" way to use and enjoy public waters (or lands). One group may be adamant about "no motors" and another is just as vociferous on the other side. Use issues like this are frequently fights over subjective amenity values: My form of use is better than yours.

Often the battle is ideological, waged by deep-pocketed special interests, rather than actual on-the-ground or on-the-water users. In an egalitarian society, prohibiting one set of users in the name of subjective values often

doesn't sit well with the broad public (and elected officials). To camouflage these motives, the amenity interest can be transformed into claims that the "other" users are destroying the environment, as that argument can get real public and political traction. Whenever these battles break out, it is crucial to separate the wheat from the chaff in the form of determining what are bona fide physical resource-conservation issues (water quality, habitat protection, clean air) as compared to subjective amenity concerns (wilderness experience, solitude).

The Everglades Park/Florida Bay plan fight included these elements, with some activists simply wanting to bar motorboat use to preserve their amenity interests in large areas open only to canoes, kayaks, and paddleboards. Obviously, flats anglers—reliant on motorboat access in the Bay—took a different tack. I would argue that the angling interests were amenable to motorized closures and restrictions where necessary for resource conservation (saving the sea-grass beds), as opposed to "protecting" someone from the sound or sight of an outboard engine. The final compromise Everglades Park/Florida Bay GMP reflects these considerations, and there is no doubt that comparable issues will emerge during preparation of the sanctuary and refuge plans.

Regulations and restrictions on forms of public use to protect or enhance experiential or amenity values are legitimate and not uncommon, especially on public lands in the western United States. For example, Alaska's Gates of the Arctic National Park, a very remote nine-million-acre unit (Yellowstone is two million acres), includes a specially designated multimillion-acre area within the park boundaries where only a handful of campers/hikers are allowed each year. From a tangible resource perspective, the severe visitor limits are not necessary to protect the tundra, water quality, fish, or caribou. The restrictions were purposefully designed over 30 years ago to assure that the area remains barely visited. People who get the limited permits venture into the restricted area knowing that they are among a tiny number in a vast wild landscape; they value deeply this subjective experience. Protection of this specific amenity value was publicly disclosed, debated openly, and deemed important enough to be written into

NPS rules. I know because I approved the rules as Assistant Secretary of the Interior in 1987.

Closer to home now, the No Motor Zone within Everglades National Park is in large part created to provide amenity values to those visitors (including me) willing to make the special effort to go into the zone and abide by its restrictions. All of us are free to be advocates for amenity-based limitations on public use of public lands and waters. The only caveats, in my opinion, are that the purposes of the restrictions must be explained clearly—that proposed restrictions are not sold on the basis of bogus environmental impacts—and that the ensuing debate be transparent and substantive. The public deserves no less.

Anglers just want to go fishing and be left alone. After all, we're not bothering anybody, are we? Complicated agency planning procedures and complex federal and state laws epitomize the headaches to be ignored. Unfortunately, such attitudes are a luxury that anglers, especially flats anglers in the Keys, can no longer afford. Activists, agencies, and other interests can be, or are, hostile or indifferent to fish and fishers. Failure to engage and failure to act to protect our interests are merely the slow road to destruction.

Many in our ranks consider themselves dedicated conservationists who practice low-impact angling, taking pride in careful catch-and-release tactics. The growing animal rights movement doesn't care (which I know from having litigated against these radicals for most of my professional career). As far as they are concerned, tormenting fish for selfish pleasure is a major sin. The fact that anglers (and hunters) pay for wildlife conservation doesn't matter. Recently a "green" publication included an article putting these attitudes on full display. It stated, unequivocally, that sport fishing constitutes torture and is immoral. Catch-and-release anglers were identified as particularly heinous by virtue of repeated torture. The article noted too that catch-and-release advocates proclaim belief in conservation, but this was dismissed as "stunning hypocrisy."

> "Torture: The action or practice of inflicting severe pain on someone as a punishment or to force them to do or say something, or for the pleasure of the person inflicting pain. That right there is a good description of sport fishing."—*Earth Island Institute Journal*, May 10, 2018

Every new study or article claiming fish possess self-awareness (I'm not kidding) or feel serious pain is another arrow in the radicals' quiver. They may not prevail in running us out of business in this generation, but we should be fearful about what's on the horizon.

Rapidly changing demographics are creating an ever-more-urbanized populous completely disconnected from the natural world. Standing up for fishing and conservation measures to help fish are likely low on the priority list for this growing mass of people.

The increasing number of "people" issues, mostly related to crowding and competing uses but including bona fide impacts on the natural environment, are already exerting unwelcome influence on our sport. These issues and impacts require that flats anglers elevate our commitment to courteous, responsible angling, conservation of our fisheries and habitats, and more engagement in unavoidable government regulatory plans. Otherwise, I fear a bleak future for the pursuit of bonefish, tarpon, and permit.

CHAPTER 4

The Places

The fact that bonefish, tarpon, and permit live in colorful, wonderful places is a big part of their allure. More than one writer has noted that if bones were caught in nondescript brown-water sloughs, they would rank way down the list of desirable gamefish. Fortunately, all three inhabit some of the most unique corners of the world. Mexican fish can be pursued almost in the shadows of ancient Mayan ruins. Far into the Pacific Ocean, spectacular atolls featuring white beaches, tall palm trees, and surf crashing on island-ringing coral reefs are home to countless bonefish (and other flats critters such as trevally). The Bahamas possess endless flats with a magical mix of blue, green, and turquoise waters.

Within the United States, the Florida Keys are famous for their funky vibe and the great 108-mile drive down the Overseas Highway. Over 40 bridges, one up to 7 miles long, span gorgeous flats and shimmering, pastel-colored waters terminating in "Key Weird." A not-too-long boat ride from the Keys enables an angler to penetrate deep into the mysterious mangrove jungles of the Everglades. Redfish aficionados travel to the vast Louisiana marshes, Cajun country, home to interesting people and great cuisine—a crawfish boil, anyone?

Home Waters

Home waters have a rich allure. Familiarity builds layers of memories and provides deep knowledge of nuances that are often the key to success. The mature appreciation of oft-visited waters is very different from the curiosity and briefer excitement created by trips to new locales. A great philosopher once observed, "There's no place like home."

This is all new in the saltwater world. Full-fledged flats fishing is only a post-WWII phenomenon, and its literature, legends, and myths are in nascent stages at best. Compare this to the trout world where fly-fishing literature begins almost 2,000 years ago in Roman author Claudius Aelianus's *De Natura Animalium*, written in the 2nd century CE (or AD); he referred to angling for brown trout in the Greek mountains. British fly-fishing literature begins in 1496, and Izaak Walton's *The Compleat Angler*, including how-to fly-fishing details, was penned in 1653. Relatively modern English trout writers extolled the virtues of the Hampshire chalk streams 140 years ago. In the

The uniquely named Dog Dick Flat, in the Middle Keys, holds bonefish and occasional permit.

147

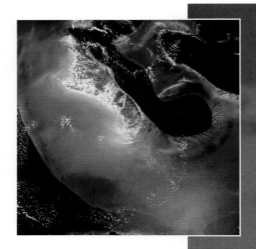

A satellite image depicts Andros Island and the mile-plus-deep Tongue of the Ocean (the dark blue) along its east—or oceanside—shore. (NASA photo)

United States, paeans to northeastern waters in New York's Catskill Mountains or Pennsylvania's Poconos appeared not long thereafter.

Trout literature is long with evocative prose about home waters and home pools, many of which were given names now well known. It doesn't take much reading to learn of the famous Junction Pool (where the Beaverkill and Willowemoc Rivers meet in the Catskill Mountains), Fox's Meadow on Pennsylvania's Letort Spring Run, or the Millionaire's Pool on Idaho's Henry's Fork. I suspect Aelianus's ancient Greek fly fishers gave pet names to their favorite pools. Flats fishers have some catching up to do.

The first two specially denoted flats spots in the Keys—not named for an adjacent geographical feature—were likely The Pocket and Hommell's Corner. Jimmie Albright named the former, which is in fact a watery pocket created by a twisting bank in the Islamorada backcountry. Tarpon would swim along the bank, get stuck in the pocket, and turn to swim out, where they could be intercepted easily. As for the latter, Captain George Hommell was figuring out tarpon migration patterns in a Lower Keys basin and discovered a bend in a sizable bank that would funnel the fish. He fished this bend, or corner, a lot, and other guides seeing him there often referred to it as Hommell's Corner. Sixty years later, both names still stick.

Most locations get named prosaically after nearby cays or islands such as Loggerhead or Sugarloaf Shoreline. Geographic features such as capes and points lend their names to fishing spots such as Cape Sable or Snipe Point.

Others have functional names such as Apte's Gap, discovered by guess who, which is a twisting channel between two islands providing a boating shortcut for those who know how to run it without going aground or destroying a propeller.

Proximity to human-created features can be the name source. The Dump derives its moniker from a nearby old landfill. And in the Middle Keys there is the Egg Farm. A long time ago a local person raised chickens and sold eggs, and a stretch of water adjacent to the farm was a good spot to intercept migrating tarpon. There hasn't been a hint of chickens or eggs here for over 35 years, but the sand strip remains the Egg Farm for veteran anglers and guides.

Descriptive names are part of the mix. A long run with a mottled coral/sponge bottom used

The Old Seven Mile Bridge, west of Marathon, built in 1912, glows in the early morning sunshine.

by tarpon is the Mottled Highway. Nearby, another long strip with some yellowish sand is the Yellow Brick Road. And near Marathon, an east–west sandbar divides an oceanside tarpon path. The fish are found inside on high water, and outside when the tide drops. Tarpon are highly visible and easy to fish to when they cross over the bar at mid-tide stages. Surprised that this spot is The Crossover?

Mishaps on the water are memorialized too. There is a nice little spot not far west of Key West named the Lost Key Flat. A former ace Key West guide was fishing the flat edge for tarpon and time came to change flies. The new fly was secured, he thought, in the pliers while he pulled hard on the shock tippet to tighten the knot. Somehow the fly popped free, snagged

the boat keys, and sling-shotted them overboard. Oops! Fortunately, a friend was able to liberate the backup keys from the guide's truck and run them out to the stricken boat.

Fishing incidents created many of the names. Monster Point in the Lower Keys will not be found on any chart or map, but I guarantee that every smart guide knows exactly where it is. Stu Apte named it years ago for the quality of the tarpon it held in the spring. Much the same is true for nearby Tarpon Alley. The tarpon there can be exasperating, what else is new, and on my last visit I had three big poons ease up to the fly and do everything but eat it. Bonefish and permit are found on Bus Bergmann's Chicago Flat. One of his clients caught a big permit there with a prominent facial scar.

A typical backcountry Keys flat beckons anglers on a calm summer day—good conditions for tarpon and bonefish.

Bus and the client called the fish "Al Capone." When Bus saw it again later, on the same small rocky flat, he decided "Capone" was still hanging around "Chicago" and a name was born.

Most intriguing are names of unknown origin or lineage. My personal favorite, in this category, is the Dog Dick Flat in the Middle Keys—a nice spot for bones and the odd permit. A Steve Huff client named it, but no one in and around Marathon can remember why.

Personal names, known by only a couple of folks, round things out. Most of us assign such names to the spots we fish. These pet names, if you will, are also convenient shorthand. Three seasons ago I was exploring with my spouse in the boat, and we discovered a little bar that gets used fairly regularly, on the right tide, by spring tarpon and packs of smaller permit. Rather than call it "the bar near Tripod Bank," I dubbed it Jeannette's Bar. Short, sweet, and a pleasant reminder of the day we first found it.

These personal names also provide an extra level of "ownership" and intimacy to your home waters. None of us may actually own, and exercise exclusive possession rights over, flats, bars, and basins. But we do become deeply attached to specific spots we fish as often as we can and grow to love—and upon which we bestow a personal name. Bird-hunting author Mark Parman notes that this kind of direct relationship constitutes the form of "ownership" defined by early fish and wildlife/environmental author Aldo Leopold in his famous 1949 "Land Ethic" essay.

Expectations, and closely related satisfaction, are often a function of different places we fish. Decent conditions on the Andros Island flats should enable a pair of capable anglers to catch in a day eight to a dozen bonefish from 2 to 5 pounds; that level of expectation has been built over 20 years. Fewer and it's a tough day, unless you were targeting only the big boys and willing to give up the smaller fish. Meet these expectations and you feel good back on the dock drinking a cold Kalik. Home in the Keys, a "dozen bones to the boat" taken sight-fishing would be cause for major celebration—break out the 21-year-old rum! Our bonefish expectations in Florida are significantly lower, and fewer fish are needed to assure a satisfying day.

Establishing realistic expectations is a major part of the education of a flats angler. Most Keys guides have a story that goes like this: A pair of guys watch the "Chasing Silver" videos or the classic Billy Pate tarpon tapes (or new shows like "Silver Kings") depicting lots of spectacular fishing action. In reality, the videos/shows are a distillation of days—or weeks—on the water. They also depict the best of the best in terms of angler skills and action. The newbies envision getting on the bow and immediately catching multiple numbers of big tarpon. When it doesn't happen, grumpy dissatisfaction seeps in. Beginners should not let their expectations be set by these films or comparable magazine articles.

To catch a good Keys tarpon on your first trip is a major feat. Most beginners don't feed one in their first three or four days on the water. Twenty-five years of our Tarpon Camp indicate that it usually takes a rookie four to six days on the water, with decent conditions and a good guide, to catch that prized first fly-rod poon. For a lot of people, it takes two or three trips to make that happen. Two years ago, my son Alex needed day four to get his first (and second) on the fly rod. He did well before then, feeding six on his first three days. Getting the hang of setting the hook without instantly breaking the leader took, shall we say, a little adjustment.

The vagaries of chasing tarpon also create incessant debate regarding what constitutes a good day of fishing for the big poons: catching a fish or having lots of chances? Captain Bus, Joe Kelley, and I struggled one day, with the tarpon having vanished. All the good backcountry spots were simply empty. Finally, in late afternoon, Bus spotted one laid-up fish, I made one cast, the tarpon eased over to take the fly, and 15 minutes later a fine 80-pounder was boatside. Hallelujah. Was that a better day than seeing a thousand poons swim by the boat while you make a hundred casts and never get a bite? Take another sip of your añejo rum, think about it, and let me know. I sure don't have a hard, fixed answer.

And expectations regarding permit? Are you kidding? I never expect to catch another one

and it's the only way to remain sane pursuing the black-tailed devils. If you think you have a real chance, repeated heartbreak is coming your way. Dampen those expectations and consign yourself to be an angling Flagellant (a religious sect that wandered medieval Europe whipping, or flagellating, themselves in penance for their sins). When certain celestial bodies line up (rarely), you might actually catch one. This will carry you so far beyond your dismal expectations that angling rapture will light your soul.

Living in the Keys provides superb home waters that are a precious annual destination for many of my angling friends. Humans, however, have a hard time taking Dorothy to heart and remembering "there's no place like home." The grass is always greener on the other side of the fence. In my case, my two favorite "other side of the flats fishing fence" places are not very far away—maybe 120 miles to the east, in the case of Andros Island, and no more than 30 miles north to the Everglades. Both are unique, wild places that can offer exceptional fishing: Andros for bonefish, the Everglades for tarpon and snook among others. Each place warrants a special look.

Andros Island

The world's largest expanse of bonefish flats surrounds a sprawling, mysterious, sparsely populated island a mere 150 miles from the glittering neon and glass skyscrapers of Miami. Andros Island, the largest of the Bahamas, offers unparalleled angling for bonefish in a largely wilderness setting. It is famous for both numbers of fish and bona fide double-digit trophies. Largely unappreciated is Andros's unique geology, colorful history, and charming people that add rich texture to the angler's experience.

Andros extends over 100 miles from Morgan's Bluff on the north to a tangle of bonefish-infested mangrove island flats off the south end of the island. Just beyond is Cuba. At its widest, Andros is 40 miles across and encompasses more land than all of the other Bahama islands combined. To the west, across the indigo Gulf Stream, sits Florida and its crowded Gold Coast. In contrast, Andros has a population of only 8,000 scattered in a thin strip of small settlements along the island's eastern edge.

On the West Side of Andros Island, a big bonefish streaks off and Captain Kiki Adderley gives a thumbs up.

Nearly 90 percent unpopulated, the big island possesses a strange and varied terrain pocked with blue holes and caves connecting the sea to vast inland bays and lakes. From the air it looks more wet than dry. The unique geology creates a highly diverse and productive marine environment.

Andros is the exposed remnants of ancient coral reefs that started growing over 65 million years ago in the Cretaceous period. In the intervening eons the Great Bahama Bank, upon which Andros is perched, grew to nearly 3 miles thick. The coral prospered during eras of higher sea levels and then became exposed when sea levels declined. During geologically recent ice ages (with so much water frozen in glaciers and sea levels 400 feet lower than today), all of the bank's rocky coral skeletons were exposed land. A form of highly erodible limestone, the skeletons were dissolved by water and weathering to create Andros's network of caves, blue holes (over 225 have

been mapped), and seemingly infinite crannies, nooks, and pockets. Some are genuinely spooky. I fished near one where the falling tide sucked water down a small blue hole in a highly audible and visible whirlpool.

Karst is the scientific name for this honeycombed subterranean landscape. The giant rocky sponge also holds a vast underwater lens of fresh water, which makes Andros inhabitable, as there are no other sources of fresh water except rain. In odd spots, freshwater springs seep into the seawaters, creating golden-hued water with a slicker feel. Sixteenth-century mariners discovered these springs and used them to collect precious waters for trans-Atlantic voyages. Spanish Wells, home to noteworthy bonefish flats, is one of these areas.

Off the island's uninhabited west side, the shallow waters of the Great Bahama Bank extend for 50 miles. This vast shallow sea terminates at the eastern edge of the Gulf Stream, providing a reminder of the origin of the name

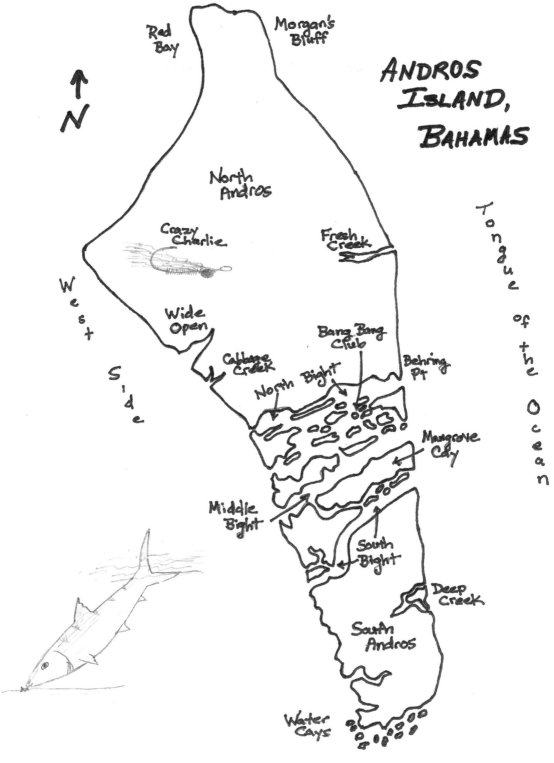

Andros Island is the biggest island in the Bahamas and only 150 miles southeast of crowded south Florida.

Bahamas. The Spaniards labeled the area the Baja Mar (pronounced "baha mar"), or "shallow sea." Anglicized, it became Bahama. Along the western shoreline are innumerable bays and creeks that penetrate far inland, providing habitat for uncounted bonefish as well as tarpon. Among these is the "Wide Open": a big, funnel-shaped, marl- and sand-bottomed bay prized as "Land of the Giants" for producing enormous bonies to 15 pounds or more.

The east side of Andros is radically different but also unique. Only 1 mile offshore, a long barrier reef fringes the full north–south length of the island. Jagged corals reach the surface, and foaming white waves crash incessantly on the shallow rocks. The water then plunges to over a mile deep into the Tongue of the Ocean. Diving the "wall" of this reef is high sport for scuba enthusiasts, and the deep blue, crystal waters host tuna, wahoo, marlin, and other pelagic species. Inside the reef are green waters over miles of golden coral and sand flats patrolled by legions of "ocean bonefish": olive-backed, aqua-finned speedsters (dead ringers for their Florida Keys cousins) that pack a real punch on the end of a fly rod. Bonefish also

The three Andros Bights and the West Side, including Wide Open Bay, are a vast, colorful, and watery bonefish wilderness.

use the deep waters outside the reef to spawn around full moons November through March. The Tongue is so deep that the US Navy has used it for years to test secret submarine technology from a set of Atlantic Undersea Test and Evaluation Center bases along the eastern shore of Andros.

Even though Andros is referred to as one island, it is in reality a sprawling archipelago consisting of three primary islands and countless small cays and islets. North Andros is the largest, bounded on the south by the North Bight—a long twisting bay that bisects the archipelago connecting the Tongue waters to the West Side. Next is Mangrove Cay, bounded by the Middle and South Bights. Each of these waterways also bisects the "island" and is home to almost endless productive flats. South Andros lies below the South Bight. Once a flats skiff heads west into the Bights, civilization ends in a bona fide bonefish wilderness beyond comprehension. The fish are plentiful and exhibit pale silver colors as they meander over pale, soft marl bottoms. I have fished Andros regularly for nearly 25 years and have visited only a tiny percentage of the productive flats.

Inland, Andros is covered in thick pine forests, cabbage palms, scrub red mangroves, or dense black mangrove jungles. Wild pigs roam the dense woods, and colorful wading birds—wild flamingos, reddish egrets, great blue herons—line the shorelines. The egrets are especially entertaining, pursuing fleeing minnows with a comical wings-spread, running high step. Brightly colored neotropical songbirds and charming bananaquits flit among the trees.

Local lore adds Chickcharneys and the Lusca. The former are half-man/half-chicken creatures 3 feet tall with a wicked mischievous streak: think Bahamian leprechauns. The Lusca is said to inhabit the deepest blue holes, transiting dark underwater passages from the Tongue of the Ocean to inland lakes. A giant octopus, half

The Andros archipelago features a colorful array of wild birds including regal ospreys , comical reddish egrets, charming bananaquits, and striking flamingos.

octopus/half eel, or half octopus/half shark (depending on the "eyewitness"), it ensnares unwary boats and swimmers.

The human history of Andros is similarly fascinating. Columbus made his 1492 landfall in the Bahamas (the exact location is debated), encountering the Lucayan natives. However, enslavement and diseases quickly eradicated these people, and the islands were uninhabited within 30 years. Lucayan artifacts have been found on North Andros by Morgan's Bluff and Caves, and on South Andros by the Stargate Blue Hole.

Amerigo Vespucci (who "gave" his name to America) is reputed to have sailed along the east coast of Andros in 1500, creating the first European map of the island. The Spaniards referred to it as Espiritu Santo ("Holy Spirit"); they were very much into religious names, calling the Florida Keys Los Mártires ("The Martyrs"). Ponce de León apparently used the map to sail by the island a decade or so later (and it may have been his sailors who named Spanish Wells).

It is likely Andros remained without a human population for the next 150 years, until the arrival of "privateers," or "pirates": the former if you learned English history, the latter if your teachers were Hispanic. The privateers were granted letters of marque by the English Crown authorizing them to prey on Spanish treasure ships carrying gold and silver from Peru and Panama back to Spain (making them "pirates" for those on board the Spanish vessels). Englishman (and privateer) Henry Morgan established settlements on the north tip of Andros that still bear his name. Later, English privateers Benjamin Hornigold, Henry Jennings, and Edward Teach or Thatch (aka Blackbeard) took control of Nassau in 1706 declaring it the "Republic of Pirates." The notorious, violent Blackbeard was voted in as magistrate, and pirates flocked to their new haven. The British Crown tolerated this as long as the pirates (er, privateers) were targeting Spanish vessels and the occasional French ship. But things got out of hand, and in 1718 King George I dispatched Admiral Woodes Rogers and a fleet of seven Royal Navy ships to restore order. Blackbeard fled to the Carolinas, and on December 12, Rogers sent nine pirate leaders to the Nassau gallows, breaking the republic.

The American Revolution spawned the next wave of settlement in Andros. American Tories loyal to the British king fled to Andros, bringing with them their slaves. By 1788 there were 22 white families on the island along with 132 black slaves. Thirty-three years later, groups of escaped slaves and Seminole Indians (fleeing

The feared and notorious Blackbeard (Edward Teach or Thatch) was a leader of Nassau's ill-fated Republic of Pirates.

the first of the Seminole Wars) left Florida to sail across the Gulf Stream to the northwest side of Andros. There they created the Red Bay settlement. In the ensuing years, hundreds more did the same, adding to the communities that still exist.

In 1807 Britain outlawed the slave trade and in 1834 abolished slavery within its colonies, including the Bahamas. This rendered the Bahamas a magnet for slaves escaping from the United States and ensured that captured Africans in slave ships wrecking in the islands would be granted freedom. The result was a growing free African population that held on to their culture. This cultural influence is alive and well in Andros.

Nearly 140 years later, the Bahamas secured independence from the British. A leader in that fight, and first prime minister of the new Bahamas government, was Androsian Lynden Pindling.

This tangled cross-cultural history is mirrored in arguments over the origin of the island's name. Following British dominion over the islands in the late 1600s, Espiritu Santo was dropped and the island referred to as "Andros," seemingly in honor of the English governor of Barbados, Sir Edmund Andros. However, in 1782 other British maps denoted it San Andreas or St. Andrews. Some contend that the name is Greek in origin.

The archipelago sustains a rich marine environment. Big pink conchs are found crawling along the flats, easily harvested by hand. Taken ashore, a machete is used to cut a hole in the beautiful shell, a knife is used to snick the animal's connection to the shell, and the big snail-like creature is pulled out. Along the shorelines discarded shells pile up—the same shells that sell for $20 a pop in the United States. The tasty, but rubbery, white meat is a great delicacy and served as ceviche, cracked (fried), in fritters, or part of conch chowder. It's one of the great attractions of fishing Andros. Spiny lobsters are abundant, and underwater rock ledges teem with groupers and snappers. Many islanders subsist on these riches or earn a living commercial fishing.

Bonefish are also on the local menu. Encountering an Androsian or two setting hand lines on a sandy shoreline is not uncommon. While our guide poled us around a set of lines

Colorful pink queen conchs yield a delicious snail-like creature that is an Andros culinary staple—especially when washed down with a cold Kalik beer (the name comes from the sound made by Junkanoo cowbells).

guarded by a local woman, the water erupted as a sizable bone grabbed a conch bait and hit the end of the heavy line. A major tug-of-war ensued, ending with a good fish dragged flopping onto the beach, where it was grabbed—and shown to us—with gusto. Some might wrinkle their noses, but fly fishers who inadvertently kill a few fish following even the best catch-and-release practices shouldn't begrudge a local the occasional bonefish dinner.

Spongers are seen diving or spearing throughout the Bights. In fact, the spongers are usually smelled first, as piles of drying sponges stink like hell. Brown/yellow loggerhead sea turtle are profuse. Pods of dolphins cavort in crystal-clear waters. Giant stingrays flap along or lie buried in the mud, showing only their eyes and a vague outline. Unusual creatures are present too in the form of big prehistoric sawfish with their fierce chainsaw-like bill. And bonefish are everywhere—up and down the full length of both coasts and throughout the three Bights.

Andros is one of the first places where it dawned on someone that guiding anglers to catch bonefish just might be a profitable enterprise. Guided fishing for bonefish started in the

1930s in the Florida Keys and about the same time in Andros. Local stories claim the wealthy Mellon family built the Bang Bang Club on Pot Cay in the North Bight in the 1920s. The apparent original purposes were to escape Prohibition and shoot white-crowned pigeons (the first "bang"). The second "bang" was more colorful: Male Hollywood stars of the '30s visited to shoot, accompanied by aspiring actresses "auditioning" for leading roles. But as anyone who has poked around Pot Cay knows, it is surrounded by fine bonefish flats. While Zane Grey was popularizing bonefishing at the Long Key Fishing Club in the Keys, it's probable one or more Bang Bang Club guests inquired about the bonies swimming by the dock. One thing

Many Androsians live off the sea by fishing
and sponging.

led to another, and guided bonefishing on
Andros was born.

It took the full-scale development of saltwater fly fishing in the 1960s to kick things
into high gear. Chasing bonefish and tarpon
in Florida acquired cachet, and legions of trout
anglers wanted the thrill of trying for fish that
really fought back on the end of a line. Given
Andros's bonefish riches, it was only a matter
of time before someone decided to take advantage of it. In 1968 the legendary, late Charlie
Smith opened his first lodge on Andros: Charlie's Haven, located at the mouth of the North
Bight at Behring Point. It opened the doors
to the Andros fishery but was lost to a fire in
1983. Later he acquired the Bang Bang Club
and made an effort to revitalize it.

Charlie was a grade A character who knew
where to find bonefish and invented the Crazy
Charlie bonefish fly. As previously noted, it
was called first the Nasty Charlie but Orvis
reputedly didn't like the name and changed
it to "Crazy." My wife, Jeannette, and I visited
him in 2012 when he was still living at the

Bang Bang Club. He was out of groceries, and
our Mangrove Cay guide Captain Leslie Greene
asked if we were OK with a "care package" run
for Charlie. I had been there before, but this
was new for Jeannette. Charlie welcomed us at
the rickety dock, provided a tour of the dilap-
idated buildings, showed off his pet sea turtles Juicy and Lucy, spun a few big bonefish
tales, and gave Jeannette a bonefish tongue.
She was charmed.

The Andros fishery expanded in the mid '70s, and the first generation of modern-era North Andros guides became prominent: Rudy Bell, Errold Brayman, and Ivan Neymour. In the following decade, Rupert Leadon opened the Andros Island Bonefish Club, also near Behring Point. He was a larger-than-life character and his club was initially a family affair, with most of the guides being Leadons—brothers and sons. My first day fishing Andros was with Rupert. In the following years, I managed to be in a skiff with four other Leadons. Lefty Kreh was a regular at Rupert's.

Today Andros hosts a number of bonefish clubs or lodges located on all three primary islands. These range from the superb, upscale Mangrove Cay Club to small DIY guest-cottage operations like the funky Seascape Inn, also on Mangrove Cay. The Mangrove Cay Club is run by a wonderful set of folks (and friends) reflecting the human and cultural crosscurrents baked into the big island's history. Liz Bain was a successful accountant in Toronto, Canada. She ended up on out-of-the-way Andros, meeting and marrying Bahamian Alton Bain. They ultimately built and run the Mangrove Cay

The late, great Charlie Smith (here presenting Jeannette with a bonefish tongue!) ran the now-derelict Bang Bang Club—amid great bonefish flats—in its final days.

Lisbon Creek's wharf, and the abandoned old mail boat upriver, mark the south side of Mangrove Cay.

Club. Their local partner and outstanding chef is Iyke Moore. He's originally from Nigeria and found his way to Andros over 25 years ago.

Down the road at Seascape Inn is another unexpected pair of people: Joan and Mickey McGowan. They're entertaining Brooklyn expats (Mickey is working on a multiyear shoeless streak) who decamped to Mangrove Cay 20 years ago to build five seaside cottages and a rickety stilted beach bar/restaurant among rustling palms and lush sea grapes. A fine bonefish flat lies a few feet from the cottage doors, and wading after early morning tailing bones followed by one of Joan's fine breakfasts is always alluring; others prefer the afternoon angling followed by an adult beverage.

Most of my Andros time has been spent on Mangrove Cay, the smallest of the primary islands. A single road courses 8 miles along the east edge of the cay, lined by pastel-colored buildings in varying states of repair, from Moxey Town (or Little Harbor if you're not a Moxey) on the Middle Bight to Lisbon Creek nestled on the South Bight. Midway, somber ruins of an 18th-century great house lurk among a tangle of tropical growth. Tropical fruit trees appear along the road—limes, mangoes, and sapodillas. Lisbon Creek has a deep-water wharf where the big, blue steel mail boat, the M/V *Lady Kathreina*, pulls in once a week to deliver goods and freight to the cay. A weathered sign announces "Welcome to Mangrove Cay: Fishing Capital of Andros." Farther up the creek is the abandoned, rusting old mail boat.

People are unfailingly polite and ready with a friendly wave and smile. Kids wear maroon uniforms to school, and the stucco churches are crowded on Sundays. As only 900 or so people live on Mangrove Cay, traffic is sparse and potcake dogs (the local name for mutts) sleep on the road. Gaps in the roadside palms, Australian pines, and sea grapes reveal sandy trails leading to the beach that fronts the cay. Small fishing boats will be anchored or pulled up on shore, usually next to piles of old conch shells. And wadeable bonefish flats can be found by each of these trails. Standard procedure is to bicycle to these spots or hire one of the three local taxis (call Harry, Patrick, or Rhoda) to take you there.

Back on the road are a handful of little cafes and a couple of conch stands. My favorite was

You will find Rolle's Restaurant near Lisbon Creek along Mangrove Cay's single road.

Aunt Bea's Café, presided over by a formidable Bahamian lady who fussed over and delighted my then 10-year-old daughter Victoria many years ago. Reggae music or the sharp cracks of serious dominoes reveal one-room bars. There are even a few small, sometimes open restaurants where the menu is whatever can be acquired on a given day. One evening land crabs were my only choice—not bad but I'll stick with spiny lobster.

Mangrove Cay is a special place, and as you know, I proposed to Jeannette there—but only after she caught her first bonefish!

An angler visiting Andros has a broad set of choices regarding the kind of bonefishing they want to pursue. The North Andros lodges fish mostly oceanside flats between the island and the reef, probe Fresh and Stafford Creeks, or bounce their way north out to the Joulters. These are a set of sandy cays out in the ocean with thousands of bonefish and numbers of hungry lemon sharks looking for a hooked bonefish meal.

South Andros lodges focus on oceanside flats; the vast set of remote Curley, Grassy, and Water Cays flats off the southern end of the island; and big inland bays such as the Little Creek complex. South of Mars Bay, a deceptively narrow Tongue-side creek mouth leads into a watery maze of interior bays, creeks, and channels that eventually run out to the west. Local knowledge is essential for successful navigation, and guides escape to this great interior fishery when winds blow hard from the east. Bonefishing off the south end (an hour-long boat ride from the end of the road) can be so good—for numbers and big fish—that anglers and guides will brave rough ocean waters to get around High Point and its abandoned naval station. Stiff winds can be dangerous, and an occasional boat founders in heavy seas. Among the innumerable cays and islets is "Lost Creek Cay"; locals fear to venture there because it might be a sacred spot for the extinct Lucayans or Taino Indians. As one guide explained, "Strong juju—come too often spirits get angry, recognize you, and bad things happen." One angling pal survived fishing there (it was incredible) but has been unable to get any local guide to return. For years South Andros had a reputation for staggering numbers of 2- to 4-pound bones (true),

but the guides there have figured out where to find the big boys too.

By my lights, the Bights of Andros are the heart of the Andros fishery. "Bight" is an old nautical term meaning a curve or recess in a coastline or a ship's rope—apt descriptions of the three Bights that twist and curve through the archipelago for 30 miles like a thick rope. Portions narrow to a few hundred yards, and other sections are miles-wide bays with an invisible far horizon. The palette of tropical colors is breathtaking, with infinite shades of aqua, blue, and emerald. Scattered cays and islets fill the Bights, and innumerable bays and creeks branch off into the mangroves, palms, and pines. There are countless bonefish flats throughout.

The North Bight marks the south shore of North Andros, and boats run its length from Behring Point on the east to Little Loggerhead

The eastern mouth of the Middle Bight, where bonefish abound, opens to the Tongue of the Ocean; Gibson Cay sits on the left (looking east).

Creek. It gets the most fishing pressure, as it is readily accessible from a number of the North Andros lodges as well as Mangrove Cay, but even then, boats are far and few. Guides focus on soft-bottomed, scrubby mangrove shorelines with names like the Dressing Room, Blue Creek, Joel Point, and the North Shore. I've always been enchanted by Jump Overboard Cay. Pot Cay and the Bang Bang Club sit in the North Bight near a broad channel that comes in from the Middle Bight. Bonefish run the gamut from 2-pound schoolies to bona fide 10-pounders.

The Middle Bight begins between Big Wood Cay and Mangrove Cay, with pretty Gibson Cay and its beautiful coral and sand flats guarding the mouth. Running in a west-southwest direction, the Middle Bight exits to the West Side by

Red Shank Point. There are great flats along its full length, with many opportunities for big fish. The justly famous complex of Moxey, Little Moxey, and Fever Creeks is found across the Bight from Mangrove Cay and constitutes the "home waters," so to speak. Well-educated bonies cruise these hard-bottomed flats—fish that can break down the most veteran anglers.

Proximity to the deep Tongue of the Ocean means there are lots of sharks on these flats. Most are lemons, also in search of bonefish. The lemons have gotten smart and know that the presence of flats skiffs means a chance to nail a hooked, struggling bone. In recent years, big lemons will frequently follow a boat down the edges of the flats and check out wading fly fishers too—a little scary but not a real threat. The occasional bull shark is:

Clear water and marl bottoms make it easier to spot bonefish in the Andros Bights.

NOV. 23, MOSTLY SUNNY, 80, WIND E 5–10. A change of underwear experience on the Gibson Cay flat. Opted to wade the big flat on low water, and along the N edge ran into a giant school of bones hanging in the channel. Many of the bones were on top and looked like rising trout; our guide told us the fish were "bibbling." [We now realize this was a pre-spawning aggregation.] A few big, dark sharks were shadowing the bonies. These bibblers didn't bite but plenty of fish were also up on the flat willing to jump on a well-placed Gotcha. I was lining up on a five-pack of nearby cruisers when movement—75 yards out in the channel—caught my eye. A 7-foot-long bull shark was on the surface, lit up, and racing in my direction with rigid, locked pectoral fins—a sure sign it was planning to run down something and eat it. It took a nanosecond for me to realize I was the target. Things dropped into super slow motion and I calculated instantly I couldn't outrun the shark, motion and stirred up water would likely make things worse, and my only option was to stand stock still and be prepared to kick the fish and/or poke it with the fly rod when it got close. The shark zoomed in; when it was right in front, I kicked and jabbed the fly rod, felt resistance, the bull made an instant U turn, threw water all over me, and steamed back into the channel. The whole episode lasted about 5 seconds. Then the adrenalin kicked in followed by the shakes—and I checked to see if my underwear was dry! The guide and other angler, standing 100 feet away, later told me they were thinking about how to save me from bleeding to death. ●

Farther west into the Middle Bight are loads of named and unnamed flats, including the entrance to Honeycutt Creek. Follow it south and east and you pop out in the Lisbon and Russell Creek systems feeding the South Bight. My spouse loves the Middle Bight:

FEB. 11, CLEAR, 70–75, WIND NW 5–10. Capt. Leslie, Jeannette, and I left the dock on a cool February morning under a flawless blue sky. A few miles down the Middle Bight, Leslie spun the skiff into a bay with a very hopeful name—"Thousand Tails." Jeannette was first up; Leslie unlimbered the pole and the hunt was on. Under perfect light and transparent water, two- to five-pound bonefish were on the prowl, in 1s, 2s, and 3s and highly visible on the light bottom. The fish were also hungry, and every good presentation got rewarded with a quick take and the sights and sounds of chartreuse backing whirring off the Abel Super 7. Leslie began a game—he gave us a vector like "fish between 12 and 3" and a prize to the angler who next found the bones. Jeannette's eyes were in full gear and she was nailing the fish (of course, I maintained she had an advantage being on the bow). She also had her A game and I wasn't about to break a run of great angling fortune. Two and a half hours later she took a break after hooking 15 and landing 10.

Between Mangrove Cay and South Andros, the South Bight snakes west in a winding, tortuous path. The ocean-influenced flats are a stunning collection of bright sand and golden coral flanked by thick black mangroves.

Crystal-clear waters reveal bright orange and red starfish, purple sea fans, aqua trunkfish, sea cucumbers, and shadowy cudas, as well as bonies. It is also the narrowest Bight and features a big blue hole near the west end run-out. The South Bight long had a reputation for small fish only, but I beg to disagree.

My first Andros 10-pounder came from a Lisbon Creek flat, and there is one secret spot where I have been perpetually humiliated by a group of big boys that easily reach double digits; Captain Greene named the biggest "Bonezilla," which has defied all attempts to be hooked and caught. Shorelines on Linda and Pigeon Cays are highly productive. Farther west, the remote Miller Creek system is a magical place full to the brim with usually willing 2- to 6-pound fish. The water can be so clear that fish appear suspended in the air.

A typical Bight fishing scenario has a skiff paralleling a shoreline lined by low, scrubby mangroves. The angler cons the bow with an 8-weight fly rod (maybe 7 if it's calm), a 10- to 14-foot leader tapered to a 12- or 15-pound-test tippet, and the tried-and-true Gotcha (red or

A spectacular morning in the Middle Bight: Captain Leslie Greene and Jeannette proudly hoist bonefish number 10 from Thousand Tails Bay.

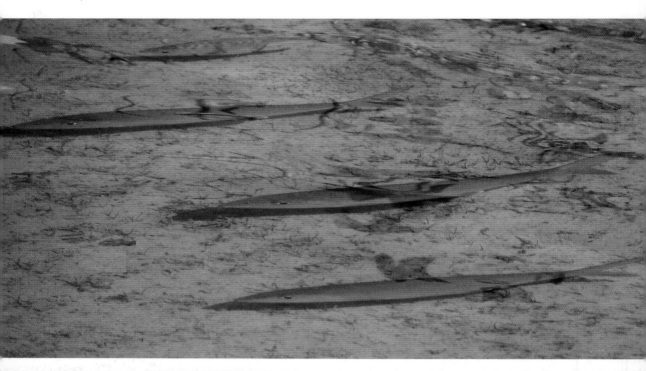

Even the "gray ghost" has a hard time hiding in the clear, shallow flats of Andros.

classic pink) in size 2 or 4 (probably used 90 percent of the time).

Most bonefish will be ghosting along the shorelines in shallow, clear waters over light-colored marl bottoms. Tailers can be spotted close in, often among flooded mangroves, and the trick is to figure out where the fish will exit the red roots so you can intercept it with the fly.

But you must also look outside in the greener, deeper water, as bones, especially the bigger

One of many airplane wrecks marks a drug run gone wrong on the wild West Side.

ones, will move in from the depths. Spotting these is always tough. Most of your shots will be at singles, doubles, or triples, although schools of 10 or more show up often enough.

Get your fly in front of all of these fish, and a take is a good bet—when conditions are right. Sometimes the conditions aren't right—or you're hexed:

FEB. 13 (FRIDAY NO LESS), MOSTLY CLEAR, 75, WIND CALM TO 5. I'm not usually superstitious but today's miscues and bad luck may change that. Ran W to Joel Point and right away the shoreline revealed a wagging silver tail that resolved into a fine five- to six-pound bone. Capt. Peter [Leslie's brother] set the skiff and we watched to determine where the fish might emerge from the flooded 'groves. The exit became apparent, out went a 60-foot cast, the #4 Gotcha plipped in eight feet ahead of the fish—which fled in terror. Damn. It's calm, we see more tails, so off comes the bead-chain-eyed fly to be replaced by an unweighted tailing fly. No sooner have I cinched the knot than Peter looks out seeing a trophy bone oozing from outside. He spun the Dolphin; I get a great shot to 1 o'clock.

As the water is three feet deep, I led the fish by 10–12 feet hoping the tailing fly would sink—it does not. It hovers, the big boy swims over to investigate, scrutinizes the suspended fly, and bolts. Damn again. Peter insisted we go back to a weighted fly in case another biggy appears, so I knot on a fresh #4 RHG. Sure enough, another inshore tailer shows up, lead the fish by 15 feet, and it cruises near the waiting fly. When the fish is three or four feet away, I try to make a slow retrieve—but the fly hangs up on a piece of coral. The bone stares at the immobile fly and when it popped free the panicked fish bored off. Oh well. ●

If Andros featured only the Bights, it would be more than good enough. But the island includes the most magical place to pursue *Albula vulpes*: the wild West Side. As previously noted, the West Side stretches uninhabited for over 100 miles, fronting the enormous shallows of the Great Bahama Bank. Running west through the Bights, there are four exits where the land peels away and nothing but tropical waters and a distant watery horizon remain in view. Colors are spectacular, and the clouds and sky reflect luminous aquamarine and emerald waters.

Captain Kiki Adderley and angler hunt the West Side for trophy bonefish.

The shoreline is an inhospitable mix of cabbage palms, scrub, and stunted mangroves. Little curly-tailed lizards scamper about and odd big-eyed, bluish land crabs appear. Get too close to shore and evil green-headed flies—doctor flies—buzz out to draw blood from exposed sweaty flesh. The remote location attracted rum runners during Prohibition and cocaine cowboys in the '80s. Wrecked airplanes litter the area, marking drug deals gone bad. Trade winds rattle through a deserted bonefish lodge on a remote sandy beach. The owner, his two-man crew, and their boat vanished mysteriously, with their fate still unknown.

Bonefish abound in near-perfect habitat with myriad creeks connecting vast inland bays to the open sea waters. Schools of 2- to 5-pound fish patrol the shorelines, and it is possible to stake out and let the fish swim to you throughout a tide. Probing slightly deeper waters provides opportunities at 6- to 9-pounders. The big attractions are the monster 10-pound-and-more bones that give the area well-deserved fame. There is extra excitement when the flats skiff planes out of Little Loggerhead Creek's narrow mangrove-lined channel, makes a sharp turn north, and heads for the West Side flats of Cabbage Creek, River Goose, the Wide Open, the Big Mangrove, or Barbara's Cove.

Just north of Cabbage, River Goose runs inland. The narrow, winding, blue-green channel runs a long way between steep marl banks lined with ragged cabbage palms and

bow when a monster bone loomed into view. The guide positioned the boat, the angler delivered the fly, the big fish tipped down, and Paul stripped tight. Ms. Bone exploded and roared off with backing disappearing at an alarming rate. Twenty heart-stopping minutes later Paul and the guide were cradling an enormous 32 inches to the fork, 18-inch girth, roe-laden fish estimated at 15 or more pounds. A lifetime catch. Another friend, fishing Andros for his 50th birthday, scored back-to-back 10-pounders in the Wide Open.

I've had my shots at giant bones but have had to "settle" for a mere trophy:

FEB. 21, CLEAR SKIES WITH SOME AFTERNOON CLOUDS, 80, WIND E 10.
With perfect weather we had to run west. Leslie steered us through the Middle and North Bights on the hour-long run to the Wide Open, and we pulled into the south shoreline to start the hunt. Plenty of school-sized fish were present and the skunk was off the boat, multiple times, in pretty short order. Decided it was time to upgrade so went to a slightly larger, heavier fly (a #2 George's Special) and slid out into deeper water in search of Mr. Big. The good Captain put me on a couple of good fish that wouldn't play. But we persisted and soon enough a trio of coke bottle green bones oozed in from the little channel. As they neared, it was evident these were good-sized fish with the lead critter a real horse. It took some poling to set up a good intercept and my cast targeted the biggest bone. The fish spotted the fly, started for it, but the smallest trailing fish dashed ahead and pounced. Set the hook, the fish took off, but Leslie and I were bitching "Damn, the small one ate the fly." Bitching didn't last long, as the fish kept running and running. It took a turn for the shoreline and the mangroves and pressured it hard to turn back. At one point the bonefish was plowing mud trying to break off. Leslie pushed hard for deeper water, the knots held, the hook stayed put, and our "small" fish was boatside—29 inches to the fork with a 17-inch girth. His expert eye decided "12 pounds." I asked in wonder, "How big was the big one?" Leslie offered "15 or 16." Only on the West Side. ●

mangrove thickets. The tall, thick greenery hems the view. Dolphins porpoise up and disappear. Sliding through tight turns, egrets and herons lift squawking from the thickets. It feels like entering a Joseph Conrad novel. A last sharp bend breaks into the open, revealing a vast set of shimmering inland bays and coves and miles of scrubby mangrove shoreline.

The waters—Flamingo Bay and Turner Sound—are home to vibrant pink/orange wild flamingos, big tarpon, and countless bonefish. Most of the water is only inches deep, and safe navigation requires local knowledge and steely nerves.

Farther up the coast sits the famed Wide Open, holding the best concentration of large bonefish in Andros—if not the world. On a flawless May day, Paul Latchford was on the

The smallest bonefish of a Wide Open trio turns into a 12-pound trophy.

The island fishery has been an incubator for fine bonefish flies. Charlie Smith's Crazy Charlie revolutionized bonefishing by adding bead-chain eyes to get the pattern down to the bottom where the fish feed. Later, Jim McVay concocted the famous Gotcha at the Andros Island Bonefish Club as noted previously. Fifteen years ago, the Mangrove Cay Club guides wanted something a bit darker and tied the fly with bright red thread, rather than coral pink, and added a gold flash tail—the RHG. It quickly became the standard there, is usually tied on a size 2 or 4 hook, and probably accounts for 90 percent of the bonefish caught from the club. Let me add that it works like a charm in the Keys and has also caught good numbers of Florida permit. However, there are differences among the Andros fisheries. A friend fished the Joulters bringing along his Bight collection of bigger, heavier dressed flies. The North Andros guides hated them and switched him to smaller, lighter models. In contrast, my friend Jim Reinertsen regularly fishes South Andros and the Little Creek complex. He added big

red eyes to the RHG drawing bonefish from many feet to snap up his pattern. This Gotcha variation—the big-eyed redhead—is dubbed the "Susan Sarandon."

I am a little worried, though, about some of my Andros angling brethren. Fly-naming conventions are skewed in a certain direction: the Blue Boner, the Burning Bush, the White Sex Death. A fly-tying table sits adjacent to the bar at the Mangrove Cay Club. Rum-inspired patterns include the "Dolly Parton" tied with two very large bead eyes and tipped with a bit of red nail polish. There are some apparently lonely fellows fishing the island's flats!

The incessant search for killer flies becomes important when the fish aren't so willing. Small tan/cream yarn crab flies (miniature Merkin style), on a size 4, have been a lifesaver on many skittish fish. Rather than the long, slow strip used with Gotchas, tiny twitches are the order of the day. Other Andros standards are Clousers in Gotcha colors as well as chartreuse/white, and Greg's Flats Fly. George's Special, referenced above, is an unusual bluish

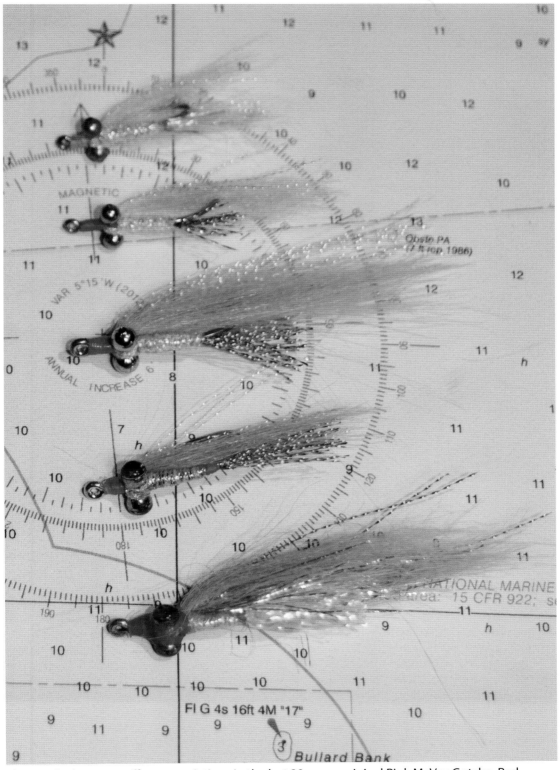

The Gotcha has spun off many variations in the last 30 years: original Pink McVay Gotcha, Red Headed/Gold Tail Gotcha, Red Headed Super Gotcha, Lead Eyed Red Head, and Big Eyed Redhead Gotcha, aka the "Susan Sarandon" (from top).

Wild flamingos take flight in Flamingo Bay.

fly that frequently works when all others fail. George Conniff showed up with this unique pattern (my apologies to the unknown inventor of this fly) about 15 years ago: blue Kreinik flash body, tan craft fur wing, tail marked with two vertical bars (one black, one red), silver bead-chain eyes, and red thread affixed to a size 2 or 4 hook. Only God knows what the bones think it is, but sometimes otherwise grumpy fish will fight to eat it.

Andros has also been instrumental in BTT's research on bonefish reproduction. With insufficient bones left in the Keys to study spawning behavior, BTT turned its attention to the Bahamas and painstakingly put together the pieces that finally revealed the secrets of the bonefish life cycle. The adult fish assemble near their home flats on the waxing moon and begin to migrate along the shorelines to aggregation sites proximate to deep water. Some fish will transit the Bights from the West Side to the Tongue side on the east. Vast schools containing thousands of bones can be found, often on the surface engaged in gulping down air. The first time I saw it on a November afternoon, as previously noted, the guides called it "bibbling." Turns out the fish swallow air and hold it until nighttime, when they swim out en masse into water 200 feet deep or more and dive deep. As explained earlier, water pressure compresses the internal air, helping to squeeze eggs out of the females. The fish then bob back up to near the surface and expel the eggs where circling males release their milt, and the mixed cloud of eggs and milt results in fertilized eggs. Note to fly fishers—bibbling fish don't bite.

The pre-spawning shoreline migration, however, when the bones head for their bibbling aggregations can produce spectacular catching:

NOV. 12, CLEAR, 80 DEGREES F, WIND 5-10 ENE. George Conniff and I searched for bones in the North Bight with Chris Leadon

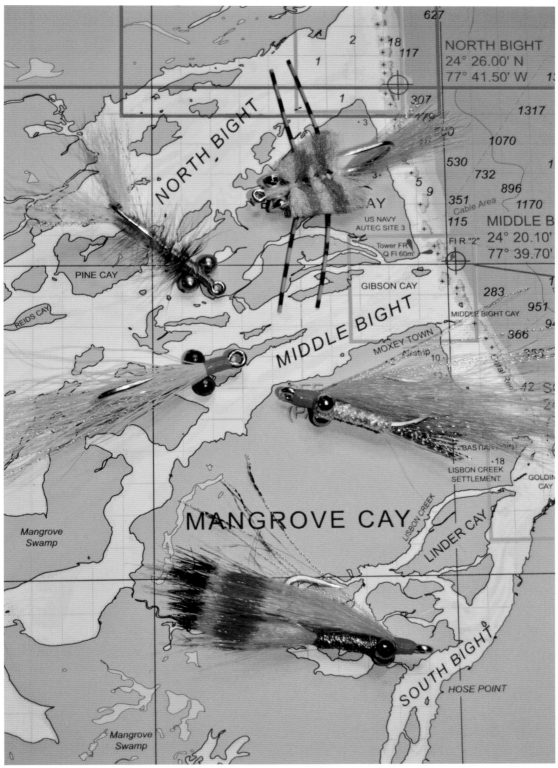

A Gold Merkin size 4, Red Headed Gotcha size 4 (and 2), George's Special size 2 (and 4), Chartreuse/ White Clouser size 4, and Greg's Flats Fly size 4 (clockwise from top right) are among the recommended flies for fishing the Andros Bights and the West Side.

Thousands of Bahamas bonefish assemble in a pre-spawn aggregation before swimming out at night into deeper waters to spawn. (Courtesy of Robbie Roemer)

[the then head guide for the Mangrove Cay Club]. It was a tough morning even though conditions were beautiful with a light warm breeze and clear skies. Took an early lunch break near Pot Cay and then Chris ran us west to a remote mangrove shoreline dubbed "The Highway." He put me on a nice tailer by a little marl point and it jumped all over my #4 RHG. But while landing the fish, a nice school swam by and we looked north up the shoreline to see another pack of bones swimming our way. For the next three and half hours, school after school of bones cruised the shoreline with as many as four schools visible at one time. The fish were plainly on a mission and followed a precise track as if yellow lines were painted on the marl bottom. George jumped out of the boat and set up in ankle-deep water 100 yards above us. Capt. Leadon set the boat so we could both fish and cover a small patch of seagrass 50 feet out which all of the bones were crossing. We

quickly developed a routine: spot an incoming school (or George would call down to us "Incoming!"), Chris put his fly on the inside right of the patch, and I cast to the outside left. When fish got to the patch, we told each other in cadence "Strip, strip, stop . . . long strip" and both lines would snap tight. Doubles and triples were common, a few fish hit the six- to seven-pound mark, and we stopped counting after we had collectively landed 75 bonefish. Simply unbelievable. When we left at 4 p.m. to run back to the Club the fish were still coming.

It ain't always so good. Bad weather is the primary culprit. Andros bonefish hate bad weather.

The fish, especially those in the Bights, depart the shorelines to feed in big groups out in 3 to 4 feet of water; the digging in the soft marl bottom kicks up lots of mud that discolors the water. Yellow Cay is surrounded by great flats that can produce very big fish. We poled the length of the south shore one crummy day, seeing only one or two super-spooky bonefish while counting two dozen large "house" muds a couple hundred yards offshore. If only those fish had been on the shoreline!

Windy, cloudy weather also makes the fish very skittish, running from flies and refusing even the finest, most stealthy presentations. And long periods of chilly winds empty the Bights of bonefish that apparently seek refuge in deeper haunts off the island's coasts.

The three worst conditions are a stiff northwest wind, a persistent southwest or west wind (even if gentle), or very high pressure. Heavy northwest winds that come with cold fronts are poison in Andros. The West Side will be churned into a muddy froth, as will most of the good Bight shorelines and bays. Plus, cold fronts mean exactly that, and wading a lee-side ocean flat when it's 55 degrees and blowing is not exactly how we envision bonefishing in the Bahamas.

West winds are deceptive in that most of the island is fishable, but the fish simply hate it. They largely leave the shoreline flats, and those that remain are damn near impossible to catch. The only times I've been skunked—when we could get out—have been under the dread influence of a west wind.

The high-pressure hypothesis was offered to me years ago by a veteran Andros guide. A day would look good, with scattered cumulus clouds, decent sunlight, and, say, 15 mph winds from the east or northeast. But if the barometric pressure was up in the 1020 to 1028 millibar range, Katie bar the door. Bones would exhibit the same rotten behavior associated with west winds—maybe not as bad, but more than bad enough. This theory was confirmed on a recent trip. The barometer reading was 1024 mb and plenty of fish were on the flats. But they suffered serious lockjaw; at one point 15 consecutive bones looked at and

Stormy, windy weather, announced by a starched out Bahamas flag, often drives the bonefish off the shallow flats to feed in big unseen schools in deeper waters, creating discolored patches of water known as "muds."

refused well-presented flies. The why is a great mystery, as many reputable fisheries biologists contend that fish do not feel these kinds of pressure changes. I'm no biologist but there is more than enough anecdotal evidence to let me respectfully disagree.

Many anglers, me included, are consumed by the effort to schedule trips during periods of good weather. Almanacs are consulted, annual weather averages studied, and moon phases considered. Conventional wisdom posits April and May as the prime months. March is windy, June and July are supposed to be too hot, late summer/fall is plagued by tropical storms and hurricanes, and the winter months are beset by miserable cold fronts. Andros lodges book up quickly for spring dates and struggle to sell

trips November through February. My advice is to pay more attention to moon phases and tides and simply roll the dice on the weather.

With nearly 30 visits to Andros under my belt, I can report that the single worst trip was a week in May that featured steady 20 to 25 mph winds and clouds; the best was a November visit with six days of perfect weather and hordes of willing bones. My best big-fish visit was in February when a cold front blew out our first two days, but the remaining four days were spectacular. And a late-June trip produced excellent angling at the mouth of the South Bight, as flood tides brought in temperate water from the Tongue of the Ocean.

Mangrove Cay guides believe bigger bones like cooler waters and that more small fish occupy

the flats as the weather warms up in April to June. It's late May in the Keys as I write this, and today is the 21st consecutive day of clouds, rain, and wind that have utterly hammered the annual tarpon run. You can never predict the weather very far in advance, so don't even try!

Tides and the moon are a different story. Andros enjoys diurnal tides, meaning there are usually two high and two low tides each day, generally six hours apart. Every tide stage, high or low, will vary a bit. Andros is also a bit like the Keys in that when the tide is high on one side, the tide is at ebb on the other. Water seesaws through the Bights. This enables the local guides to find almost any tide stage they want somewhere. And the tides to avoid are the highest and the lowest. Big, high water at Andros, associated with full and new moon "spring" tides, frequently floods the scrubby mangroves, allowing bonefish to swim deep

into this flooded jungle to pop snails and small crabs off the spidery mangrove roots. It is frustrating to stare at dozens of cruising, tailing bones deep in the groves where it is impossible to get at them. Conversely, very low tides drain good flats and push the fish out into mudding depths. The West Side is especially sensitive to very low tides, keeping anglers far removed from feeding fish.

Many prefer fishing the neap tides associated with the half or quarter moon. The mangroves don't get flooded and shallower flats don't get drained. But like all fishing "truths," there are caveats. Bigger tides mean better currents and more water movement that often prompt the best fish to come out and feed.

So you can only roll the dice and hope you don't get poor weather. Fortunately, though, there are some ways to counter the bad-weather influence. As noted, the Bight fish are very sensitive to bad weather, but their Tongue of the Ocean–influenced buddies at the mouths of the Bights act more like Keys fish. Maybe more-stable water temperatures or better water clarity (the soft-bottomed Bight flats mud up in wind, while the hard-bottomed oceanside flats stay clear) is the reason, but "ocean" bones will be out and feeding even in poor conditions. How-ever, these are highly schooled bones that could teach a thing or two to their Keys brethren. In my opinion, tailing bonefish along Fever Creek (on the north side of the Middle Bight) are the second-most-difficult bones I've encountered (Hawaiian bones are the freakiest):

FEB. 21, HEAVY DECKS OF CLOUDS, WIND NE 15. In the afternoon Capt. Micah was poling us along the Fever Creek shoreline. Got a couple of shots but couldn't get a fly anywhere near the skittish fish so I asked him to let me wade on the incoming water while he poled George on the south edge. Worked a couple of tailers on the sand bar but casting to the fish was impossible. Any fly that landed within 15 feet caused the fish to boogie off the flat. Reached the corner formed by a jagged brown coral bar and spied a big tailer working slowly from one little sand depression to the next, exposing a thick olive back as it crossed the shallow bars. Crouched and crawled into an intercept position and guessed which sand hole it would enter. Knelt and quietly put the little #4 golden crab fly in a hole nearly 20 feet ahead of the fish. Watched the big tail wave up 10 feet from the fly but when the tail went down the bone disappeared in the miserable dark light. Then a break—the tip of the dorsal showed in the hole with my fly. Gave it two small twitches, the dorsal flared, and the bone tailed on the fly. Stripped tight, the fish exploded racing for deeper water. I scrambled up, got the fly line on the reel, backing clattered out the guides, and I breathed a sigh of relief only to have the line go slack. Damn! Fooling this big one under these conditions was a victory in itself. ●

Andros is 99 percent bonefishing, in contrast to places like Ascension Bay, Belize, or the Keys where bonefish are part of a mix including permit, tarpon, snook, redfish, or other spe-cies. There are odd sightings of permit, espe-cially at each end of the Bights and reportedly

Wading Fever Creek is sometimes the only way to salvage a day too dark and windy to fish from a flats skiff.

Interview with
CAPTAINS STEVEN "KIKI" ADDERLEY AND LESLIE GREENE:
Andros Island Bonefishing

Captains Kiki Adderley and Leslie Greene have been wading or poling the vast bonefish flats of Andros Island for over 30 years. Both grew up on Mangrove Cay—the center island in the Andros archipelago; Leslie was born there. Each jumped at opportunities to become bonefish guides nearly 20 years ago. Leslie started guiding in 2001, Kiki a year later. For many years, Leslie was the head guide at the Mangrove Cay Club before going independent. Kiki has been the head guide there for the past five years.

Both Leslie and Kiki spend hundreds of days each year searching for bonefish (and the occasional tarpon) on the innumerable flats found on the Tongue of the Ocean side of Andros, in all three Bights, and along miles of the uninhabited West Side. Beyond their incredible knowledge, they are fine gentlemen and a joy to fish with. It has been my good fortune to have fished with them for almost 20 years and I couldn't think of anyone more qualified to talk about Andros bonefishing. I interviewed them during my most recent visit to Mangrove Cay.

Why did each of you want to become bonefish guides?
   Leslie: Growing up here I heard all the stories about the fish, the fishing, and the chance to meet people from different parts of the world coming here to chase bonies. The few older guides had this lingo about the "clock," how to pole and position a boat—I was fascinated and always wanted to try it.
   Kiki: I loved being on the water and started commercial lobster fishing after high school. The bonefish thing sounded far more interesting and was a way to stay on the water, hunt for the fish, and meet other people with the same passion. When there was an opening for a guide at the [Mangrove Cay] Club, I jumped at it.

What's special about fishing Andros?
   Kiki: There are endless flats and habitat areas and miles and miles of watery beauty. Plus, with some effort, you can always find new, more beautiful areas to fish. Bonefish can be everywhere, including the big ones that make Andros famous.
   Leslie: I agree. Lots of water, lots of opportunities. I would add there is a tradition of good guides on Mangrove Cay. There were a few guides here starting as far back as the '30s. Early fishing was with conch baits and such, but it was still bonefishing.

What's special about chasing bonefish?
   Leslie: The hunt and tricking a spooky fish in shallow clear water into eating something that's not natural. Visitors come here because they either share the same passion or want to try it. It makes me very happy to share the flats world with these people and guide many of them to their first bonefish.
   Kiki: It's much the same for me. Putting clients on fish and getting them to enjoy the thrill of catching a bonefish—if it's number 1 or number 100. Sharing the joy with the first-timers is a special thrill.

Can you describe the bonefishery around Mangrove Cay?
   Kiki: There are really two sets of bonefish here—the ocean fish, found on the east side flats and in the mouths of the three Bights, and the Bight/West Side bones. The ocean fish are darker, greener, and stronger than paler, silvery bones found back in the Bights and on the West Side.

Why is that?
   Kiki: The ocean bones get more pressure from local fishers, see more sharks, have to

defend themselves more. Bight fish are a little more relaxed.

Leslie: Oceanfront fish have to swim harder to escape the sharks. It makes them stronger and warier. You're always telling me some of our ocean flats fish are harder to catch than your Keys bonefish.

You're right about that. What about the Bight/ West Siders?

Leslie: They are the same fish, with many of them moving in and out of the Bights and along the West Side flats. These fish are usually easier to feed.

Are there seasonal differences in the bonefishing here?

Kiki: Absolutely. Bigger fish are on the flats in the winter months and can be found inside the Bights as well as the West Side. Many of

these are 4- to 8-pounders with the occasional 10-plus-pounder in the right spots. Spring and summer find more fish on the flats, but most are 2 to 4 with the odd 5- to 6-pounder. The fall can be excellent, with lots of bones migrating along the shorelines before spawning and bigger fish reappear as it cools off.

Leslie: Fall fishing has another benefit—less fishing pressure and a lot of the fish haven't seen a fly for months. The migrants also want to feed and tend to move hard just before the first cold fronts. Once it cools the bigger fish come out like our friend "Bonezilla."

Why does everyone focus on the spring fishing?

Leslie: The more stable weather conditions make for good fishing, and there are usually lots of fish around too. In fact, good weather at any time of the year is more important than the season in terms of catching fish.

A pair of superb Andros guides and gentlemen: Captain Kiki Adderley posts guide/ angler assignments; Captain Leslie Greene displays a West Side tarpon.

What makes a good client?

Kiki: A client willing to listen and learn. Some need to learn new skills, some need to change bad habits. We can help them catch fish if they listen. I really like a client who is willing to ask, "Fill me in on what I'm doing wrong."

Leslie: Listening to the guide, having patience, and appreciating the whole experience—not just the numbers of fish caught.

Kiki: We also want the clients to realize the fish are very important to us. Good fish handling and good releases help us sustain the fishing.

Comments on casting skills?

Leslie: Reasonable distance, say a real 40-foot cast, and accuracy are valuable. Speed is not key, as we can usually see bonefish from 100 feet or more, allowing reasonable time to get set. A decent 40-foot cast will catch plenty of fish here.

Kiki: That's right. But some folks show up with bad habits—up and down casting strokes, too much wrist. That doesn't work when there's wind—and it's usually blowing here. A nice tight loop with that 40-foot cast will handle the typical breeze.

How about seeing the elusive gray ghost?

Leslie: If you can see the fish, making an accurate cast is much easier. Otherwise, we can talk a client into an invisible fish. But if he or she sees it, it is so much better. I like to teach folks to look through the water, see the bottom, and look for movement or shadows. Spot the shadow and if it moves, it's a bone—or maybe a barracuda.

Kiki: Don't focus on seeing the fish, look for that light gray moving shadow. One other trick is to cock your head like a dog to change the polarizing angle in your sunglasses.

Leslie: I tell clients to look for that gray/silver shadow when in the Bights. On the ocean flats, look for more green. But movement is the key.

What's your advice on tackle and rigging?

Kiki: Standard 8- and 9-weight outfits. Leaders in the 9- to 12-foot range or longer if you can roll them over. There's no need to go lighter than 12- to 16-pound-test tippets.

Bonefish are not really leader shy, and you can fight hooked fish harder and get fish in quickly with the heavier stuff. Less-tired fish have a better chance with the sharks.

Leslie: I have nothing else to add except longer leaders can be very helpful when it's calm and fish are skittish.

What are your suggestions on fly patterns?

Leslie: My go-to fly is the Red Head Gotcha in a size 2 or 4. Sometimes it helps to tie them with a puffier body. The backup flies are the Pink Gotcha, a Spawning Shrimp, or Clousers in tan/white or green/white.

Kiki: I've gone back to the original Pink Gotcha in the same sizes. I like it best under brighter conditions. The Red Head seems to work better with clouds and lower light.

In the Keys, a short, brisk strip emulating a darting shrimp is the standard retrieve. You guys like a long, smooth strip. Why?

Leslie: Fish want to chase the long-stripped fly and it makes them want to grab it. Guessing it looks like a shrimp going away. The longer strip also keeps the line tighter to the fly—you get better hookups.

Kiki: It's very helpful for beginners who don't see or know that the fish ate the fly. They have a hard time setting the hook with the short-strip retrieve.

Any parting thoughts?

Leslie: Client expectations are an issue. There is a lot of market hype about catching dozens of fish a day or routinely getting the big trophy fish. A new angler can have a fine day, catch some nice bones, and be unhappy because he didn't catch 20 or get a couple of 10-pounders as promised in the ads, articles, or videos. Those great days are always possible, but most of my return clients appreciate the difficulties, the weather issues, and the need for skills only developed over time.

Kiki: Anglers should enjoy the pursuit, being out on the beautiful flats here. Once they catch a bonefish, the pressure should be off so they can share the joy being on water chasing these great fish. ■

along the northwest shore, but no one goes to Andros specifically for perms. No one really goes for tarpon either, but the big silver kings are there. The best place for a tarpon ecotour is the blue hole near the west end of the South Bight. Fish can be frequently found rolling in the deep hole. We arrived one day, saw no activity, and the guide fired up the outboard to run little circles in the hole. This woke up packs of 40-pounders that popped up immediately, rolled once or twice, and then went down. This went on for a while, but the fish were in their frustrating "roll and dive" mode in which bites are damn near impossible.

In our early trips, we also encountered an odd poon or two out on the West Side, cast at them with bonefish rigs, and managed an occasional bite. But 12-pound tippets don't last long with big tarpon. I decided the only option was to bring along a rigged-and-ready tarpon rod on each outing. It collected a lot of proverbial dust until Captain Greene was poling us along the Willis Creek shoreline on a November afternoon. Two large, dark forms appeared 100 yards away. We dismissed them as sharks, but Leslie poled closer, looked harder, and quietly directed, "Get the tarpon rod!" A pair of 70-pounders swam into range and fish number two pounced on a 2/0 Black Mouse. Drove home the hook and the fish laid on the surface, shaking its head mystified about what was sticking it. A good five count later the tarpon figured something was amiss and took off in a series of foamy jumps. Kept up the pressure and took the skiff and big fish to shore, where Leslie and I jumped into the water for the requisite hero shot with my first Andros tarpon.

Five years later up Cabbage Creek, we encountered three separate 40- to 50-pound poons. Each jumped all over a fly, each stayed buttoned, and we managed a rare tarpon triple. Tarpon aren't plentiful but they're there.

Another Andros fishing sidelight is nighttime shark fishing. Some of the clubs have docks or bulkheads proximate to deeper water where the sharks patrol. Mostly lemons, nurses, and blacktips, but there are also mean big-shouldered bull sharks lurking about. When we first visited the Andros Island Bonefish Club in the 1990s, one of the guests appeared on the back deck, overlooking hard-flowing

Cargill Creek, shouldering heavy-duty 80-pound conventional tackle. A chain leader held a BIG hook, and a huge bloody chunk of fish meat was impaled on it. The bobber was an empty white Clorox jug. The rig was heaved into the tropical darkness, landing with a hearty splash. And then the waiting began. One rum went down the hatch, so our angler ambled back to the bar for a refill, asking us to man the fort and set the hook if something ate his bait. Sure enough, the guy walked away, the big gold reel began to wail, and the Clorox jug headed out to sea. One of us manhandled the rig and flipped the reel into gear. The thick rod bent over, and a big, unseen sea creature doubled its departure speed. It didn't last long, as the line parted like a .22 going off. Oh well. So, we returned to our rum and fishing lies. Half an hour later here comes the Clorox jug swimming upcurrent and disappearing into the upstream darkness.

At the Mangrove Cay Club, evening sharking is a very visible pastime. After dinner the dock lights are turned on, illuminating the bottom out to 35 feet from the dock. The fish carcasses, lobster shells, and such from dinner are pitched out, hooks baited, and rods placed in holders. Anglers freshen their rums, light up a cigar, and begin the vigil under dark starlit skies; green nav lights blink on the far side of the Middle Bight. Before too long the first shark zooms into the lights to inspect the offerings. And if conditions are right, three or four boys in the brown suits will be swimming about. Eventually one of the waiting baits gets gobbled, and Mr. Shark blasts off for the darkness. The person on the rod is subject to lots of running commentary about their fish-fighting skills, or lack thereof. One busy evening we chummed too much, leaving too little fish for bait—and the sharks were thick. We stole into the kitchen and liberated a pound of bacon, which was greedily devoured by a big lemon. Chef Iyke was displeased the next morning, as were the other guests when the bacon ration was skimpy.

Fishing from a club or lodge is more than angling—it's a social experience. A return to the dock at day's end allows anglers to gather, grab an adult beverage, and recount the day's successes and failures. A good time is had by all. However, the close quarters of a flats skiff

Andros also has tarpon, primarily on the West Side and in places like Cabbage Creek; Captain Greene showed me where they live.

can put a premium on amiability and social skills. An eight-hour day in a 16-foot boat can expose tensions in a hurry, especially when conditions get tough. Suffering through such days with a smile should be part of every flats angler's skills.

It's harder when the troubles are inflicted by an inept guide. The Achilles' heel of most saltwater lodges is the depth, or lack thereof, of the guide staff. Many have a couple of "A" guides—competent, knowledgeable, patient, and amiable; guides with whom a day on the water is a pleasure even if the bonefish are contrary or nonexistent. Down the guide roster, quality often drops like a rock. A short-handed North Andros operation once recruited the owner's 18-year-old nephew from Nassau to play guide. The very nice kid invited us into the boat and promptly asked, "Where should we go?" Given it was our second visit to the island, we had no answer, and the outlook for the day went south.

Another F Troop "guide" sort of knew where to go but was clueless on how to pole. Bonefish would appear at 100 feet and the guy on the bow would get ready to cast, but when the pole whanged the boat a couple of times, the fish would flee. After this happened a few times, our guide observed, "Bonefish be spooky, mon." No shit, Sherlock! A brief discussion

After dinner it's time to go shark fishing on the Mangrove Cay Club dock.

"I don't need you men!" Jeannette bailed out of the skiff to catch a bonefish from the shoreline.

cured this problem, but our captain kept setting us up for shots to 12 o'clock and failed to spin the stern to let the backcast clear him. We'd wait for the nonexistent turn, he'd yell "Cast!" and then complain loudly when he got hooked. It went downhill from there.

Mangrove Cay guides have been almost uniformly good (except for one who lit up a joint during lunch one day). Captains Leslie Greene and Steven "Kiki" Adderley, with whom Jeannette and I have fished regularly for nearly 20 years, are wonderful guides and have become good friends. Leslie was the head guide at the Mangrove Cay Club and is now fishing independently; Kiki holds the Mangrove Cay Club top slot. I was in the boat with Kiki on his first morning guiding. We worked a Pine Cay cove with slick conditions and silver tails waving along the marl shoreline. He quietly maneuvered the boat from tail to tail and we boated half a dozen fine bonies to 6 pounds for a memorable day.

Other days can be a test. Kiki had piloted Jeannette and me to the West Side to intercept schools running a shoreline. Unfortunately, a brisk northeast breeze sprang up, blowing over Jeannette's casting shoulder, making it hard for her to make the needed casts. Everyone was getting frustrated, and after she blew a few tries and Captain Adderley and I sighed a little too loudly, she commanded to be taken to shore. She hopped off the boat, said "I don't need you men," marched to a little point (where the casting angle was better), and promptly caught a pair of bonefish.

Captain Greene revealed unknown skills as a marriage counselor. Our first three days at the Mangrove Cay Club had been a bust, watching it blow and rain. Day four dawned bright and calm, and we raced down the Middle Bight to

Captain Leslie guides Jeannette to a big bonefish, and our marriage is saved!

the mouth of Honeycutt Creek. Bones were out in force, and Jeannette took the bow. However, she was rusty after the three-day layoff and missed a number of shots. I was the culprit this time groaning a bit too much, prompting a displeased spouse to shove the fly rod in my face declaiming, "I'm not putting up with this!" As the day wore on, she adamantly refused to get back up, and my two-year-old marriage wasn't looking good. Leslie shot me a stern look meaning "keep your mouth shut" and went to work cajoling Jeannette to try again. Finally, she relented and got back up. I put a sock in my mouth, and Leslie guided her to an excellent pair of bonefish. Smiles broke out, and our marriage was saved.

Pursuit of bonefish opened the magical world of the Andros backcountry. With rare exceptions, only anglers and local fishermen venture into these pristine waters. Few, if any, Nassau tourists know about Bights, blue holes, the West Side, or the Tongue of the Ocean. And none of them appreciate the warmth and hospitality of the Androsians. Those of us fortunate enough to be regular Andros visitors learned that we came for the fishing but got so much more.

An Angler's Everglades

The Everglades evoke a wide range of reactions. For some, Marjory Stoneman Douglas's poetic River of Grass, flowing miles wide and inches deep from big Lake Okeechobee south down the Florida peninsula, comes to mind. Others see vast saw-grass prairies and mysterious dark waters under gray cypress strands. An urbanite driving from Miami to Naples grumps about a lot of nothing along I- 75/Alligator Alley or the Tamiami Trail while whizzing by at 80 mph. Many think of a big swamp filled only with alligators and mosquitoes behind the glitter and neon of Miami and Palm Beach. Nationally, the Glades are a potent symbol of our ability and resolve (very different things) to right environmental wrongs.

Lots of south Florida visitors think only of mainland Everglades National Park, unaware that the park, at the southern end of the historic Everglades, makes up only a quarter of the remnant Glades. The complete historic system begins near Orlando and the Kissimmee

A foggy sunrise over remote Whitewater Bay in Everglades National Park.

The Everglades, a vast, watery, wild area hiding behind Florida's Gold Coast, have been degraded by mismanagement of the freshwater flows from Lake Okeechobee. Historically, fresh water flowed from Lake Okeechobee to the Everglades and Florida Bay, but water diversions directly to the Atlantic have starved the Glades and Florida Bay of critical, clean fresh water.

River flowing south into Lake Okeechobee. Water spills from Lake O to meander south through 100 miles of saw grass, little islands (hammocks), cypress strands, and finally the dense mangrove jungles edging Florida Bay and the Gulf of Mexico.

The typical park tourist drives south of Miami, turns west at Florida City, crosses miles of big flat tomato fields, and enters the park at the visitor center. Most take a short ride to Royal Palm and the Anhinga Trail, catching glimpses of gators and wading birds in weedy freshwater sloughs. A few more press down the main road, crossing the tongue-in-cheek "Rock Creek Pass, Elevation 3 Feet" (a bit of National Park Service humor) on the way to the Pa-Hay-Okee overlook providing long views of the freshwater marl prairie. Those not in a hurry to get back to Miami, or on to Key West, may drive the remaining 30 miles to Flamingo and road's end. Flamingo perches amid the mangroves on the southern edge of mainland Florida, looking south across the expanse of salty Florida Bay.

Anglers come to and appreciate the Glades differently. Virtually all of the Bay is within

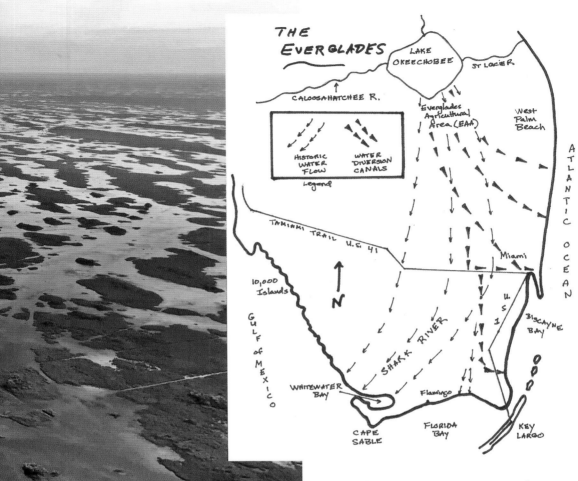

THE EVERGLADES

LAKE OKEECHOBEE

ST LUCIE

CALOOSAHATCHEE R.

Everglades Agricultural Area (EAA)

West Palm Beach

HISTORIC WATER FLOW

WATER DIVERSION CANALS

Legend

TAMIAMI TRAIL U.S. 41

10,000 Islands

N

ATLANTIC OCEAN

Miami

U.S. 1

BISCAYNE BAY

GULF of MEXICO

SHARK RIVER

WHITEWATER BAY

Flamingo

KEY LARGO

CAPE SABLE

FLORIDA BAY

Everglades Park. In fact, the park's southern boundary, 20 miles south of Flamingo, is an aquatic line running parallel to and a bit north of the Keys and the Overseas Highway from Key Largo to Long Key. Florida Bay is an integral part of the Everglades, being the receptacle of water that can flow all the way from the Kissimmee. The Bay is full of small mangrove cays, getting more numerous as you push northeast. Between the cays are huge flats, many of which are drained dry by the tides—not good places to be stuck. Channels are few and far between, and many are unmarked. To make matters worse, modern GPS devices can be very wrong about parts of the Bay. I've nervously steered my boat through winding narrow channels while the GPS insisted I should be 50 feet to the right trying to run on exposed sea grass! Matters are complicated by "pole and troll" zones where running an outboard is prohibited. And boaters now have to pass an online course on navigating the Bay to secure a boat permit to operate there. Too many clueless boaters have run over too many flats. Aerial photos of parts of the Bay show flats crisscrossed with propeller scars.

Ecotourists, and similarly inclined anglers, love the Bay. Dolphins and manatees are common. Sea turtles, mostly brown/yellow loggerheads, abound. Big sharks run flats edges, and prehistoric-looking sawfish appear. Stilt-legged wading birds are found throughout, including stunning roseate spoonbills and elegant great blue herons. Ibis with their odd curved red bills probe flats for crustaceans. Winter months find big rafts of large orange-billed white pelicans. Black-crested, bright white royal terns perch on channel markers.

(Clockwise from bottom left): The Everglades and Florida Bay, despite severe environmental degradation, still support a diverse array of wildlife including sea turtles, ospreys, roseate spoonbills, and white pelicans.

Most of the "backcountry" flats fishing from Islamorada and Key Largo for tarpon, bonefish, snook, and redfish is conducted within the confines of Florida Bay and Everglades Park; these park "visitors" never see an entrance station or a ranger. Much the same is true for the western edge of the Everglades. The 50-mile-long reach of wild black and red mangrove-choked islands from Chokoloskee and Everglades City to sandy Cape Sable (the end of mainland Florida) are also part of the park. These waters—where the Glades meet the Gulf of Mexico—are prime for snook, redfish, and tarpon, among others, and reached by long boat runs. I consider these two areas to be the "outside" zones of the Everglades saltwater fishery. And it offers a lot more than the glamour species. A chum bag and some bait make it easy to keep rods bent all day with a potpourri of species: snappers, jacks, ladyfish, sea trout, black drum, groupers, catfish, and sharks, to name a few.

The "inside" waters are just as fascinating. At Flamingo, a long, narrow canal runs north for about 4 miles to exit into Coot Bay. A channel on the far side winds through the thick, green subtropical forest, opening onto the main event: Whitewater Bay.

A spectral dead tree reflects in the water of Whitewater Bay.

Apparently named for the long white foam streaks kicked up by stiff northwest winds, Whitewater Bay features mostly shallow (5 feet or less) tea-colored waters; the color comes from the tannins in mangrove roots. The sprawling bay covers nearly 50 square miles, branching off into a watery labyrinth of seemingly endless bays, coves, and creeks including famous spots such as Hell's Bay. At its far northwest end a set of channels connect it to the Shark River—the main freshwater outlet for the water that flows slowly down the River of Grass. Snook and tarpon are the main attractions. Snook can be almost anywhere along endless miles of wild green mangrove shorelines. Big poons will flood Whitewater Bay, often as early as January when the weather is right, providing outstanding opportunities to stalk laid-up fish when the Keys' tarpon run is still weeks or months away. Tarpon that hang out in the Everglades' tannin-stained waters take on a unique coppery hue.

Navigating with modern GPS devices is bewildering enough; how the pioneers found their way in—and out—is a mystery. Herman Lucerne was one of the pioneers. He came to Florida City after World War II and started exploring these inside waters not long thereafter. For many years he kept a houseboat in Flamingo and used it as base to probe the fishing mysteries of the Glades. Lucerne, aka "Mr. Everglades," unlocked the area for many famous anglers, such as Stu Apte and Flip Pallot, showing them its outstanding fishing. Hell's Bay was a favored spot, and Lucerne claimed it got its name because "it was hell to get into and hell to find your way out" and he's absolutely correct! Hurricane Andrew took Lucerne's life, and to honor all he had done for the area, the Herman Lucerne Backcountry Fishing Tournament was founded in 2000; proceeds support Everglades and Florida Bay conservation.

Southwest of Whitewater and north of East Cape Sable, another system of "inside waters"—mostly unnamed lakes and bays—stretches 15 miles on a mostly east–west axis. Lake Ingraham is a major feature in the area, accessible via boat from the south and the north, where it exits into the Gulf of Mexico. Tides pour in and out of Ingraham, and a strong incoming flow from the Gulf looks like rapids in a river. Adjacent to the lake is the

A canoe or kayak must be portaged a short distance to reach Everglades National Park's No Motor Zone.

No Motor Zone, another large area where only self-propelled craft, such as canoes and kayaks, are permitted by NPS. Access takes work, as a canoe gets strapped onto a flats boat at Flamingo (or the Upper Keys), followed by a long slow run to the East Cape canal. The boat is moored, and the canoe is unloaded and portaged over the plug in the canal. Launched on the north side, a couple of miles of paddling reach fish-rich waters. The place can be heaven for small tarpon, snook, and reds.

These Everglades waters, outside and in, are still eminently fishable because the Glades themselves, despite terrible abuse, remain uniquely productive. Historically, nearly two million acre-feet of clean fresh water flowed through the Everglades every year, exiting into the Bay where it mixed with Gulf of Mexico salt water, creating an immensely rich estuarine environment. The dense untouched mangrove jungles and Bay sea-grass beds hosted untold quantities of shrimp, crabs, oysters, and forage fish to feed legions of predatory species (our gamefish). Bays, coves, and creeks tucked in among the mangroves provided boundless nurseries for small fish of all species.

This ecological system was wholly misunderstood and unappreciated until relatively recently. Florida's pioneers saw only a pestilential, stinking swamp that if drained would support and sustain valuable farming and land for settlement. Efforts to dry out the Glades by damming, ditching, and diverting its copious waters started in the 1880s.

Hamilton Disston was a Pennsylvania industrialist who apparently fell in love with Florida during an 1878 fishing trip. In 1881, he purchased four million acres, mostly in central Florida. He envisioned "reclaiming" lands around Lake Okeechobee, including portions of the Everglades south of the lake, by draining the waters to the Atlantic Ocean. Canals were dredged and some lands dried out, but the job was too large for a single entrepreneur.

In 1905, Governor Napoleon Bonaparte Broward got into the act. He promised to create an "Empire of the Everglades" by draining it so the "fabulous muck" there could become rich agricultural lands. He envisioned "convert[ing] what is now unsurveyed waste land into a state asset more valuable than all lands now under cultivation" in Florida. A massive canal from the south side of Lake Okeechobee to the New River at Fort Lauderdale was the centerpiece of the drainage scheme. He didn't succeed, but his proposed canal largely exists today as the North New River (L-35) canal.

Miami was a culprit too. Few realize that the city was built first on a natural, coral/sand ridge between the Atlantic/Biscayne Bay and the historic Everglades. Lands occupied today by Miami International Airport, Doral, and adjacent communities were a giant wetland drained by a beautiful, clear-water stream—the Miami River (now a polluted, industrialized gunkhole). There was a narrows in the river and a rapids with enough flow for Ferguson's Mill (just east of today's airport)—very hard to imagine looking at contemporary Miami. The river was dredged and widened in 1909, destroying the narrows while draining and drying the lands to the west—another bite out of the original Everglades.

At the same time, the advent of commercial plume hunting made the Glades ground zero for one of America's first national wildlife conservation battles. Feathers for women's hats became a huge industry in the 1880s. Demand was insatiable and prices high, particularly for the exotic subtropical birds inhabiting south Florida. Roseate spoonbills, pink flamingos, dazzling white great egrets, blue and white herons, and many other birds sported uniquely shaped and colored feathers that milliners had to have.

A very tough bunch of men went to work satisfying this demand by slaughtering thousands upon thousands of these birds; one year over 130,000 snowy egrets were killed. Money poured into remote, ramshackle little villages at Chokoloskee, Everglades City, and Flamingo. Stopping this industrial-scale slaughter was a primary factor in the 1886 founding of the Audubon Society. President Teddy Roosevelt created the National Wildlife Refuge System in 1903 to establish sanctuaries for the birds. Legislation was passed banning plume hunting, especially the heinous practice of killing birds on nests. However, enforcing the new laws was difficult. In 1903, the American Ornithological Union and the Florida Audubon Society hired Guy Bradley, a former plume hunter, to enforce the restrictions in the Everglades. Two years later he encountered

Hundreds of miles of drainage canals sluice fresh water out of the Everglades to be dumped in the Atlantic, drying up and killing the Glades. (Courtesy of Dr. Stephen Davis, Everglades Foundation)

three men shooting up an egret rookery near Flamingo and ordered them to stop. They shot Bradley dead. The incident galvanized public opinion against plume hunting and made him a conservation martyr. Today you can catch tarpon near Bradley Key just west of Flamingo.

Another assault on the Everglades commenced in 1921 when construction began on the Tamiami Trail, a highway bisecting the Glades to connect Tampa and Miami (hence Tamiami). The two-lane highway, today's US 41, was constructed by digging a canal and using the fill to create an adjacent elevated roadbed. When completed in 1928, the road became a major dam blocking vital north-to-south water

The first of two Mod Waters bridges, completed in 2013, breaches the Tamiami Trail "dam," allowing more fresh water to reach Everglades National Park and Florida Bay. (Courtesy of Dr. Stephen Davis, Everglades Foundation)

flows into what is now Everglades National Park. It doesn't take a very high "dam" to block a river that is only inches deep.

Fifty years later, the damaging effects of the Tamiami Trail were recognized and plans were started to breach the dam. Complicated negotiations in the '70s and '80s (which I was part of in 1985–88) led to congressional authorization of the Modified Water Deliveries Project ("Mod Waters") in 1988. The federal and state governments would fund construction of major bridges on the Tamiami Trail to allow water to flow more freely under the highway into the park. Everyone declared victory—prematurely it turned out. The actual construction and funding were not approved until 2008,

wonder why the Everglades and Florida Bay are still struggling?

Death-dealing hurricanes in 1926 and 1928 contributed to the Everglades' ailments. Both storms flooded areas around Lake Okeechobee, with the '28 storm being the worst. A small 4-foot-high mud dike had been built around the lake's south shore to start drying out the lands there for agriculture and settlement. Of course, the dike acted as another dam, impeding the River of Grass. Rain and strong south winds in the '28 storm breached the dike and sent floodwaters pouring south into towns like Clewiston. Over 2,500 people drowned. The catastrophe created pressure for a bigger new dike and work started on it in the 1930s, culminating in completion of the Hoover Dike in the early '60s. Water flows out of the lake into the Everglades were now really cut off.

With land south of Lake Okeechobee drying out and available for agriculture, in 1948 the Everglades Agricultural Area (EAA) was established. The 700,000-acre EAA converted over 25 percent of the historic Everglades into an agricultural area with industrial-scale cane sugar cultivation.

Approximately 500,000 acres in the EAA are controlled by two companies: U.S. Sugar and Florida Crystal.

The year 1948 also saw federal approval of the Central and South Florida Project under the aegis of the US Army Corps of Engineers. It was the grand plan to replumb the Everglades, keep the EAA lands dried out for sugarcane, and dry out more Everglades land—west of Palm Beach, Fort Lauderdale, and Miami—to facilitate development.

By the mid-'60s, replumbing of the Everglades was almost complete. Most of the water coming out of Okeechobee was sluiced to the Atlantic Ocean by the Hillsboro, North New River, and Miami canals. Every drop of water sent to the ocean was a drop denied to the Glades and Florida Bay. Farther south more dikes and ditches diverted waters from the beginnings of the Shark River, exacerbating the drying out of this great hydrologic system. The last structural indignity was completion of the C-111 Canal in 1965. It finished draining the areas west of Florida City and on the east edge of Everglades Park to facilitate tomato farming. Water that should have gone down Taylor

and then it took special congressional action to bypass court rulings: A federal court held that the environmental impact statement for the project (to improve the environment) was deficient! In 2013 the first 1-mile-long bridge was opened, but water has only recently begun to flow under it. Construction on an additional 2.5-mile bridge, to further facilitate water flows into the park, was finished in 2020. Over 30 years elapsed between original authorization of the project and on-the-ground benefits. Any

Slough to northeast Florida Bay got shunted east to the ocean. All of this starved the Glades of vital quantities of fresh water. The National Academy of Sciences' Everglades Committee estimates these water diversions cut off over 40 percent of historic water flows into Everglades Park and Florida Bay.

At the same time, a water-quality crisis was erupting. Decades of agricultural runoff north of Lake O had filled it with excessive amounts of phosphorous. The taxpayer-subsidized sugarcane companies were also backpumping phosphorous-laden water into the lake and into the Glades as well. Turns out that water with more than 10 parts per billion (ppb) of phosphorous changes the water chemistry and vegetative growth in the Glades. Invasive species such as cattails take over and crowd out the native species. Excessive nutrients, like phosphorus, flowing into Florida Bay also trigger algae blooms, the source of noxious pea-soup waters that kill sea grass, along with forage and predatory fish. A bitter Clean Water Act legal battle started in 1986 that culminated a decade later in a historic court-approved settlement prescribing that water sent to the Everglades would contain no more than 10 ppb of phosphorus.

Recognition that these water quality and quantity problems were killing the Glades and Florida Bay underpinned the cooperative Everglades Restoration Acts enacted in 2000 by the federal government and the State of Florida. The two statutes authorized the Comprehensive Everglades Restoration Program (CERP), which is a set of projects designed to get more clean fresh water into the Glades and remove many of the canals, dikes, and ditches that prevent the water from flowing smoothly south into the park and then the Bay. Unfortunately, progress has been painfully slow, and the Everglades still teeter on the edge of irrevocable adverse environmental changes. To make matters worse, Okeechobee is still heavily laden with phosphorus and when it begins to fill up (and overtop the now-leaky Hoover Dike), the dirty water cannot be sent to the Everglades because of the water-quality settlement. Instead, the fouled waters get pumped east down the St. Lucie River and west down the Caloosahatchee, polluting and killing those two systems. So, failure to restore the Everglades is now indirectly destroying two other valuable estuarine systems.

Everyone knows precisely what needs to be done: more water storage and water cleaning capacity south of Lake O; blowing out the canals, dams, and dikes impeding water flows through the Glades; and putting the C-111 water back into Taylor Slough. Even if CERP is fully implemented, Florida Bay will still receive only 65 to 80 percent of historic freshwater inputs. But the political will and funding to move ahead on CERP has been missing, and most of the crucial projects are languishing. Florida's new governor (as of 2020) is saying the right things and ordering the right actions. It remains to be seen if the orders are followed.

This sorry story should make every angler angry. Knowing how outstanding the Glades fishery remained into the '80s is testament to its resilience and how staggeringly good it must have been before it fell prey to this litany of calamities. And even though the Everglades fishery is diminished, it remains good enough to entice anglers, especially during tarpon season. A day or two of warm, calm conditions in January will push big tarpon into Whitewater Bay. The early fish can be aggressive in the tea-colored waters, and anglers, including me, try really hard to be there when this happens. Catch it right and a memorable day is in the offing. Unfortunately, the window of opportunity can be very short, and never open in my case, as the fishing shuts down hard when normal winter weather and stiff northwest winds return:

JAN. 22, CLEAR, 75, WIND A.M. SW 10, LATE A.M./P.M. NW 15. Capt. Alex Zapata called to report lots of willing poons in Whitewater, the weather guys predicted gentle E winds, so we met in Florida City at 0 dark 30 for the drive to Flamingo. It was still cool running the canal to Coot Bay and then thru to Whitewater. Bright skies provided some optimism, but winds were already veering around and picking up contrary to the forecast. Before too long whitecaps and foam streaks were marching across the Bay. Free jumping tarpon were plentiful, but the fish weren't laying up and impossible to see in the deteriorating conditions. That forced us to lee shores and still no fish. Finally, late in the afternoon we stumbled upon a few tarpon in a little cove but the wind and dropping temps precipitated lockjaw. One of these days Whitewater is going to come through for me—maybe. ●

The siren song of the No Motor Zone is very hard to resist when prized warm, calm winter days come along. You fish here in the bow, usually a canoe. Warmth kicks the snook and redfish into gear, and a key is to find water clear enough to see the fish before you bump them. Much of the area consists of shallow bays with soft mud bottoms that winter winds can churn into a muddy mess, rendering sight-fishing problematic, to say the least.

Snook fishing in the No Motor Zone can also be very different from the normal tactics used on the linesides. Typical fly rodding for linesides throughout south Florida entails blind casting into tangled mangrove shorelines. It's a real casters' game, as inches make the difference between bites and zippo. The fish tuck up under the mangrove roots and overhanging branches, and the fly must get back in there to be bit. The bounce, or skip, cast is a crucial part of the angler's arsenal; a sidearm throw delivers the fly a couple of feet short of the target, and the bug bounces or skips off the water, getting under the groves. Tricky but not impossible, and a well-placed fly can earn the distinct popping take of a hungry snook. No Motor Zone linesides also love the mangroves, but a goodly number can be found cruising super-skinny open waters. Angling to these fish is on par with targeting tailing bones:

FEB. 25, MOSTLY SUNNY, 80, WIND CALM TO SSE <10. Launched the canoe at the canal mouth and paddled N a mile or so passing a dozen crocodiles sunning on an exposed mud bank. Creeping by big crocs in a 12-foot canoe was more than spooky. Baby tarpon were rolling but snook and reds were our target. The first pair of coves were too muddy, and we bumped a few fish. We could see a little in the next one and located a nice snook prowling in eight inches of murky water. Got the floating white Mini Mouse (1/0) in front of the fish, waited until it got close, bumped the fly, and the lineside sucked it in. Feeling the hook, the fish took off plowing across

the shallows, getting well into the backing. The snook never jumped (too shallow?) but gave me a good running head-shaking tussle. Don lipped it and pegged it at seven or eight pounds. Pretty neat. ●

Snook and even largemouth bass turn up in the multitude of rivers and creeks that feed Whitewater Bay. Dark, narrow channels wind deep into a jungle-like environment, and an appearance by the Creature from the Black Lagoon would not be a surprise. Some spots are much too tight for a fly rod, but the snook are more than willing to hammer small plugs and jigs flipped near the thickets. The farther north you penetrate, the closer you are to fresh water. That gets announced by dark green largemouths appearing to nail a topwater fly or lure.

Highly prized linesides are found in the "outside" waters as well. In fact, the waters around Chokoloskee, fronting the Gulf of Mexico, likely have the finest snook fishery in Florida. But it's a bit far for us Keys guys, so we hit Florida Bay for *Centropomus undecimalis*:

JULY 28, CLOUDS AND WIND. We were sandwiched between Tropical Storm Dean and Hurricane Erin—making it difficult. But the boys and I bounced our way into the Bay, finding a sheltered channel near Dildo Key; we could see the big Flamingo radio tower to the N. When told our location, the guys started snickering and I realized my 11- and 9-year olds [they are 38 and 36 now] knew what a dildo was. Shocked me more than a bit. Fortunately, the fish got us refocused, as the channel was full of hungry 5- to 10-pound snook. Lobbing in pinfish did the trick and we managed a dozen hard-running, leaping fish. Action stopped when we ran out of bait. ●

South Florida snook have taken hits in recent years, with the January 2010 record cold killing thousands of fish. Prompt fishing restrictions and closures by FWC, and a bit of normal weather, caused the fish to bounce back quickly. Then a pair of water-quality crises hit the fishery: first, in the form of the 2015 Florida Bay problems, and second, with a devastating 2018 red tide along Florida's west coast. Fortunately, it looks like the snook are

Everglades National Park's No Motor Zone features big American crocodiles, skinny-water snook, and very tight waterways among thick black and red mangroves.

recovering again (but how often can we dodge these bullets?).

Big tarpon are the main attraction of the "outside" fisheries. The Gulf portion features a series of rivers emptying from the Glades into the salt, including the Chatham, Lostman's, Broad, Harney, and Shark. Chatham is known for the location of Edgar Watson's place. Reputedly a notorious killer, he was gunned down by his fearful neighbors in Chokoloskee in 1910. Peter Matthiessen told the story in his excellent novel *Killing Mr. Watson*, later incorporated into a larger superb book, *Shadow Country*. A. W. Dimock was fishing for and catching tarpon from a canoe in Lostman's, Broad, and Harney in the 1880s—all recorded, including unbelievable glass-plate photographs, in his *Book of Tarpon* published in 1911. Tarpon fishing in the area can be so good that tournament anglers and guides will make the two-hour boat run from Islamorada to reach these waters during the Gold Cup or the Hawley tournaments. The 60 miles from West Pass (the northwest edge of Everglades Park) to East Cape is the last truly wild stretch of Florida coastline. Myriad cays and islands thickly overgrown with tall black mangroves and a mix of other tropical trees are utterly uninhabited.

Florida Bay is a more famous and readily reachable tarpon locale. The big fish appear first in late January in the deeper (20 feet) waters off Cape Sable and its sandy wild beach. As it warms, the fish spread out to the southeast and can be found in famous basins and along bank edges with names whispered reverently by tarpon addicts: First National Bank, Palm Lakes, Sandy Key, and Oxfoot Bank, to name a few. If the weather cooperates and an angler can intercept a push of these early migrants, spectacular angling can be had. Tarpon will often roll in, literally, on an incoming tide, busting mullet en route. Early season, happy, feeding poons are a great combination and well-placed flies quickly elicit foamy, gulping bites. Angler Paul Turcke and Captain Ponzoa found such a combo near First National early in the 2015 season and boated 10 big tarpon in two days.

This "early season" lasts into April. However, conditions need to be right and the fish in the right mood, as always, to assure success. George Conniff and Captain Bus hit it right one afternoon at Oxfoot. A number of tarpon had moved in and laid up. Despite murky water, they found enough fish for eight good shots and hooked seven—a spectacular batting average. Bus, Alex Good, and I returned the next day with the same weather and almost identical tides and found more fish, but couldn't buy a bite. George figured we failed to provide a proper sacrifice to the tarpon gods.

Looking for laid-up tarpon in murky Bay waters can create odd visual challenges. Fish

Still mornings in Florida Bay, during all four seasons, frequently reveal rolling, sighing tarpon.

Laid-up tarpon can be difficult to see in Florida Bay's naturally off-color water—mistaken casts to manatees are not uncommon.

are often hard to see, and anglers and guides strain to pick up a bit of color or the shape of a tail and discern which way a fish is facing. Throwing at the tail doesn't earn bites. We spotted a bit of gray, poled closer to investigate, and the color grew to sizable proportions—a laid-up monster. A well-directed cast earned only a boil of water, and a large round-tailed manatee undulated away to rest elsewhere.

These experiences and others demonstrate that Bay tarpon too can be fickle, and taking advantage of the often-short windows of opportunities is critical:

MARCH 25, CAPE SABLE, SCATTERED HIGH CLOUDS, 80–85, SLICK CALM IN AFTERNOON. Bus and I ended up off East Cape surrounded by wads of rolling tarpon. Unfortunately, they were in the roll and dive deep mode and showing zero interest in our offerings. I was ready to slit my wrists. Bus counseled patience, thinking a pending tide change might get the poons to float up high and give us some good chances. An hour later the current slacked and sure enough the fish came up—just as the other boats departed and left us gloriously alone. Bus then located a pair of laid-up fish at 2 o'clock facing to 12. I put a 1/0 Olive Mouse/Toad about 10 feet ahead, let it drift closer, and then a long slooooooow strip. A tarpon eased up, turned on the fly, and gulped it in. Set the hook, the 75-pounder launched immediately 40 feet off the bow and raced off. A knot in the fly line hit the rod guides and popped off the top two sections of the four-piece 11-weight. Backed off the pressure, reeled in the tip sections, partially picked out the knot, and the tarpon surged off, this time with only the tip section dangling on the line. Got it back, Bus finished untangling the knot, we reassembled the rod and got down to fighting the fish—a real cluster foxtrot. Renewed pressure got more jumps then we had her boatside, got a good look, and broke her off. We now looked around to see numbers of other laid-up fish and a few surface cruisers. Taking turns on the pole (and

Rolling tarpon in Florida Bay are often heard before being seen.

my poling abilities in 15 feet of water are piss poor) we fed five more in short order, jumped two, and got two. When it shut down at 5 p.m., we made an incredibly beautiful hour-plus run S to Marathon across mercury slick Florida Bay colored silver/orange by the setting sun. ●

The advance of spring gets the migratory Bay tarpon on the move. Wads of fish swim south. Some filter past Man O' War Key and work into Rabbit Key Basin north of Islamorada. Many of these poons eventually end up swimming through Jimmie Albright's "Pocket" by Buchanan Bank. Others track the west side of Nine Mile Bank, bouncing off the 1st, 2nd, and 3rd Points on the way to the Channel Two, Channel Five, and Long Key bridges in the Keys. In recent years, however, the numbers of tarpon swimming these traditional routes have diminished. No one knows precisely why, but many point fingers at the water-quality problems that afflict the Bay.

The Bay also includes a population of resident big tarpon that can be pursued year-round. East of Flamingo are very shallow bays where redfish are the usual quarry. It is not uncommon, however, to find tarpon, particularly in the fall months when more than usual numbers of mullet (a big baitfish) are present. Tarpon of 100 pounds can be found in very shallow water shadowing the frisky mullet.

Casting to a 5-foot-long fish with a big, broad back and upper tail lobe sticking above the water is pretty damn exciting. The fish are sensitive in the skinny water, and I have yet been able to hook one. Friends have reported awesome bites and lots of flying mud, sea grass, and water when one of these super-shallow poons feels the hook.

Florida Bay and the remnant Everglades remain wild, mysterious, and intriguing. Big crocodiles eye passing canoes, manatees (so ugly they're beautiful) surface unexpectedly, dolphins herd mullet in shallow bays, and great birds stalk the vast mudflats and roost among myriad mangrove cays. Dense jungles of black and red mangroves remain impenetrable. The fish are still there in numbers to make anglers smile and bring them back year after year to chase the silver tarpon or find the furtive snook. Sadness and anger seep in when you realize how spectacular it must have been not too long ago before the River of Grass was dammed, diked, and diverted and the Bay pushed to the edge of death. You owe it to yourself to fish the Glades and the Bay. Develop your own appreciation of this special place and at least see it before it's gone. With a little luck, that special angler's appreciation might prompt you to join the ranks of those dedicated to restoring the Everglades system to some semblance of its prior greatness.

CHAPTER 5

The Passion Never Dies

Taking the bow of a flats boat can be transformative. The angler joins a select club tuned in to a unique shallow-water world teeming with fascinating life. Only adherents know that the real bonefish doesn't go on a grill, a tarpon isn't caught for the dinner table, and a permit is not a fishing license. Like any subculture, we have our uniforms, special lingo, heroes (unknown to outsiders), and organizations to join. The fraternity (and women are included) is still pretty small, and only one or two degrees of separation exist among most of us.

Chasing the big three of the flats is a labor of love. Others, including any number of ex-wives, call it addictive. The addiction, I prefer commitment, arises from the perpetual challenge presented by the environment as well as the fish—the wind blows too hard or not at all, waters are below the magic 70

Mike Lawson closes the deal with a Keys backcountry tarpon. (Courtesy of Mike Lawson)

degrees or a parboiling 90 degrees plus, clouds cover the sky blotting out visibility or a naked sun broils everything on or in the water. Or squall lines spit out dangerous waterspouts.

Fish are just as uncooperative, most of the time. Then comes the rare day when the stars align, the weather and water are right, and the fish are there and for a change ready to eat. At that point, the angler better be prepared to make the cast, set the hook, clear the line, and catch something. A doctor friend tells me we are hardwired to do things that trigger the release of adrenaline and dopamine. Seeing and having a chance to hook the fish must release a good dose in my system, and getting one of the big three on the line kicks my natural drugs into high gear.

Difficulty makes it stick-to-your ribs fishing. Those fortunate enough to have caught a few permit can tell you a detailed story of each and every one. And tarpon are never part of a stringer of commonly taken fish going home for an everyday fish fry.

British trout-fishing author G. E. M. Skues wrote a masterful short story capturing the value of challenging angling: Mr. Theodore Castwell, member of an exclusive fishing club, is a dedicated angler but a less than exemplary human being. He passes away, finds himself before St. Peter, and as one fisherman to another, asks for his Heavenly assignment on a fine trout stream. Mr. Castwell awakes in a lovely meadow next to a gorgeous small river full of hatching mayflies and rising trout. His guide is a dour fellow. A big trout is rising on the corner, and with one cast, the fish rises and is caught. And damned if another big one starts rising in its place and Castwell catches it on one cast. And another shows and is caught. And another, and another, and another. An exasperated, bored Castwell asks the guide, "May we move on to the next pool?" He answers with a firm "No" and Castwell mutters "Hell!" "Yes" says the guide.

Flats fishing is rarely easy, and it makes us hone our skills and elevate our game in order to succeed. The fish are genuine trophies that are hard-earned and all the more precious because of it. In turn, we care (or ought to) about these fish and the habitats that sustain them.

Animal rights critics, contending that catch-and-release fishing is torture, argue we should just look at the fish and still care about them. As I wrote in *Seasons on the Flats*, looking—or voyeurism—is no substitute for actual immersion in the flats environment and physical interaction with the fish. Being a successful predator requires that we learn the nuances of the fish's environment, where the fish will be and when they will be there—what will influence their willingness to bite, how to engage their primordial instincts and elicit a strike. That in turn makes us pay attention to seasons, weather, tides, and the availability of prey. Each time the fish fool us by not appearing or not eating triggers more questions about why and why not, leading to learning and greater appreciation for the environment as well as the commitment to conserving it. Interaction, not mere voyeurism, breeds the kind of passion essential to keeping the flats, the fish, and flats fishing alive for the next generations.

Teddy Roosevelt and company made this very same connection 140 years ago when they founded America's wildlife conservation movement. TR and his pals were committed hunters, and the passion engendered by their pursuit of big game became the cornerstone of successful conservation. Principles of fair chase were reflected in fishing and hunting seasons and rules and regulations, and required licenses and stamps paid for wildlife research, professional management, conservation, land and water acquisitions, and game wardens.

This same model is at work on Florida's flats fishery. Dollars provided by anglers via licenses, federal excise taxes on fishing tackle, and taxes on motorboat fuel are funneled to the Florida Wildlife Commission, which regulates fishing for bones, tarpon, and perms and engages in critical research on these species. Publicly funded research is matched by privately funded research conducted by the Bonefish & Tarpon Trust and its partners. This work is supported by anglers—not lookers.

It raises the question: Is there value or purpose in our flats angling? I submit the answer is a resounding "yes." There is internal, personal value in the form of recreation, triggering fascination, and the variety of social benefits enjoyed by anglers. Externally, none of the animal rights activists, carping from the sidelines about fish torture, contribute a dime to the essential work of fishery conservation

An Atlantic waterspout snakes down from a squall line, looking ready to take you to Oz.

A fine Keys bonefish is ready to be released—part of the partially recovering Keys population.

and research. None of them are on the front lines in the fight to restore the Everglades and Florida Bay or conserve bonefish, tarpon, and permit in key locations in the Bahamas, Belize, Cuba, or Mexico. They are not making annual pilgrimages, covering decades, to the Keys to "look" at tarpon swim their ancestral tracks. Genuine fisheries conservation—rather than empty virtue-signaling about fish torture—is the legacy and value of the angling community.

This kind of utilitarian answer, however, is not going to be enough to defend our fishing heritage. Anti-fishing activists are in fact radicals arguing that it is simply immoral to catch and release fish. They argue that real-world pragmatism and facts about funding conservation and research merely distract attention from this fundamental moral issue without providing a counter. I agree but note that there are inconsistencies inherent in the animal rights philosophy, which sells itself as a better way for us to interact with wildlife and nature. In fact, humans must reject nature and natural predator-prey relationships to be "moral" per the activists. The animal rights movement posits that any animal or fish capable of feeling "pain" is vested with "rights" entitling the animal or fish to not be harmed, hurt, restrained,

or killed. There is, however, a catch. Animal "rights" apparently operate only in relationship to humans. When a shark eats a red snapper, it would be idiotic to charge the shark with murder. But if you kill the same snapper, the animal rights philosophy labels you a murderer. This reveals that the motive, not the deed, is the crime. The snapper is dead in both scenarios, but the result is "immoral" only when the fish dies from human action. So, if humans act "naturally," consistent with our role as an evolved apex predator—and eat the fish—that is an immoral act. A philosophy so antithetical to human participation in the natural world is not only foolish but poison for sane conservation policies. Academics describe modern urban America as suffering from "nature deficit disorder" and alienation from the outdoors world (thanks laptops, tablets, and iPhones) as a source of behavioral problems. The anti-natural animal rights philosophy is either a contributor to or symptom of this disorder.

It is worth noting that the radical animal rights doctrine is very different from traditional concerns regarding animal welfare. Animal welfare focuses on humane treatment of domestic animals, arguing human morality requires that pets and livestock not be subject to abuse and cruelty, hence the creation well over 100 years ago of societies for the prevention of cruelty to animals. These well-established, widely accepted ethical precepts are a far cry from investing animals—domestic and wild—with rights.

The bottom line is that angling has value and purpose. It connects us with the wild world and provides incalculable personal benefits, and the passion for the fish and fishing translates into crucial conservation. Catch-and-release angling is not torture. A tarpon's brief encounter with an angler is nothing compared to the dismemberment and death meted out by a great hammerhead or sinister 10-foot-long bull shark.

We have absolutely no reason to be ashamed of what we do as long as our angling practices are constrained by fair-chase principles and we remain committed to giving back to the environment as a small payment for the benefits we derive from taking the bow in pursuit of bonefish, tarpon, and permit.

Commitment to conservation is also essential unless we are content to be the last generation able to enjoy fishing on the flats. Being just a user is unsustainable knowing what we know now about the multiple threats to the

fish and the habitats upon which they depend. The still-great Florida Keys fisheries are substantially less productive than when pioneer anglers and guides like Stu Apte, Bill Curtis, and George Hommell took to the water. Fortunately, we now possess the knowledge enabling us to arrest the downward slide and restore, at least in part, the fisheries we have been able to enjoy and cherish for more than 6 decades. Whether or not we have the will to do so is the crucial question.

I prefer to be an optimist but not a wearer of rose-colored glasses. Within the Caribbean basin, we know enough about bonefish spawning, life cycle habitats, and connectivity among populations to map out an effective regional conservation strategy. Maintain or improve water quality, conserve pre-spawning aggregation sites as well as spawning sites, ensure that adult mortality is within sustainable limits (stop wholesale netting of sexually mature adult fish and engage in the best catch-and-release practices), and protect the sheltered bays and creeks occupied by young bonies. Correcting egregious water mismanagement in Florida and restoring the Everglades are not simple chores. The Bahamas has created

A healthy "green" tarpon swims away, none the worse for wear, after a brief nonlethal encounter with a pleased angler.

large national parks to conserve and protect bonefish habitat, but enforcement is always an issue. In Belize, Cuba, and Mexico, convincing poor, hungry people to stop netting fish—so we can catch them instead—is no easy task.

Twenty years ago, we barely knew bonefish were in trouble and were clueless about why. Now the diagnosis is complete, and the fish doctors can prescribe the cure. Are we capable of implementing it? Only time will tell, but at the very least we must try and try very hard. And to mix recent campaign slogans, I'm betting "Yes we can" and "Let's make flats fishing great again."

Angling is inherently an optimistic enterprise. Every cast is made with hope that this one will get the bite. Even hard-bitten, somewhat cynical permit aficionados carry a huge reservoir of hope, otherwise the fickle, fiendish black-tailed devils would grind them down. Rather than lament what has gone wrong, the better course is to focus on the fine angling that remains. The glass is half full. On this point, Stu Apte has offered excellent wisdom: Today are the good old days of tomorrow. Hit the water, get on the bow, pursue the fish, and make your memories for tomorrow. Every venture on the flats is a learning experience, and every outing provides a chance for one of those magical days that will be recounted, cherished, and polished lovingly for years to come.

Bitching about what's been lost and throwing in the towel is a one-way ticket to bitterness. In fact, people have been writing off the Keys flats fishery for over 50 years, claiming the fish are gone, the flats are destroyed, and wall-to-wall anglers have destroyed the whole experience. Obviously, the Keys have suffered a litany of environmental woes, water-quality crises, and flats carved up by ignorant boaters and jet skiers. Even so the fishery remains extraordinary and can serve up extraordinary days that demonstrate anew the need for and value of fighting vigorously to conserve and restore the fish and their habitats:

May 28, 2020, Middle Keys, Mostly Clear, 85–90, Wind SE 10–15. When Capt. Scott and I planned to poke around outback—and take a break from ocean tarpon—we had no reason to consider or expect the almost impossible—a Double Grand Slam. At 8 a.m. Scott found a small shrimp hatch and rolling, feeding small tarpon. Quickly put two in the air and took the hook out of #3—a jumping 10-lber. With the sun up, time to look for bonies. Found a batch on a nearby light-bottomed flat and by 10 a.m. we had boated a trio of 3-lb. aqua-finned speedsters on the #2 Red Head Gotcha. It's so great to have our bonefish coming back even if still a bit small. The next flat had a surprise—a bunch of permit. Two fish did everything but eat the Gotcha then Scott set me up on a happy group of 4 or 5 perms 60 feet away at 2 o'clock. Got the fly there landing it quietly, started stripping, two showed interest, and one charged ahead to grab it. Hallelujah. Cleared the line and pursued as the permit charged across the flat. Both of us stayed quiet and focused—no cheering, no congrats, as we knew not to tempt fate. Then disaster loomed. The fish beelined for a sunken tree, left over from Hurricane Irma, and Scott maneuvered the boat while I dipsey doodled the rod to keep the permit and line clear. It worked, got 50 yards past the snag, when Mr. Perm reversed course and headed back for it. More deft work kept it clear then Capt. Collins tailed it—a very nice 10+-lber—and a Slam.

Now we were playing with the house money and agreed to use the rest of our day (it was only 11:30 a.m.) to check new spots, explore. Had lunch and off to a flat to see if it held some of the resurgent bonefish population. It did but more importantly another permit cruised in at 3 o'clock, showed it the Gotcha, and a series of strips/stops/long strips enticed a highly visible bite. Couldn't believe we had another perm on the line. This one bored for deeper water, flirted with another snag, and before long Scott had it in hand—another 10+ fish. Wow.

What to do next? In the midst of our options discussion, Scott mentioned he'd never had a Double Slam on his boat—and I certainly never sniffed one. That sealed it—had to try for the impossible so off to the ocean for migrating tarpon. Buzzed from the Gulf to the Atlantic and found a good spot open. Rerigged for ocean poons and here came a nice string. Unclipped the anchor, Scott poled to intercept, and the second cast got a middle fish to lift up, slide to its right, and suck in the worm fly.

All I could think was "Don't screw this up." The fish danced around the boat, ran off, then back at us. Scott had to spin the stern and I had to keep the line off him. Fortunately, the tarpon then ran inshore and we chased. Scott implored "Don't jump, don't jump" and the fish ignored him three or four times. Finally, it tired, pulled it close, and had the leader on the 50-lber—caught! A Double Slam. Now we traded high fives savoring something no angler/guide team could ever expect. A fishery that can still serve up a day like this is worth fighting for. ●

Never discount the selective nature and therapeutic value of great angling memories. I've kept a detailed angling journal since high school (now up to 28 notebooks!) and looking back through them reveals much about how we remember things. My friend Joe Kelley and I were talking about a set of summer days in the Keys over 10 years ago, and he recalled it being a great trip focusing on a bunch of big willing tarpon we got into in the backcountry. We put down our adult beverages and dug out the journal volume with the entries for the three-day trip. Day one was cloudy and windy with rain blowing in late in the afternoon—and no fish. Day two was worse—we spent most of our time hiding under bridges to escape curtains of gray rain and sizzling lightning. Rain and squall lines persisted the next morning, but around noon the storms moved out to sea, leaving behind a solid pewter sky. The wind dropped and it was calm, slick, and humid. Captain Albert announced there was a good spot to check for tarpon, and he was right. The short afternoon was spent stalking laid-up fish in water like a sheet of mercury. We hooked four or five, landing a pair of big girls. Ran back to No Name Key, moored the boat, and walked down to the pub for a cold one. Joe and I remembered that superb afternoon—our brains had deep-sixed the miserable two-and-half-day lead-up.

Success on the flats is fleeting, and the less-productive days (I won't call them bad) greatly outnumber the former. It's the price we pay—very willingly in my case—for the good ones. Poor luck is accounted for colorfully in a variety of means. Lack of mojo is one explanation; bad juju is another. Captain Bus coined my favorite—BOHICA, short for "bend over, here

Permit number one of a rare Double Grand Slam (two bonefish, two permit, and two tarpon on fly in one day)—proof that the Florida Keys fishery remains extraordinary and worth fighting for.

it comes again." Repeated references to karma are so pronounced, I suspect a goodly number of Keys guides must be closet Hindus. Following a run of excellent fishing days a few years back, Captain Ponzoa warned that I was due for some bad karma. He threatened to ban me from his boat until the bad stuff passed. I laughed then, but a multiyear permit-less streak followed, as did some horrible spring tarpon weather. When poor weather and poor angling come our way, we hope we're paying advance dues for good days to come. The fear is we're paying for previous good days and our karmic account is still underwater, so to speak.

My fascination with fish, created as a 7-year-old watching yellow schoolmaster snappers and aqua cowfish under an Islamorada dock, has influenced my life more than I could have imagined. Becoming an angler was the next step and took me into a world of color, curiosity, fascination, intensity, passion, and interaction with great creatures. The passion put me on a professional path that led to a career in natural resources law and to becoming a senior federal fish and wildlife officer, chairman of an international fishery commission,

The body of flats fishing literature continues to expand.

A Keys September sun sets between spidery mangroves.

and a Bonefish & Tarpon Trust officer. There is nothing unique about this trajectory. My guide friends took essentially the same path to building a life with fish and the flats, and places like the Keys, the Everglades, or Andros occupying a central place in their lives. Fishery scientists probing the mysteries surrounding bones, poons, and perms share curiosity and passion with anglers. In a crazy, crowded world, lively transparent flats and wary fish are a clean, bracing, mind-cleansing challenge worthy of embracing as often as possible. A life built around the flats is a pretty good choice.

Trout and salmon have engendered the same kind of passion and commitment for centuries. The passion for these fish and their environment is notable for spawning a great body of literature. Flats angling is beginning to do the same. Forty years ago, flats fishing books were almost nonexistent. Lefty Kreh touched on the flats and bonefish, tarpon, and permit as part of his 1974 book and a few years later Kreh and Mark Sosin produced the first book focused on the flats, and that was about it. Now a plethora of fine authors are producing flats angling literature on par with the trout guys: Brown, Burke, Cardenas, Cole, Dombrowski, Fernandez, McGuane, Mill, Olch, and White, to name a few. I hope that a contemporary 25-year-old budding devotee of bonefish, tarpon, and permit will be able to contribute to this body of work a generation or two from now. It will happen if our love and fascination for the fish, fishing, people, and places creates the commitment to conservation that enables our successors to enjoy tomorrow what we cherish today.

INDEX